George E. Yoos
Simplifying Complexity.
Rhetoric and the Social Politics of Dealing with Ignorance

George E. Yoos

Simplifying Complexity

Rhetoric and the Social Politics of Dealing with Ignorance

Managing Editor: Magdalena Randall-Schab

DE GRUYTER
OPEN

Published by De Gruyter Open Ltd, Warsaw/Berlin
Part of Walter de Gruyter GmbH, Berlin/Boston
The book is published with open access at www.degruyter.com.

ISBN: 978-3-11-045056-9
e-ISBN: 978-3-11-045057-6

Bibliographic information published by the Deutsche Nationalbibliothek
The Deutsche Nationalbibliothek lists this publication in the Deutsche Nationalbibliografie;
detailed bibliographic data are available in the Internet at http://dnb.dnb.de.

Managing Editor: Magdalena Randall-Schab

www.degruyteropen.com

Cover illustration: © Ali Heshmati

To my wife Mary Johanna Yoos

'In the perception of the false, there is truth. In the understanding of ignorance, there is intelligence.'

A verbal statement made by J. Krishnamurti, an Indian Philosopher

Contents

A Preface on Aims

This book is a unified collection of *essays* in the rhetoric of the sciences and technologies discussing a multitude of ways of framing and modeling. The book is organized around a set of themes embedded in a listed set of quotes in the appendix that encapsulates my thoughts on simplifying complexity and the consequent oversimplifications of the simplifications made of the apparent complexity.

These essays center on three basic concerns about my own analytic and interpretive methods that I recently developed in reflecting on the complexity that I found in my own experiences in using different frames of knowledge that I have encountered in my overall long life experiences and my sustained inquiries into the methods that I once used 1) in the teaching of high school sciences, 2) in my teaching of rhetoric in undergraduate communications studies course work, and that 3) I used in a variety discipline areas in the teaching of philosophy. These three methods are based on three narratives that illustrate for me my present way of looking at the way we communicate with each other from a perspective that I have adopted, which was named and modeled by a good friend Preston Covey, and labeled by him as 'the wells of ignorance'.

The narratives of these experiences illustrate three propositions about scientific, humanistic, and rhetorical communication:

- The interpretation of what we think, say, and do is a matter of *context and background knowledge.* (Dan Sperber)
- We negotiate with others what we think is knowledge by making *appeals* and *responses* to each other by *noting* and *reminding* what we think we know. (Ludwig Wittengenstein)
- We use *conceptual dyads and triads* rhetorically *to interpret* as best we can clearly and simply what we think we know and understand. (George E. Yoos)

Coming to terms with ignorance, I suggest, is the key to understanding what we think of as knowledge. It is gained through the processes of falsification of each other's beliefs. We gain understanding through our oral interpretation of visual script and frames and models that are purported to be representations of knowledge claims. The aim of the book is that through the use of visual frames and models and through lists of contrasting and correlative distinctions it can be shown how we can create new language and new forms of graphic representations.

We use these frames and models as prosthetic, mnemonic, and attention controlling devices to produce simpler perspectives on the complications that we find in trying to understand different forms of complexity. We use these graphic forms of language to overcome our mnemonic and structuring limitations in organizing what we need to do to escape our existential ignorance (our wells of ignorance).

The book as a whole aims to display some of the means that we have of creating visual language and graphic modes that we need to simplify the complexity that we find in the different sciences, both social and physical, that we find evolving at various times and in different places and in different cultures. The book continues my attempt to explain what I have argued about before about the value of rhetoric and communications in trying to make sense about the puzzles that others find in talking about what is real and about what are the true reality based structures to be found in our world.

My personal view of life is that it is about empowerment, the elimination of ignorance, and about the joy and beauty that we find existing in the different forms of life. Thus the sciences, both social and natural, are ultimately about conceptions of values and power (Flyvbjerg, 2001) that are directing and shaping our social practices and shaping our personal forms of expertise that we use to enhance the qualities of our lives practically.

I am attempting to illustrate the creative aspects of modeling and to show how the uses of models are best interpreted and understood by looking at the sciences and technologies as *plural*, not as systematically explainable or derivable from any unified theoretical representations such as the many proposed Theories of Everything (TOES) try to do. Such devising of unified theoretical representations to my mind is a favorite metaphysical pursuit in our modern age especially to be found among theoretical physicists and astronomers.

Specifically, the book attempts to do this by surveying the different models that have evolved out of the innate biological development of the frames of grammar, logic, and the modes of orientation, and especially through the evolution of biological and socially constructed systems of numerosity and measurement that evolved and developed in the rigors of science in the different formal languages used in the various sciences and technologies.

Essentially, the book is an exercise in genealogy much in the spirit of Nietzsche and Foucault. It is about the archeology or the anthropology of knowledge based upon the study of error that historically has progressively been eclipsed and has been eliminated rationally by discovering the numerous falsehoods to be found in our cultural mythical origins. There has been a dramatic increase in what now is thought to be available as public knowledge. The book attempts to show how human action is centered in practice (*praxis*). It is centered in the human artifice of the social constructions that we have developed as the rules of thumb that human beings use to solve their practical problems of living.

The book is about how *the plurality of the sciences and technologies* that develop around the prosthetics of printed language and visual models. These help us create new models and new modes of language to help us understand and to solve our problems. In doing so the models and frames that we create become rhetorical tools in scientific and technological communication. Our understanding of some of these rhetorical tools whereby we simplify complexity is key to our clarification of the communication that is used 1) in the languages of the humanities, 2) in the new language of the sciences, and 3) in the languages of new and evolving growing forms of expertise.

George E. Yoos
Clear Lake, Minnesota, USA
May 2012

1 Rhetorical limitations in the use of frames and perspectives

Multiple conceptual perspectives help us understand public discourse as I have attempted to explain elsewhere in dealing with the complexity in of the problems of politics. Different conceptual frames help us address all sides of the issues in politics and help us see why policy argument is so complicated in its aims and purposes (Yoos, 2009). I introduced in that context a number of new conceptual frames and models that I found useful in guiding my own studies in rhetoric and argumentation, and I now propose to continue to add more frames and models as I transfer some of this rhetorical methodology to discussing the sciences and different forms of expertise.

Perspectives and frames have certain psychological limitations in using them if an audience is to understand readily what is being talked about. It was for this reason I kept most of my own model of methodological liberalism outlined in a sequence of simple triads (Yoos, 2009). The simplicity of such frames facilitates a reader's and listener's uptake to what is being said. As abstract, my models had the advantage of aggregating complexity and enabling us to see it logically and systematically.

Let me illustrate a mathematical and a geometric method of viewing complexity, which I shall call a mode of contrasts. This method I have already illustrated in the above mentioned published contexts (Yoos, 2009). It was best expressed I thought by a mathematical formula for measuring the numerical complexity of perspectives, oppositions, and contrasts in political frames and discussions. I used a simple formula to measure the number of *loci* in my model of a liberal rhetoric of practical reasons.

Contrasts are asymmetrical accounts of perspective differences. A is greater than B, and B is smaller than A. John is Mary's brother. Mary is John's sister. There are two points of view either from A or from B showing how we view these relationships as described from the two poles or perspectives. The two contrasts mark simple asymmetrical dyadic relationships and are not semantically equivalent statements. Semantically they sometimes simply logically imply each other.

My mode of enumerating contrasts then can best be illustrated by talking about the mathematical progression that allows us to calculate the numerical value of contrasts when we have a given number of contrasting terms in any frame or model. The easy way to do that is to note the mathematical progression that 'the number of contrasts equals the number of poles times the number of poles minus one.'

$$C = n\,(n-1)$$

Contrasting perspectives from ten poles thus would then equal 10 (10 − 1), which would be 90 contrasts. That is too much complexity to visualize in any form of holistic or direct attention that we might want to give to such a large complex number of contrasts. Too many contrasts would be an overwhelming amount of complexity in any piece of rhetoric.

As already illustrated, there are only two contrasts 2 (2 – 1) for a binary perspective or a binary conceptual distinction. In a triangular set of oppositions there are two contrasts for each of the three poles A, B, and C. A contrasts with either B or with C. B contrasts with either C or A. C contrasts with either A or B. Three poles times two contrasts 3 (3 – 1) give us six contrasts in all. The six contrasts between three terms as we will later show is a very natural way of thinking and analyzing things. We can see this pattern operate when we define things. We see it in how we think of a simple comparison or correlation of variables in talking about various factors in science, especially when we reduce or simplify our correlations to simple linear equations.

As a semantic note there are three terms contrasted in a logical definition, thus six contrasts to be made between three classes in a definition as in Figure 1.1.

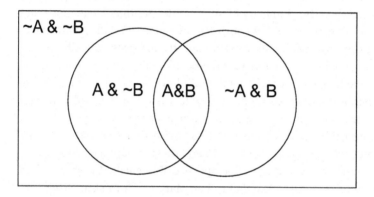

$$(A\&{\sim}B) \& (A\&B) \& ({\sim}A\&{\sim}B) \& ({\sim}A\&{\sim}B)=1$$

Figure 1.1: Venn Diagram and Conjunctive Possibilities of Combinations of two Terms and Their Complements

There is the term or the class being defined A. There is the class of which the term being defined is a subclass B. And finally there is the differentiating class C that intersects with B, the class of which the term defined is also a subclass. The division of a defining class (the class of which the term defined is a subset) by a differentiating class (another class of which the term defined is a subset) creates a class, and that class is identical or logically equivalent with the class of the term defined (thus the class of the term defined is identical with the defining class).

It is arbitrary in Figure 1.1 whether we differentiate B by C or C by B. It simply is a matter of perspective how one regards the defining class and the differentiating class in logical definitions. Foreground and background as in perspective in the visual arts are dyadic contrasts. And note that role taking in rhetoric is dyadic. The perspectives we choose to look at things depends on how we consider perspectives relevant or important. That is the principle I used in choosing the various perspectives on political argument that I presented throughout my mentioned book. Relevance and importance are key to any study of perspective that you take in looking at any policy argument, whether liberal or conservative.

The problem with essential definitions is always: 'Are they unique descriptions?', 'Are human beings (persons) uniquely rational?', 'Are human beings nothing more than persons?', 'Is a fetus a person?', 'Is a fetus a human being?'. If we are to avoid endless circling in the use of these ordinary language terms we need to avoid any specious realism and vagueness in talking about so-called natural entities as having definable essences.

Note there are many other sorts of contrasting triads especially as in the sciences comparable to those found in the logic of definition. For example in Newtonian physics, and not in Einstein's, the acceleration of a piece of mass is a function of a force applied. $F = (f)$ kma. In physics we practically apply the equation $F = kma$ in dynamics, where k is a constant depending upon the units of force, mass, and the rate of acceleration. We have thus three contrasting oppositions in the second law of dynamics between the three factors—force, mass, and acceleration - a total of six contrasts in all.

Note there is an interesting cause to the confusion that high school students have in distinguishing force and mass in physics, such as for example understanding the difference between 'a pound of force' and 'a pound of mass'. The confusion is caused by thinking that a pound of force and a pound of mass are identical units. The failure in this confusion is not noting the contrasts existing between force and mass. To understand this confusion we need to look at mass from the point of view of force and to look at force from the point of view of mass.

Importantly, and this is a point that needs emphasis, the two concepts require each other to understand the other. The two concepts are interlinked, and that is the important point that I made in discussing politics. We look at rights from the point of view of duties, and we look at duties from the point of view of rights. There is reciprocity in understanding the two concepts just as there is between mass and weight. In physics we look at force as a push or pull and then we look at mass from the point of view of a principle of inertia where we need a push or pull to overcome its reluctance to move.

Just so we need to look at rights as a privilege or a liberty that we have from a commitment or a promise (duty) that has been made. And we need to look at responsibilities as something we have created from the commitments we have made in granting people certain rights (liberties). The two concepts are interlinked in our understanding of what politics is all about.

Importantly, chemical properties are defined in chemistry by what combines with what to make new compounds. Chemical properties in this respect are chemically interlinked. Each element or compound is understood by their mutual interacting chemical properties. We thus look at the chemical properties of one substance from the perspective of the chemical properties of other elements and compounds, each defining the chemical properties of the other. Oxygen supports combustion, and certain chemicals are inflammable in oxygen. We understand the chemical properties of one from the chemical properties of the other.

But these simple examples from the sciences illustrating the use of triads are not truly representative of how we manage complexity in the scientific disciplines. Science deals with more complex contrasting states of affairs than those that are just to be found in simple examples of triads. The sciences have much more sophisticated tools for managing complexity not available in a rhetoric that specifically addresses non-specialist audiences. The sciences have mathematics and complex modes of modeling, using formal systems to assist in managing attention to a large numbers of factors and variables. Importantly, these models enable us to order, combine, and chunk together numerous elements to be able to deal with complexity logically in simple steps and in long sequences of logical inferences that are made one step at a time.

These methods of organization and arrangement used in the sciences require too much scrutiny and interpretation for the reading and the listening of non-specialist audiences. These formal methods are too much for audiences that are outside disciplines using formal systems and who are unable to handle complexity adequately except in simple sound bytes or aphoristic types of propositions expressed in dyads and triads.

Formal systems and mapping help the sciences reinforce powers of attention. They help those in the disciplines to remedy the psychological limits of memory, thus providing scientists with prosthetic, mnemonic visual aids in the use of graphics, script, or text, and that are importantly now being used in spreadsheets and computer printouts to engage attention to a great deal of complexity.

Such professional scientific disciplinary methods are too complicated to use in any rhetoric designed for non-specialist audiences. Scientists thus use prosthetic memory using visual texts to scrutinize large numbers of interacting variables or factors. They are able to do it by referencing and then making inferences, using a model or a text in a systematic way logically step by step. The sciences and the technologies have visual aids to memory generated by formal languages and graphics, and now they are being enhanced exponentially by computers. But to reiterate, elaborate proofs and elegant demonstrations are too complex to follow in any scientific explanation or argument that addresses non-specialist audiences unfamiliar with models such as a spread sheet.

Popular books by Albert Einstein that illustrate his theoretical physics are a lasting example of the differences between how professionals think in their disciplines and how they interpret their work for a general public. Given the limits of ordinary attention, the limits of short term memory, and the lack of a technical language that precise scientific terms, those who generate complex scientific argument necessarily have to resort to using a simple number of factors or variables in looking at issues in dealing with the social politics involved in the generating of the technical terms in science.

One can only deal in social political argument with the knowledge to be found in the expert disciplines by interpretations reducible to simple models or frames with simple contrasting oppositions within the constraints of usually only two or three terms. This sort of rhetorical reduction as a result of oversimplifications is often dangerous and misleading as it is prone to logical fallacies and ripe with interpretive ambiguity. We need to beware that simplifications have their own complications.

2 Aging and complexity

We find ourselves as we age bound up with new and an ever growing number of limitations in our ability to remember and to think. We begin to sense our growing stupidity as we age by what we know that we have forgotten. Our learning curve and our capacity to adjust to the new forms of expertise and technologies becomes as we age too much for us. We have a sense of becoming obsolete.

When we try to recall all that we have been through in life, for example, such as when we have forgotten simply all those people that we have been in touch with throughout our lives, the thought of it is too complex and over whelming. Our memory becomes fragmented and disparate with so much to try to recall. In old age we have much to regret. And in considering the choices we have made, not only do we have the regrets for all those past mistakes, but in our nostalgia we fancy that with what we know now that if only if then we knew what we know now, how easier matters could have been had we understood things better back then.

Besides a decline in physical strength as we age, we become more aware of our inability to engage in rigorous sustained thinking. Our powers of calculation decline. And as we as grow older as individuals we are embedded in a life framed by past personal choices and long term commitments. Even more we become aware of the narrowing boundaries of our short-term memories. We need to make up to do lists to keep from forgetting. The net result of all these complex aging factors is that we have developed personal constraints that confine us to living in a world where our attitudes and beliefs more and more are questioned about their validity and their verisimilitude as we relate to other people.

As we age we find that we existed in and lived through many new and different changing cultures. We find that we were in the past associated with different social groups. I myself had five different families. And too as we grow older we find ourselves more and more alienated from the younger generations with their new cultural ways of looking at things that are constantly changing.

There is nothing like old age to give you a sense of what it is to be stupid. And with age how many more mistakes do we increasingly make with the new contemporary emphasis on the importance of busy multitasking? Our old pop culture is dead. For me there were the twenties, the thirties, the forties, the fifties, the sixties, the seventies, the eighties, the nineties, now the first and the second decade of the new millennium, ten decades in all. Noteworthy each decade has its own historians that interpret and explain the events that happened. It is easy in old age with such complexity to slip into a willful and a self-inflicted crippling amnesia of things that we want to forget.

Much of what we think we remember turns out to be fiction. And as we age we have much more to remember, and even much more need to forget most of it. But still the complexity of our corrigible past keeps piling onto our anxious present. To keep reminiscing on so much of what has happened when we get old is just an additive befuddling set of diversions and distractions from our elderly matters of urgent concern, and especially with the brevity of time we have left to do what we can in that little time left. And besides rhetorically to reminisce and to talk about our past makes us elderly a conversational bore. Enough said!

Many of us have a need to forget. Importantly, what we need to do is clear away a free space in our thinking away from the intrusions of so much distracting diversity. We need to clear a space to help us keep in focus on what we think are important about matters at hand. And when that space has more than three items there is need to clear away the complexity that starts to be introduced when we are dealing with the complexity that starts developing when we start dealing with four items or more.

But many of us need to forget what we regret. We need to shed our regrets and to purge ourselves of worthless fantasies and lamentations that best be forgotten. Added to all these many things that introduce complex confusions in our thinking there are all those stories we tell about ourselves that we have selectively revised and idealized about ourselves and as a result we have produced distorted and errant memories. Many of our stories have been revised and retold to reshape our newly developed revised ends and purposes. Present circumstances always play a part in all our revisions of who we think we are and who we think we were, and who we think we might have been.

How many times have I found that I have been absolutely wrong about many things that I believed passionately to be true about the past? Many of my beliefs have been shattered by great reversals in my hopes for yearned and desired for expectations and aspirations. It is the condition of life to have all too many convictions of yours that others may question and that you as a result in turn will begin to question yourself. At best what we have are convictions about estimates and probabilities. Complete certainty about a great number of things is not a condition of a life.

But there is for us some certainties and truth, for we firmly believe things that have been shown to be demonstrably false. Our knowledge begins and ends in our questioning of beliefs. In this sense knowledge is the negative of what some people think of as their beliefs. Trust can never be a means of gaining certainty. Certainty comes when our beliefs are undermined. As J. Krishnamurti said, 'I can't go back. If for example I see all the religious nonsense, it is finished.' How can we go back to believing what has been shown to be demonstrably false?

And now that I am old I certainly have questionable memories and false beliefs about earlier times when I thought that I was fresh and bright and when I thought that I was mastering very many complicated things. Personally, I have forgotten all the complexity of the technology that I had to master in the Air Corps at a very young age in military service. And many of the things that I once thought I had mastered I cannot now for certain know what I knew then. I do not recall very much of it at all. Now, it is all too complicated for me ever to reconsider again and to try to understand once again what I thought I once understood. Especially, I no longer have the possibility of doing those sorts of things in those situations.

Those memories of those complex sets of facts that I once thought I knew, I had memorized with much effort and mostly by rote. But those memories of what I learned by rote learning are fading with age. All those multitudinous bits of intricate detail that I once thought were so easily to be dealt with are now obviously eroding from my brain. And the doubly dispiriting thing about it all is to think that many of those things that I once understood so well have been completely forgotten by me never to be revived in my mind in any conscious way. Most of what I read and thought I understood is now reduced in my memory to fragmentary schemes and frames. Most of what is left of all that reading that I am still able to recall is now reduced to simplified proverbs, aphorisms, and rules of thumb. It is at best a simple summary, a simple gist of all those many things of that past forgotten complexity.

Like most of us what I have read in the past has been simplified into simple conceptual dyads and conceptual triads that are common to our ordinary ways of common sense perception found in our ordinary ways of seeing things. Such are the truncated and abbreviated abstractions from past experiences that I remember aphoristically that now amount to little more than over- simplified algorithms as rules and guides to action.

It is this examination of many of my old age simplifications of past methods of exploration and inquiry that I wish now to analyze and try to come to understand so as to explore the role that rhetoric plays in the sciences and technologies in coming to terms with their own theoretical and technical terms. While reading and studying I mastered much of what I knew by devising many different interlocking frames of vocabulary relating to different structuring concepts. I used visual schemata to organize thoughts in my mind. Using mnemonic tricks I learned much additively in memory of those things that I knew in the past, and then when I found that there was little use for most of the detail that I had crammed into my brain, especially about what other people mistakenly said they knew and believed to be significant and important, all that was easily forgotten.

It is interesting how we speak of 'mind' and 'minding' in every day common speech. Note the following common locutions: 'Never mind', 'Mind your own business', 'I will keep that in mind', 'Mind the way you are acting', 'His kids never mind', 'His job is minding the store', 'I have a mind to throw you out the door', 'Keep your mind upon what you are doing', 'You are out of your mind.' Such various different locutions in using the term 'mind' raise questions about the variety of uses of the term 'mind'. Is mind a container wherein you can put things? Or is mind an action in which you pay attention? Or is mind an intention that you want to do something? And how is minding related to memory? In what sense is the act of minding mental? In what sense is it an action? Or is it simply behavior?

Note that by nominalizing the term 'minding' as what goes on in mind suggests that it may be simply grammar that has a great deal to do with how philosophers talk about the mind. Is minding what a mind does? Is it an entity or a process? Note that forgetting happens when you are not able to mind what you have done in the past.

And *reminding* is getting someone to mind what they may have forgotten or what they may have put out of their mind for a time.

Again how many historical facts in how many histories that I have read have slipped away? This forgetting leaves only the few facts that I have over time found to be significant in understanding patterns of historical change. Today few of these historical events I still find significant in my life. My list of truncated chronicles of history pretty much shape the time lines that I personally use to order my conceptions of historical time and my place relative to my present perspective, and my relevance to it. But how easy it is to forget those time lines by which we order and shape our personal concepts of history as our concepts about the past is constantly changing. Thus in shaping our knowledge of the past we do it from the present (Mead, 1932).

I remember many times in my teaching in preparing for class discussions of my texts where I was able to remember most of the details of the word passages on the pages. In my teaching I remembered for a few brief days what was said in all those texts. At the time I remembered even where the quotes for discussion if not marked were located on the page. But memory of those texts that I had so carefully read and annotated for my teaching lasted only a day or two. How little did my students realize at the time that what I said about what was said in those texts had no permanent residence in my head?

What is left of any memory of that past complexity to which I was once exposed to daily exists now mostly in my memory in no more than a few sketchy outlines and simplified models that I keep in the back of my head. They are there in mental residence in only a few short lists, some flow charts, and some useful algorithms. What exists there as reminders are numerous simple schematic triads of mediating concepts that I continue to use to simplify what I think was said in all that past complexity once exposed to in the reading of philosophy. And now too I can remember only a few mathematical schemata and a few scientific hypotheses or theories that I thought I once fully understood in teaching science in high school. Most of what I remember now is only illustrated by inaccurate summaries of historical stories about famous experiments whose details I have by now mostly forgotten. How much of what I remember now are only stories that highlight what I thought to be important at the time.

I remember vividly when I stopped being an English major of being so pleased at the thought that I could forget all those novel plots and their characters and what went on between them in dialogue that were part of the expected background knowledge needed to be a budding, well informed English literature scholar. I no longer had any need after that change in my major from English literature to philosophy for much of any such literary knowledge. What I once needed to remember about literature I could forget. What I thought I needed to know had changed and taken on a new face.

Just think of all those past times that you may have spent memorizing complex lines of thought about so many different matters and on so many different occasions. And think of all the events in our lives you have forgotten that you no longer have any need to remember at all. It is all too complex and beyond our capacity to remember very much of what we have experienced. It is impossible to remember most of what you have done in your life. And as we age there is so much more to remember and so much more to forget.

Thinking back on it, there seems to be no unity to much of it. Looking back on all of it there seems to have been a large number of random and sets of chanced events that we lived through. How much was luck a great part of it? There is no orderly organization that can be made of most of it. There is no logic or purpose to be found channeling through the length of it. There are few straight lines and consistent courses that we have taken in much of what goes on in our lives. It was very much like that in navigation training having to follow numerous dog legs flown by a fickle pilot.

Nothing in the way of a holistic theory seems to bring together any sort of unity to the diverse memories of thoughts that we have had and have forgotten, especially all that we once thought to be true and that we laboriously labored through. Brushing up on a few of those past forgotten understandings might help us in a way in old age to revive a few thoughts or two of what we once thought carefully through, but in old age one finds oneself running out time ever to go back over and review much of what we once thought we knew to be true.

Especially in old age we no longer have the time, especially the time to try to learn new things about all those topics that we stopped learning about or just ignored in the past. In my case the foreign languages I studied I did not have very much use for in my life. They died on the vine. Learning anything has its costs both in time and especially in money. And as time gets more valuable as we age, we regret the time we spent in the past on what proved to be fruitless things. Who has the time and energy when old to go back and think through much of what we once mastered and now try to re-do it or to repeat it all over again?

So much for forgetting! It is a blessing at times to wipe away useless trivia and forget most of it. But maybe in throwing away much of that trivia it may turn out that some of it may still be of some importance to us. How many household items I once threw away that I had to re-purchase. This has become now a problem for me in the writing of this book. Much of what I say that is new to me now I may have heard it before elsewhere. Old thoughts may be there still residing deep in my unconscious to rise up in me mistakenly as now a new intuition.

And when we try to see ourselves as a person living through all the multiple learning experiences that we have had, we look for some unity to help us to define what we think we know about our own life and destiny. But what we find in thinking of the totality of all our multiple experiences that we had, we find that they appear to be no more than truncated summations and narratives having little logical consistency, little direction, or singular purpose.

What we usually remember is simply an aggregation of different experiences and the multiple diversions that we encountered in the multiple opportunities that engaged us at different times in the past. When we reminisce about what we have sought and done in our lives that sense of unity that we would like to have as a person seems to be no more than an addition of a number of short skits of memories, images, synecdoche, and frames of events involving many multiple selves. We all have in our lives much to regret. Many of those past selves we once considered ourselves to be in the past we now want to deny. What is to be learned from all this is that though forgetting is a handicap, it also can be a blessing!

Again there are the problems we have in thinking about willful ignorance. And many of the stories we tell about ourselves now are a just another form of willful forgetting. Often we find the stories we tell about ourselves turn out to be quasi-fictive, stories that we do not want to be ashamed of. We like to think that we have a single time line that defines our history as just one person living in control of our lives and always sanely being on top of it.

But our conception of ourselves, what we are now, and what we have been changed day by day. We often forget the order of the events that happened to change us. We find in the summing up that we have had on the whole overall very little unity and consistent purpose in much of our lives. And part of our ignorance of ourselves is in not knowing for much of the time what we were doing, or what we did.

Happenstance and circumstances are too much a part of what has guided us. As we age we have found many reversals occurring throughout our lives. Such reversals have been mostly chancy things at best. How unsurprising is the fact that what we are now and the choices that we made changed who and what we have become. Most of it was least expected. To be least expected is simply by definition, not something that we can expect. There is little seeming causal sequence leading to the novelties that we discover in most of the changes that have kept occurring within our life.

Yet at times we can be satisfied with many of the choices that we have made even though their results were not intended. In my own life many of my failures I am now pleased to say that fortunately they happened. If not for them better things that did happen later would not have happened. For the most part we are ignorant of the consequences of our actions in life until we are fully aware of all the dirty deeds we did are fully done and no longer can be undone. Such was Aristotle's notion of happiness.

3 The human animal and its ascendance from ignorance

But there is another perspective we can take about the jumbled up complexity we have faced in times past. And that perspective is simply to see it all as just a part of that general ignorance that we all have about most all of the things that surround us. We have no notion of the scale of it, nor do we have any precise measurement or definition of it.

But in opposition to this view of mine that focuses on ignorance as a way of seeking and trying to define what we know, there are all those people who want to deal with complexity in objective and realistic terms, who think complexity as something objective and existing outside of us. They seem naturally to believe that there is a world existing outside of us, even though that world is beyond our wildest imaginations. They think of it as a definite or as a determinate world despite the fact that they have no conception of it. Nor do they have any adequate way of describing it.

Note how the terms *subjective* and *objective* have a way of reversing their meaning in ordinary ways of speaking. What is subject of concern is sometimes thought of as outside of us. And also what is subject also could be something that exists inside of us. But in another way of speaking a subject can in general said to be an object of our concern. When we are concerned about something we find in one manner of speaking that we can be both concerned about a subject or concerned about an object. Given this duality of senses of the two terms *subject* and *object*, what is both structurally and potentially definably as real can be thus thought of as a subject or as an object, something that can be within us or can exist outside of us.

Topologically then our sense of place is subjectively and objectively defined by what is fundamentally either inside or outside of us. There is an inner sense in which there is something psychological that exists within our skins. We feel our heartbeat inside of us. And what we see beyond our eyeballs is outside of us. And what we sense to be outside is the concern of what is on the inside. The problem in speaking of realistically or objectively is to decide what is the difference between what is inside and what is outside.

Note the expression 'being in touch with your feelings'. Is this a metaphor or a literal way of speaking about feelings? Note doctors, when they place their hands on you, can touch you to locate your pains. Touching in one sense as a feeling is about what is outside. It is about contact, such as two billiard balls touching. Note how figurative it is to say that billiard balls can touch each other. But note we can keep in touch by telephone. Note too how some want to talk about being in touch with your feelings. But it seems laughable to some to hear the pathetic expression, 'I feel your pain.' We all have heard it said that a man can never know the pain that a woman feels in child birth. But such a statement leads to the paradox of one never being aware of somebody else's pain when in fact we can be more or less empathic about how we feel and care about somebody else's misery.

Our experiences tell us then what we can sense of what is both inside and outside of us. Both sides are equally complex. Both sides are not very well understood as we know there are things inside and outside of us that we cannot see or feel. We have limited ranges of vision and limits to feeling. Some of us have better visions and hearings. And we find some people such as psychotherapists that have much more sensitivity to how others feel and what they themselves feel than do most other people. There are those then who are said to be in touch with their own feelings. They feel sad. They feel glad. And there are others who are more sympathetic and empathic about others. They see pain and sadness in faces. Note the problem of actors separating their personal feelings from the roles that they play.

But when we begin intellectually to extend our limits of thinking about what is inside or outside, we try to frame these regions of vision and inner feeling in physical and biological models. Optics is about what happens in our seeing of what is external. Physiology is about what happens internally. But what is there on the outside that seemingly exists outside that is completely independent of what is inside? Many hold a dualistic view of things existing independent of what is inside. That view has been described technically in philosophy as *ontological realism*. What we know according to this view is that there is something that is complex and structurally real that we can interpret and designate as being the causes and effects inside that are coming inside from the outside.

But traditionally in philosophy the view that our source of knowledge is outside of us, and that our perceptions of it can be real, is technically been called *epistemic realism*. Often this view is termed *empiricism*. It is the view that the source of our knowledge is made up of bits and parts of sensory experiences that tell us what is cosmologically structured and externally real that is the causal source of these experiences. And there are now communications specialists who hold the view that computers will eventually be able match with using its sensors and bring into itself bits and bits of digital memory that matches with the reality which is only itself bits and bits. The computer then would be a robotic epistemic realist.

However my view is, in contrast, that the complexity that we see and that we talk about in objective terms is actually a feature of our own complex linguistic, generative, innovative development. Such a development of language is both a product of our own physiological interactions and a product of our evolving culture. Our modes of communication have been shaped and formed in various types of social situational contexts. Such complexity of what is real then becomes simply a problem about the adequacy and complexity of our communications and our ways of understanding each other and our communications.

We create generatively the language we use, which in turn frames the systems of reference whereby we speak of complexity. In doing so we seem to be confronted about what goes on the inside and on the outside of what we speak of as our bodies. Complexity as we sense it in one sense then derives from our sense of the limitations that we have in communicating and interpreting the ways we have of dealing with what we think of as our world.

We find the complexity in our lives from the way humans have developed by artifice the expertise, which includes our ways of thinking using as tools complicated mathematics and complicated ways of visual mapping, especially by engaging in constructive drafting. This sense of complexity is a reaction we find in the work of experts who are able to do complex structural constructions. They find it in their models and graphics that map out their observations and inventions to be able to create their own innovative designs. We also see this sort of complexity in all those lists of details in all those charts and maps that we make. We see it in the immense variety of observations and measurements that we embed into various types of frames in order to remember and keep track of them. Our cultural world is full of such prosthetic filing cabinets.

It is in the displayed contents of communication that complexity seems to become a problem for us. We begin to be more aware of such difficulties when we generate new frames of reference and the numerous new models and mechanisms that we have invented to schematize complexity. We see this graphic complexity magnified in our thinking, especially in all those new computer programs that we design. And we see it too in the recursive expansions that we generate endlessly in all those infinite extensions that we find in the aggregated progressions that we can sum up and integrate into our mathematical systems.

We thus fail in our thinking about complexity to realize that this sense of complexity that we have about the world is mostly a sense and a product of our linguistic and graphic constructions. They are as structures generated by rules that in turn generate formal patterns that can become almost infinitely expansible. Our theories of numbers are largely responsible for much of this sense of this complex sense of numerocity in how we visualize the world in our measurements.

Those who believe complexity is something real in the world, such as we find in the work of Nicholas Rescher (1999), treat our ignorance as a failure to understand the reality of an already existing complexity in the world or universe. It is a complexity that we cannot in its entirety comprehend. Ontological and epistemic realists such as Herbert Simon (1996) and Rescher presuppose that what we are ignorant about has a definition and has features that are ultimately existentially real. Although in their view we may never know all those features of that complexity, presumptively that complexity has *a priori* existing features potentially incapable of discovered. It has features that are capable of description of what exactly actually is existing out there in the realm of nature if only we can find ways of observing it and describing it. It is worthy of note that both Rescher and Bertrand Russell have written extensively on the epistemic and ontological problems that we find the work of Gottfried Wilhelm Leibniz.

Realism such as that of Simon's and Rescher's makes no clear distinctions about what is inside or outside when it comes to talking about the complexity of what is real.

And they contend that they are able to represent and describe the ultimate external reality of it with their models and frames that they use. It is with their formal systems of logic and mathematics in all their beauty that is ultimately realistically descriptive. But they fail to realize as Kant did that human life as it has evolved has created its own forms of structured complexity. This dualistic realistic view of human artifice and thinking about an external world is incoherently expressed by Simon in his work, *The sciences of the artificial* (1996). Note my quote in the appendix where Simon presumes that what exists straight down the dark lit hall has fixed definable descriptions that he is not able to see.

And I especially have found this view expressed by Rescher (1998) in his work on complexity. Both Simon and Rescher believe complexity is something real, and it is not something that is being artificially produced by human creation, nor is it a form that is constructed through linguistic systems and through logical and mathematical languages of enumeration. But contrary to what they maintain, I contend that language and graphics are not mind-independent as I promise later to further illustrate. I shall maintain that these frames and models of reference, which they use to talk about what is real, are products of human artifice, and in that sense contrary to what they maintain. They are mind dependent. They are graphic conventions whereby people reach out and seek to understand things beyond their human limitations to cope with matters that they cannot control. That inability to cope is what helps define our ignorance.

In sum, these two authors maintain the complexity of things has a natural and real existence. These ontological realists do not think of complexity, as I am doing, as a failure we have in dealing effectively with our ignorance. For them real complexity that is external to us and internal in us is a thing that we have simply failed to develop any accurate and precise terms to describe it. I find to the contrary that there is confusion in what they think of as existing in reality. Both authors fail to clarify what it means to exist independently of subjective expression or what it means to be mind-independent. Theirs is a failure to communicate in a language about things whose usage is fraught with figurative ways of speaking, full of ambiguity, and imprecision.

The real sense of complexity I see is thus not as an objective but a subjective response to our sensations, thoughts, and feelings. It is what we encounter in the complexity of our linguistic frames and in the complexity of the human interactions that we see taking place in human communicative situations. It is this sense of complexity that generates the sense of our limitations and that seems to define the boundaries of these felt limitations that both Simon and Rescher appear to recognize. Language for them represents what is external. The failure to know for them is a failure to discover the reality of what is external. This realistic presumption is in large part just a failure to comprehend the perplexity we have in entertaining the very complexity of our rhetorical expositions and the complex interpretive ways that we use rhetorically to describe the meanings and interpretations of the applications of our complex formal and graphic systems.

Let me further examine Rescher's view that complexity is open to positive realistic descriptions of structures and patterns that he thinks of as real: 'The pursuit of cognitive objectivity - with its injunction to align our thought with our best judgment of the demands of reason - calls for a *commitment* to *ontological* objectivity, requiring *the supposition* of real-world objects whose true character is independent of what any of us happen to think [emphasis added].' (1998: 36)

Note his need to presuppose the supposition of real-world objects. That need to presuppose is simply an argument from ignorance. I want to contrast this expressed view with that of mine where no presupposition is needed. Complexity arises in the rhetorical attempts to put words and language together to describe actions and to describe the creations that we make in attempting to resolve our problems and our issues. But Rescher in contrast expresses his overall line of thought by saying instead the following:

> Complexity is a profoundly characteristic feature of the real. The world we live in is an enormously complex system - so much so that nature's complexity is literally inexhaustible. This circumstance is reflected in the inherent limitedness of our knowledge of nature; the descriptive/ explanatory project of natural science is ultimately incompletable. In fact, our recognition that reality is indefinitely complex - that its nature extends beyond the horizons that it can possibly know or even conjecture about - betokens the objective *mind independent of the real* [emphasis added]. (1998: xiii)

My contention then in opposition is that knowledge does not come from discovering what we are ignorant about in the complexity that overwhelms us. We find knowledge after the fact. We find it after we have performed our linguistic deeds. We find that knowledge through discovering first what others conjecture to be true. But then those conjectures we discover to the discomfiture of those who believe them that what they believe can be shown to be demonstrably false. What we claim to know are things that others claim to know that actually are not so. I take this to be the view of Karl Popper (2004). We discover truth by disconfirmation or refutation of things people believe to be true.

There is then a simpler explanation of our ignorance. Ignorance becomes simply thinking we know something that is not so. There is a political ground illustrating this sort of ignorance. We find it is in the politics of denial. We find this sort of ignorance in the politics of debate over what can be shown to be demonstrably false. It becomes a double sort of ignorance for people to recognize politically what they think they know to be demonstrably false, and then in turn stubbornly refuse to acknowledge their disbelief in what is true as actually false. This is a self-willed ignorance about ignorance. It is a form of ignorance that is not willing or able to question itself.

To re-quote an anonymous bit of religious cynicism that I once heard about such intellectual forms of stubbornness of willful denial from an old cynical colleague, 'Faith is a way of knowing things that you damned well know are not true.' It is simply difficult to deal with this sort of ignorance if people refuse to acknowledge what others have found them to be ignorant about. Bernard Williams (2006a) suggests that the proper way to deal with such ignorance is to **alert others** especially the audiences of such purveyors of such falsehoods that they are without question ignorant about what they claim to know and their claims are demonstrably false. To me this is the social and political value of critical thinking. It manifests to others what others fail to recognize as fallacious, and from that we then can go on to display to others how they stubbornly deny what is demonstratively fallacious.

But there is another way of confronting any ignorance that ignorantly refuses to question itself. It is about the proper rhetorical way of dealing with the ignorance of fools. Aristotle is frequently quoted to have said that 'it is demeaning to argue with fools.' Rhetorically given this quote, the proper stance to adopt towards such fools is not to talk to them. But such a form of condescension creates its own deleterious reciprocations. Elite pretensions have a way of destroying communications that are based on openness and equality as proper attitudes to take towards other participants in a conversation or discussion. Openness is necessary for politics to work. One way to deal with fools is to humor them and not to humiliate them in order to create openness to what the other person has to say.

But again there is another sort of ignorance that we all possess. It is the grand state of personal ignorance that we all have about our own personal worlds and the personal worlds that all of us live in. We can never truly know everything about our own little personal worlds. Such ignorance follows from the limits of our own bodily and psychological limitations of knowing what is going on inside of us. That world for us takes its subjective description unfortunately from our very unreliable memories and their distortions and inerrancies. It comes about from our lack of awareness of our own feelings and desires. It comes about from lack of clear definition of our hopes and expectations, and even of our true aspirations if we have any. This same deficiency holds alike for all human beings. We all alike suffer from these same personal limitations and cognitive deficiencies.

But to play the grant skeptic, and say we can never truly know anything, is disconfirmed by the fact that we assuredly know things that we were once ignorant about. And again assuredly we can know what others have been ignorant about. We cannot be skeptical about the fact that we continue to know things so long as we continue to have our wits about us in seeing what is demonstrably false. We need not be skeptical of many things so long as we continue to know how to disprove things about what others claim to know and about which we are able to demonstrate that they are totally ignorant about.

We surely know what it is to be ignorant about things that we thought we once knew. We cannot be skeptical about that. But it is an unwarranted presumption, such as Rescher maintains, that there are things that we will never fully know. 'Fully' is his way of projecting infinity into the finite and projecting it into our limited modes of knowing. Infinity takes its meaning from the properties we find in logistic and mathematical systems about progressions. It is a mere type of progression analysis that we find in mathematics that becomes useful in making aggregating and integrating summaries of calculations that approach known limits and known boundaries. But we need boundaries to interpret and to define limitations.

To grasp and understand the extent of our ignorance we need to begin to imagine the scale of expertise and its limits and the global extent of it. But that scale and scope has no defined limits and boundaries. It is on such a grand scale that we have no way of measuring it, let alone knowing how we can model it. What we know has its limits, but yet in our ways of measuring of expertise there is no sure way of measuring and defining our methods of knowing expert knowledge as our expertise is always open to innovative improvements. The expert knowledge that we find in expertise is always expanding. Given the creativity of experts and their design improvements, there will always be room for greater improvement.

Even if we are able to recognize what we know only in part only about what has been working and failing us, there is no unit we can use to itemize and quantify what are the distinct boundaries and forms of improved expertise. Nor do we in our expertise know what in the future what purposes it will potentially serve us. Expertise merges and blends with other forms of expertise. We can see where we think we have knowledge, but we also see that same sort of knowledge may exist in many other sorts and types of expertise that exist in different walks of human life existing across this planet. It is only by social aggregations and mutual recognitions of experts that we can talk about any numbers in talking about the extent of anyone's expertise.

How can we then integrate and measure any totality or any a sum of knowledge? Some expertise is personal and some of it is institutional. Some of it is locked up in trades, professions, and especially in various types of businesses. Much of it is to be found in the academic disciplines, which as disciplines keep altering, dividing, expanding and multiplying in different directions around the world. Most of this diversified expertise lies hidden from us to be found in the secrets of guilds, and much of it is held in privacy by persons and corporations for fear that others would profit by it if they revealed it.

And too there are the many complex functions and interlocking modes of production in corporate organizations with layers and layers of departments and divisions that innovatively create products and professional services that are kept hidden from spying eyes. This sort of ignorance about who knows what can potentially be revealed, but usually it is discovered to be or not to be the case only within the frames of those people who have mastered these sorts of specialized expertise to make judgments about it.

Sometimes only experts have the background knowledge that can disconfirm what some people think to be the case. Importantly too it can be shown to be the case that there are questions about those who claim to have expertise that they know about, yet they cannot describe or explain it. Certain kinds of expertise can be embedded in bodily and feeling skills. Note how many experts with musical instrumental skills have expertise as a part of their physical reaction to the music that they play. Trombone players have their sense of tone in their muscles. Pianists have the sense of tone in their touch. Violinists have their feel in their use of the bow. In such cases they are ignorant about the existence of any correct answers to questions about how they are able to do what they do so well when their performance is part of their bodily skills and inner feelings.

Some of the questions we put to experts, or some of the questions that experts ask themselves, may appear to have ways of answering them. But what they know with their bodily senses of correctness may have no ground in any physical or mechanical explanation. There may be some mechanical answers, but some of the questions that we put to experts may simply be verbal questions that seem to being going nowhere. The many who fail to see this emptiness in some questions about expert skills are trapped as a result in their own verbal confusions. All too many fail to see that their issues are merely verbal as such. It is at this point that experts run up against the limits of language in interpreting the questions they are being asked about things that they are doing. But then in the end they ground their confidence in their expertise in the results they achieve.

And again it is at this point that experts are running up against rhetorical constraints in arguing and explaining about what they are arguing for or explaining about. They are I suggest failing to come to terms with their own terms in addressing such questions (Yoos, 2009). There is thus then the ignorance of asking dumb questions and not knowing that they are dumb questions. There are questions logically and rhetorically that can have no answers. This un-answerability to certain types of questions reduces to another type of ignorance that just keeps trying to pursue questions that logically can have no possible answers.

Note that paradoxes are not simply the province of philosophers. In mathematics and logic it is part of their game. We find paradoxes in economics, physics, astronomy, biology, politics, statistics, and decision theory. And what many see as the stupidity and the futility of much of philosophy is the continuous pursuit of paradoxical questions by philosophers that logically can have no possible decisive answers. But it is not just philosophy which has a reputation for asking dumb questions. It is equally if not more prevalent to be found in many of the sciences. Many of the questions and presumptions and interpretations of scientific theory are treated as real questions, that is, as questions that have real answers in terms of what is presumed to be factually and externally real, that is, independent of mental functions.

But without language it is difficult to gain such independence. Much of institutional and professional expertise in the sciences and technologies has limits to be found in their applications not understood even by those who manage to apply them. And again too there are an almost endless number of inquiries to be found about questions that shape the grounds of research where specialists are evolving and developing new disciplines, especially developing new disciplines through interdisciplinary exchanges that keep developing and expanding around new kinds of expert knowledge.

It is at this point that rhetoric and views on communication enter into the discussion about how experts and scientists express their views about truth and reality. Since they are experts about what they do, they have rhetorically an advantage in using their technical language as their fallback position in explaining what they do, which makes it difficult for the non-expert to participate in their discussions about their alleged theoretical rectitude. But in the end they cannot disconnect the use of their technical jargon from our ordinary ways of speaking. It is in their interpretations of their own theories in ordinary language that rhetoric becomes an issue in how they interpret their theories, their meanings, and their applications.

This is especially so in the newly developing programs that they are now integrating. It is in this shaping of the different and evolving disciplines that we find a need for new and different interpretations. It is amongst those who are involved in developing new lines of scholarship and new lines of research that we find the shifts in the language we use with new and different types of interpretations, especially using new developments in the use of newer graphic models and mathematical frames as we presently see going on in the multiplication of sciences and technologies.

It is in these shifting paradigms of what constitutes a discipline that we see the new transformations happening in academic institutions that presently are becoming the important research centers around the world. It is there that we hear questions about the logic and the interpretations of their questions about what their expertise is, and it is there where we hear questions about what constitutes their disciplines. Such questions are serious questions that are notoriously open questions in academic and bureaucratic administrative considerations about what fields and disciplines need support financially within scientific and technological research institutions.

'Is what they are doing a worthwhile human enterprise?', 'What sorts of answers are being provided about the value of what they are doing for matters of social and public policy issues?', 'What questions do we need to answer to discuss the importance of various fields and disciplines in the acquisition of public knowledge?' These are questions about public policy issues that are about the maintenance and support of scientific and technological research centers. The Rand Corporation as a consulting institution illustrates how government development funds for research goes when politics is guided by corporations with a vested interest in defense policy. It is no accident that the Rand Corporation had its beginnings in the self-serving interests of the generals of the 20th Air force.

The scope and scale of these research institutions where knowledge is imbedded is spread into multiple isolated islands of distinct disciplines. And our knowledge producing institutions continue to break down over the value of what their self-serving cliques claim about their expert knowledge. It is these failing reconsiderations of disciplines and their purposes that act as a surfactant in multiplying, changing and spreading over into new and other disciplines. These new directions of inquiry then spill over and continue to break down further into newer multiple islands of newly developed types of expertise, which again become isolated from each other again into a new regime of separate islands of inquiry just as they were isolated before.

It takes only a few hours of exploration on line on *Wikipedia* to see the scope of so many different sciences and technologies, and to see the scope of so many forms of research and scholarship about so many diverse and different subjects. Such a surface survey gives one a sense of the immense magnitude of the diversity and the complexity of what many of us think of as scientific and expert knowledge. We see in it a marvelous complexity that keeps growing continually, multiplying into the various tangential spin offs from the various developments occurring within the multitude of the different disciplinary units.

Given the fact that *Wikipedia* touches only the surface of what its contributors advance as knowledge and given the fact that such articles serve the authors and the rhetorical purposes of vested interests rhetorically, rhetorically these contributors to public knowledge are seeking public resources from economic and political sources power. And, just as encyclopedias and handbooks have done so in the past, we lose all sense of the magnitude of what it is that we do not know about these disciplines rhetorically. Much of the surface spin that is spun superficially off those multitudes of topics and surveys of what is going on in disciplines reflects the need for all their own self-serving time spent by them on public relations (PR). Actually we are ignorant of most of those things these people claim to know and understand. We are ignorant of so much of what there is out there in those small inquiry groups in society. We do not understand and do not know about it, nor do we know even the extent of it, nor know what their aims are in spinning it. Not everyone wants to tell you what they are into, nor why are interested in doing it?

But not knowing about something is not the sort of ignorance where we make claims about knowing something when actually we do not. But it is the sort of ignorance such that the very scale of not knowing overwhelms us in thinking about our severe limitations in knowing things others seem or claim to know. It overwhelms us to think about the amount of all the different kinds of specialized knowledge that exists within individual minds and in the institutions that have been built around different professional specialties and vocational skills. It is an ignorance we have that we can only lament not knowing its practical limitations.

But it is a limitation we need to live with. Those who are not experts tend to shy off and are given to accepting that extensive ignorance they have about what others can do without commenting about it. It is taken for granted that there is a large scale complexity of what goes on in all those expert fields of knowledge. We tend not to question that sort of ignorance. We cannot be blamed for not having it. We tend to give experts the legitimacy that they claim for themselves. We tend to accept what they say that is going on in those professional black boxes.

Note the American Council of Learned Societies (ACLS) is only an umbrella support group that gives some legitimacy to all those doing research in those black boxes. But how much does the ACLS know about some of the emptiness of scholarship and research that is going in those black boxes that they have in their supposedly careful prior judgment sanctified as learned societies. To illustrate the isolation of learned societies, just examine the bibliographies of any of those in those specialized fields that have some recognition of legitimacy. What is striking when we examine the bibliographies of experts in other fields is that their bibliographies are empty of authors preeminently listed in one's own fields of specialization. What we find are multiple islands of inquiry and multiple fields of specialization not communicating with each other. The popular metaphor for these isolated fields of inquiry is that they are silos. I tend to think of this specialization isolation as in *Alice in Wonderland* as separate rabbit holes.

And to add to this problem about how we treat and consider expert knowledge, we have no conception of how much and to what extent that expertise we see surrounding us can be trusted. Not only do we have no conception of the extent of the number of claims, conjectures, theories, hypotheses, and histories that are accepted and held by so many that we have no way of telling whether they are wrong or even misleading. We can only say that we are ignorant of most of what their claims are, and that we are ignorant about what is true in them. And we are even ignorant of the probabilities of these specialists being right about any or all of their claims. And in many, if not most cases, we have no way of knowing how to go about efficiently to access, assess, or evaluate the results of most of it. Just think of the extent of the misconceptions and misinformation that dominates so much of the contemporary politics that appraises the importance of expertise as a source of good reasons for public policy formation.

Certainly, the computer has changed and increased our ability to access what we do not know of what would be relevant for policy formation. It has increased the transparency and simplified how to sort out and to develop new models and frames for exchanging information and it has developed new ways of verifying beliefs about this and that. But numerous societies have developed around groups of people who have a vested interest in profiting from their expertise. How legitimate is the research and scholarship that goes on in all these vested interest groups that are subsidized political producers of public policy recommendations.

But we also do not have any real sense of the extent that these vested interest research groups are overpopulating the earth, nor do we have any conception of how many have combined and have exercised their influence on the politics that frames the laws governing the uses of the expertise in so many fields. Some of these groups are private and secret. Some are hidden behind fences to protect their self-interests. There is no significant canvas we can make of all this vested interested diversity such that we cannot generalize about or give a fair estimate of the scope of their corruption of politics, nor can we give a fair estimate of the unreliability of much of what they contribute to public discourse.

We have no way of knowing about the extent of privacy that hides what so many know. We do not know the extent of how much of what is known that is protected by law, nor do we have a concept of the extent of the property rights of those who have patents or have copyrights on it. Intellectual property is something that requires lawyers to define it in the courts that interpret the laws within our different legal systems. There is something mindless about those who talk about property rights as being defined within their own legal system. Why is there so much concern for the rule of law about property? Is it that the law protects the intellectual property of so many different vested interests in different sovereign states? Note the conflicts over intellectual property that many in the United States have with what is being produced in India and China.

One supreme answer to our quest for making sense out of politics is that we seek by means of it the protection of what you and I have, and the protection of what you and I think we know from those who would want steal and profit from what we profit from the most. Note the difference in legal systems that sustain intellectual property. And note the difference between corporations existing in different societies. It is no wonder then that some want to think of the rule of law as singular entity, grounded in the laws of nature that sanction property rights. They just want to protect the form of the legal system that grants them the legal rights and privileges that they have that are derived from that self-same legal system that they defend.

The major problem that we have in our lives is in understanding ignorance and having a modest and decent sense of humility about all those things that we are ignorant about. The major problem we all have is to find what we think to be true that is actually false. That social awareness of being in error is a true demonstration of the extent of human ignorance in so far as we know the extent of the fact that so many have not escaped from it. But I have found in my desire to escape my own ignorance of so many things that what I think of as a pursuit of knowledge is not a pursuit of knowledge at all. Rather instead I think much of it is actually an attempt to escape from the ignorance that pervades our lives and our social contexts.

But Confucius's proverb that 'knowledge is knowing the extent of one's ignorance' does not seem to recognize that we have real limits in knowing the extent of it to escape from it. In a reversed way knowledge comes to us when we find our beliefs demonstrably false. We do not find knowledge by just looking for it ourselves, or in mostly deriving it with the help of others. We find it rather in the discovery that we are ignorant about much of what we thought to be true. We get knowledge in a way that it is upside down. We do not get it directly from those who claim that they know because they have good reasons to know or from those who just claim they have evidence to prove it. Actually, the case is that what people truly know they obtain it from those who were able to expose so many falsehoods about topics and conjectures that they were curious about.

This view of knowledge that I am presenting is upside down in a way. It is comparable to the way we reverse the image that falls upside down on the retina of the eye. The brain reverses it. Just so our brain reverses our way of seeing knowledge. It does not come, as many suggest, from limited instantiations or generalizations from our perceptions of particulars by induction that generates convictions about their certainty. Rather it comes from demonstrating that certain **conjectured correlations** are demonstrably false. We find it in a reverse way by finding that our beliefs thought invariantly true turn out not to be the case.

When we generalize and accept the certainty of law like repetitions of things that we observe occurring in nature, we are only enhancing our acceptance of such notions by induction from probabilities. But I suggest that we gain certainty not by probabilities, but from what we can logically demonstrate to be false such as that certain defined probabilities of observed correlations turn out not to be the case. When we observe things to be true we think that what we observe directly is something that is true of the world, but in actuality the brain has reversed it. We know that certain things are not true of the world. What we are doing instead in acquiring knowledge is finding falsehoods in our systems of conjectures and systems of belief. We are shrinking our ignorance. Our reasons for our conjectures are inherently pragmatic. But practicality never in the end can be a ground for certainty. That things always seem to work does not make for certainty that it will always be the case. What makes us certain is that if you say that it will always happen and it does not, it is surely certain that it has not worked!

4 The work of Herbert Simon on Artificial Intelligence

Much of what I have found to say in this book came about from my recent introduction by Richard Young into the life and work of Herbert A. Simon. Especially, what I have to say arises from my questioning some of Simon's presumptions about cognition that I found in reading Simon's two books: *Administrative behavior: A study of decision making processes in administrative organizations* and *The Sciences of the artificial*. Each book deals with the limits of rationality and about the problems of dealing with complexity. It is his emphasis on the differences between the conceptions of human **artifice** and **sufficing**, and his work on the different **modes of human problem solving,** especially in using **artificial intelligence (AI)** that fascinates me most. Much of what I want to say is an assimilation of his discussion and a reaction to what Simon said in the two fore mentioned books. Much of my argument against what Simon says consists of undermining his realistic presumptions behind the use of computer models that pervade his writings. In a way I am just playing another game of 'Simon Says'.

Let me provide an introductory illustration of my Simon game by using an isolated quote from Simon:

> Rationality *implies* a complete and unattainable knowledge of the exact consequences of each choice. In actuality, the human being never has more than a fragmentary knowledge of the conditions surrounding his action, nor more than a slight insight into *the regularities and laws* that would permit him to *induce* future consequences from knowledge of present circumstances [emphasis added]. (1994: 94)

Let me identify the presumptions that I find behind these *italicized* terms that I have indicated that lead to his prescriptions that I wish to challenge. How does rationality imply (suggest) (presuppose) knowledge of the *exact* consequences of choice? The second questionable presumption lies behind his talk of *regularities* and *laws*. The term *laws,* especially the term *natural law* presupposes a fixity to what happens that is always open to question. *Law* and *nature* are loaded terms in discussing questions about knowledge and the ends and purposes of the sciences.

And finally, I interpret Simon's term 'induce' to be used in an unorthodox or in an extraordinary way of speaking and to actually mean by it 'deduce', that is 'It logically allows us to *infer*.' Simon seems to be supposing in this case that rationality requires a reality of complete and fixed certainties that no one can by their limited nature cognitively attain. These presumptions I want to argue are inconsistent with his notions of artifice and suffice. The term *artifice* implies in its usage artificial constructions of novel structures and the creation of novel organizations by engineering and planning. But such products of novel design are in the last analysis understood in our ordinary ways of speaking for the most part as meaning emergent and novel creations. We find that creative design is about non regulative and unlike law happenings or events, which we through artifice want to create or generate as novel facts. *Artifice* as a term thus is a correlative of the term *creativity*. It is in the contrast in the use of these two terms *creativity* and *artifice* that we discover the antinomies created by their contrasting uses.

Contrary to Simon's presumption there is still another kind of ignorance I want to contend that frames our existential situation. There is a past that we are oblivious to, and there is a future too about which we are likewise oblivious. We have no adequate concept of the fate (*Kismet*) of ourselves and the universe. It is in a way a form of folly to predict anything without an adequate concept of what is being predicted. There is ignorance in the folly of trying to explain everything, especially as we can have no conception of what constitutes 'everything'. TOES, fail to predict why and what is living and emerging. The creative artifice of life is not something that is predictable or subject to preconceived designs as to why it occurs.

It is this sort of complexity and change coming from human artifice and invention, especially from those computer programs developed in Artificial Intelligence that appear so creative that continue to befuddle us. AI in developing innovative models and frames for use in the everyday life of business, academic research, and for the organization of the political world, as Simon says, should be tested to be shown to be applicable or proved (empirically verifiable) to be successful. Artifice in AI is more than the randomized uses of mathematical or logical algorithms. It is innovative change that makes optimal conceptions or completely logical rational predictions of the certainty of optimal possible worlds quite impossible.

We have no conception of the scope or scale of what goes on in the actual world especially about the risks that are taken in it by all too many people at the present time in the high tech world. They in the developing forms of expertise are doing so many things differently, and these things are sometimes as we later find even detrimental to our culture. They now are using different models and programs to create and to produce poisons, pathogens, biogenic toxic modifications, and destructive mechanisms especially nuclear weapons that potentially are in the process of destroying the planet and making it unfit for life.

However, ignorance of what we have forgotten and ignorance of things we have experienced does have an object that helps us define in one sense what it is to be ignorant. That sort of ignorance is simply an ignorance of facts that have happened. But when we speak of *ignorance* we need to be aware that the term has different senses, especially when ignorance turns out to be about things that no one knows about, and especially about what no one can even talk about. It is this sort of ignorance about what we can never know that raises the paradoxes of talking about things that are indefinable. And much of what happens in the world is often indefinable.

What are the boundaries by which we can verbally distinguish these difference degrees and senses of ignorance? How are these senses of 'ignorance' related, that is, if they are related? In speaking of ignorance there is a lack of awareness of the immense complications that we find in attending to so much. There is ignorance of the shifting and changing detail that we find in our lives or in our personal worlds. But there is an all-important sense to the term *ignorance* in that we are ignorant by the limited means we have in communications where we lack all possibility of definition of the terms in the languages we speak.

There can be no definition of what we cannot presently know about especially those things yet to be created. To define what we create would be to create that something before we have created it. There too also is ignorance that has no self-awareness. When we try to escape such possible subjective ignorance by communicating with others, we find that there is also ignorance in those persons with whom we communicate, which helps us know something about them and the world. Sometimes this fact can be easily demonstrated. We thus are bounded by others with their own personal deficits that sometimes constrain us in finding out what we don't know and what it is that we think we too are ignorant about. Ignorance is equally in a way the existential fate of us all. In an ideal way to be human is to try in various ways to eliminate it. It is hoped for in both science and philosophy to eliminate mysteries about ourselves and about the world we live in.

There have been empirical confirmed limitations discovered by psychologists about the brevity of our memories in what we learn and what we have to forget. But some of these limits we know can be transcended by the developments of new schemes and mnemonic devices that create external resources or prosthetics to help us remember. These devices help us simplify and clarify things that we might be able eventually to understand. And they help us do things that we are able to do better and more efficiently and productively in doing things we want to do.

To acquire such knowledge our civilization depends on the external memory of written languages, and especially now on visual representations using graphic and mathematical languages that aid us in escaping some of these psychological limits and deficiencies that limit our knowledge and mastery of events. We are able in the way we communicate with each other to explore the ignorance of others and are able to find why they are ignorant, and in doing so we are able to find in our own little abyss what we too are ignorant about. These explorations and mutual clarifications about what we do and say to each other are limited and constrained by our language use and the various ways of we have of displaying to others the implications of what we say and what we visually display so as to communicate better with others. It is in this sort of context that the politics of language use and usage comes into play.

Let me at this point suggest a distinction to be made between *oral* and *graphic language* where by graphic language I would mean written or printed language. Such an assimilation of the visual makes both literature and our scripted expository prose just variants of graphic artifacts. But graphic language then is not simply just the printed word. It includes drawings, pictures, maps, charts, and graphs. It includes the drawings of geometry as well as the formal scripted languages of symbolic logic and mathematics. I wish to use this distinction between oral and graphic language later to show just how and why our interpretations of what people are saying in oral and written language is open to different questions about the interpretation of both our and their usage.

Usages I maintain are socially and politically constructed. Likewise, I have defined technical usages of language as standardized professional social constructions of graphic usage. There is a social politics that creates not only technical vocabulary but also devises formal mathematical and logical representations and that equally defines the rules and modes of construction in using schematic visual frames.

There is thus a social form of politics for expertise, for the professions, and for the sciences and disciplines that rank and structure the way we define our ways of dealing with the practical matters of the world. This politics is not only a quest to eliminate misinformation but also a quest for power and the achievement of accepted values. Not only is there then a politics that standardizes our spoken and written languages, there is a social politics to all our graphic languages, especially our formal logical and mathematical languages. And it is this social politics that guides the use and usage that is at the heart of our understanding of the aims and modes of rhetorical action that tries to reach mutual understandings in communication.

5 Circular thinking and linear exposition
Circling around a point to discover the point

When we think of a circle we think of a return to a point. When we think of lines we think of queuing. Circles are confining, but lines give one a sense of liberty and of freedom.   E. B. White defined democracy as standing in line. When we get in line we customarily need first to get to the end of the line. Lines give one a sense of equality. We have no special social privileges as individuals do in queuing starting from the rear of the line. We do not return to any point unless the line returns to the original point of origination.

And when we get in that line and that ends in the grave there are no special exclusionary privileges from such a fate. In thinking about thinking we also get in a line whose terminus of our thoughts are to be discovered as we move down that line. We need not necessarily know our destination unless someone has been down that line before and tells us what lies ahead. Thus linear thinking without knowing of what is ahead is lining up all of our ducks in a row on our route to discovery.

But circular thinking always revolves and then returns to the same point. It is cyclical. What is interesting about circles is the perspective we have from each and every point on the arc of a circle. It is simply a different set of orientations. With lines we go simply to the next spot ahead with only our hoped for and wished for expectations. Our perspective is always looking forward. But in circles we can surround each other with the perspectives of others.

I was listening to a discussion about sports on TV recently, and one speaker asked the other, who supposedly was a so called expert about baseball, 'Is baseball as a game different from other sports?' What struck me about this discussion was that the speakers were circling through the various ways they wanted to use their terms: 'What is a game?', 'What is a sport?', 'Is baseball truly a game?', 'Is it truly a sport?' And again, 'Are not games and sports nothing more than different forms of entertainment?', 'How is baseball just a merely a game-show or a performance, or an entertainment?' And when we are listening to the news, 'Is it really just news, or is it just a game-show, or a form of entertainment just like baseball?'

What appears to be going on in these sorts of exchanges in questioning about what is truly the case the discussion is not about making any points about facts or about what is true of the world in any absolute sense. Rather the participants are circling through each other's vocabulary using their preferred uses of words such as *game* and *sport* in the contexts in which they prefer to use them so as to make their own judgments about social value and political practicality. In sum they are talking about how they are using words and then in turn using their preferred uses of their terms to make judgments or appeals to others to make policy judgments using the senses of terms they use to make appeals to their audiences.

It has struck me that each individual has his or her personal language that differs from the language of other individuals. The major problem in communication is to interpret the meaning of each other's own personal language. Each person's language is very much like the development of each other's DNA. It consists of fragments of our ancestors' DNA. So it is the case that our personal language consists of fragment of meanings derived from the interpretations of persons we encounter who speak the same cultural language we speak. Language thus is anchored in the individual language we learn and use as we develop the personal and individual language we speak that is an amalgam of many different speakers.

Note all the nonsense spouted about who is a *liberal*, a *socialist*, a *racist*, *conservative*, or even just a *Christian*. All such terms haves no precise meaning in ordinary discourse. Each of these terms as used in contemporary politics have loaded or emotive senses of just how much value additive priority people want to give to each term as we personally use them in their contextual uses of them in dealing with each other. Note comparably how such questions about terms arise in political discourse about *justice, equity, fairness, compensation*, and *what one owes another*.

Such discussions of abstract terms usually involve the same sort of verbal circling 'Are you happy?', 'What is happiness?', 'Is happiness a brain state?', 'Are you happy only after the fact?', 'Is happiness to be free from misery and pain?' Such questions are about the different ways that people choose to give meaning and value priorities to the uses of such terms in the language they develop for themselves such as they learn to speak and develop new meanings for words for such things as *happiness, misery, pain, pleasure, bliss, contentment, satisfaction, euphoria, being fulfilled*, and *goal satisfaction*.

You can name the other synonyms for *joy* to enlarge this circle. How can you talk about life without ranking and relating to these synonyms and antonyms? How can we without thinking of them as correlatives define and distinguish how we use these terms in communicating? And importantly we need at least one term in such clusters of synonyms and antonyms to stabilize positively our meaning contrasts in our coming to terms with the others (Yoos, 2009).

What people are doing in circling through distinctions and differences between our uses of words is interpreting their own pattern of uses of them. And when we interpret them we discover the vocabulary that people want to use to talk about how they want to relate to each other, and again about how best in what terms that they should want to relate to one another. Usually in their attempted definitions and prescriptions of use, or what they might think of as usage, they are trying to give technical definitions of such terms without the social contexts and without the power and authority that legitimize standardized uses of technical terms.

They are not about seeking conclusions about what is the case, but they are discussing how they want to talk to each other about their meanings in their dealings with each other. They are seeking language to talk about the conclusions they want to agree upon by agreeing on the language that they want to use in expressing the conclusions that they have mutually arrived at in talking about the matters at hand that concern them. They are seeking agreement about how they should be talking and the words they should be using to make a point that is at issue or that is about a contention between them. The great mistake that they often are making is in presuming that their terms are amendable to precise definitions of essences, or essential forms of typical types of things. What they are presuming is that there are fixed natural paradigms and exemplars for the words that we or they use.

What we think we know requires that we know the language that we use to talk about the things that we think we know. We need to construct the language out of usages to talk about what has not been experienced before. Especially this is the case when we talk about what we know that turns out not to be true. To reach accord or agreement we also have to come to an agreement about how we use and interpret visual schemata that we create for expressing what we think that we know. Not only do we need to come to terms in the printed word with the way we express what we think we know, but we also have to come to terms with the uses of pictorial and mathematical representations that we use to interpret what we think we know in our ordinary ways of speaking about them.

It is this creative construction of language in science that marks the progress in the sciences. It this awareness of meaning shifts in the language of science in the manner of Ian Hacking in his work *The social construction of what?* That also marks the work of Evelyn Fox Keller in her work on nature-nurture debates. As she says:

> Interpretations (or descriptions) are cashed out in experiments, with different interpretations leading to the design and execution of different kinds of experiments. When successful, they point the way to observations of different kinds of phenomena, which, in turn, are taken to lend credence to the interpretations that generated them in the first place. It is this sense that, even under a realist view, one can say that language 'constructs' knowledge. By simultaneously facilitating certain research trajectories, and foreclosing others, descriptions shape the construction (articulation) or the edifice we call scientific knowledge. (1992: 177)

Sometimes we need to simplify the complexity of what we are talking about to find simpler words to use or to use simpler visual and formal graphical representations to come to terms with our understanding of so much of the complexity that in our lives we for the most part encounter. In mathematics and in the sciences and especially in technology, visual representations do in a useful way simplify, or even sometimes oversimplify, much of what we think of as knowledge and truth. Such mathematical and technical models and frames are perceived as excessively complex. Most of them seem to be intuitively beyond our immediate ability to grasp their linked patterns and complete structures. But so long as we can explore the complexity of them with the rules that generate them we find our trips through them can lead to finding extraordinarily highly complex structural patterns that may be prove useful in mapping our practical applications in the use of them.

But such formal complex models have an underside and a dark side in their uses by the various sciences and technologies when we interpret their technical language interpretations in common sense terms, especially in interpreting the rules used to generate them in ordinary language terms. What is important then to see is how visual representations can like the terms of our language produce false or oversimplified representations of what seem infinitely complex experiences. In the end what we seek is not rational knowledge in our rational linguistic and graphic frames, but knowledge of our ignorance that we are able to discover when we misrepresent our convictions by misrepresentations of measurements and orientations that we introduce in our linguistic and graphic frames in trying to warrant their scientific validity.

Just as we orient ourselves by turning our line of sight around the point on which we stand, so we equally circle in our language finding the right words to make our point. Note that the most stand pat point of orientation for any individual is looking outside from inside. The next individual stand pat point is in the orientation we have of looking straight ahead. We stand fixed on something staring at it that lies out on our horizon that is straight ahead. Such is the act of pointing. It is an act of linear extension. It is the way our noses go. 'Follow your nose. Straight ahead!' But even then we can have no knowledge of our true orientation if we have no knowledge of whatever it is that we see out there outside us that seems to be positioned in front of us straight ahead. And if something is blocking our view such as a hill, a building, or a tree, how is it possible to establish any horizon as a distant line surrounding or circling us that is lying before us straight ahead?

In standing still a horizon nevertheless is necessary to indexing or orienting ourselves to what is straight ahead. And it is looking straight ahead at a point resting on a horizon that is at the very basis of what is thought as our sense of direction when we are standing still on what is assumed to be level or flat surface. Our true orientation or heading is on that line on that presumed level plane moving toward the horizon that we face that is straight ahead. But if a line determines a plane, how do we know the plane we stand on is flat and level? It seems all too arbitrary as lines and planes mutually define each other.

But to have awareness of our orientation or our sense of direction, we also in our orientation need to make comparisons with other directions. And in looking straight ahead without looking around we have no conception of our orientation without reference to what is about us or around us, nor do we have any conception of the other things that are related to what we are directly seeing if we do not turn our head. Consequently, unless we move forward, up or down, or turn on our situated spot we have no sense of direction in reference to anything. We are static or stable on a spot which has no definite referenced location. Note in sports in track we get 'ready, set, go'. Note the multiple uses of the verbs 'set' and 'run' in our English Language Usage. The variety of contexts of their variety of uses indicates that these imperative verbs are a basic psychological frame by which we frame track experiences in running.

Likewise from another point of view when we describe what we see from where we stand just looking straight ahead, we have no conception of what it is that is directly out there in our line of sight. Just as in radar when I stopped the directional line of the radar sweep on a blob of light straight ahead, I had no conception of what it was that was straight ahead unless the sweep of the radar continued to turn and redirect my perspective or orientation back to that seeming static blob of light. When we look ahead to see an object out there while focusing on a point, we are also focusing on our straight ahead orientation.

But note when we change our line of sight from straight ahead to the line of sight that we find when we turn our head towards the direction of our right arm, we have created a new orientation that is a quarter of a turn to the right, or as we will illustrate later that it is a clockwise motion. To do this turn is simply to follow the Drill Sergeant's command, 'Right face!' We turn to the right and then face it. Note the word face is the command, and right is a description of how to execute the command. Commands are a description of what to do and the order to do it!

Thus rotating and facing to the right is an angular rotation which enables us to measure the change of our bodily rotation. Four right turns make for a return to our original line of sight. Angular rotation is simply an alignment of parts of our body with lines of sight. Equally our standing straight and looking down gives us another angular rotation of up and down, which again are rotations that give us balance while looking straight ahead. Note how our ordinary ways of talking about seeing outside, seeing straight ahead, and about our bodily rotation, right and left, up and down help us in ordinary language interpret, and eventually technically help us, to define our orientations and our balance. The following Figure 5.1 indicates how our four turns to the right generates our sense of angular measurement based as they are upon four right turn rotation.

We use our index finger to orient ourselves either to our line of sight facing straight ahead. Or we can use our index finger to point to our right and then we turn to orient ourselves to see our pointed finger now oriented straight ahead that was once oriented to the left. We turn our attention as we turn always to the right, again and again as we keep turning rotating to whatever we want to face. Note that turning around in rotating backwards is two right turns to the right or two left turns to the left.

Note the symmetry in a complete rotation. Rotation is how we measure angles. The sum of four right turns is equal to a single rotation. Turning and pointing are the ways we organize attention on any level plane. And if we lie down on our left side pointing and facing ahead, we can then point with our right arm straight up. We have entered into three dimensions simply by rotating from a stand point either standing or lying on the ground. And if we stand up again after lying down, we can again look up and down, either up and down from our perspective of looking straight ahead. Note we have difficulty looking up when standing up. We get dizzy looking up at sky scrapers.

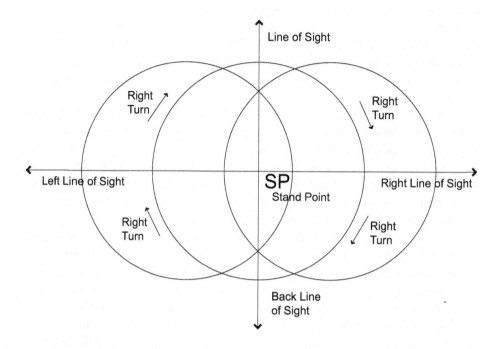

Figure 5.1: Angular rotation

Thus, pointing and turning to our right either lying on our side or standing up frames the whole sphere of our direct attention. But note though we can point and aim and turn around in three directions straight ahead, to the right, and up, we have no biological sense of where we are in space accept for three factors 1) our sense of weight, 2) our balance, and 3) our horizon. We have only a sensuous frame of reference, but no direct indication or any sense of our location. Note that this way of talking about orientation is embedded in the ordinary language that we speak.

But note that this way of speaking can change for those who live at the foot of a mountain who have a mountain as a point of orientation on the horizon. The mountain becomes a point of reference as we turn and rotate in reference to it. How easy it is to know your orientation when you live directly south from a mountain with a sharp peak as a point of reference to determine what is north. It has always been difficult for me to sense the direction of the compass points living in a valley where a mountain has no precise compass direction to be able to orient ourselves in using it. I found this to be the case in State College, Pennsylvania, when I was in school there in the service during World War II. I never quite knew the direction of Mt. Nitany that stands and splits two valleys that merge into one valley at State College. Roughly in my mind the valleys were running towards the southeast. But I had no precise conception of their compass direction.

But note there are other ways of speaking of orientation depending on the language we speak. In aerial gunnery there was a clock orientation language. Planes could be coming in twelve o'clock high or low, three o'clock, or three o'clock high. 'Nine o'clock low, and six o'clock high.' Another language of orientation can be determined by directions of north, east, south, and west, which again like right and left and straight ahead can be the language of a different sort of compass. Note again as previously mentioned that farms in the Midwest were laid out with surveys that drew lines based upon compass headings at the time which varied with local magnetic variations, so what was said to be north was not true north as measured by the directions of the fixed stars that could be determined by the rotation of the celestial sphere.

Thus the fundamental stance we take on orientation depends on the ordinary language meaning for direction that has developed in different contexts depending on the evolution of our language and the location used in talking about orientation. Location always requires a standardized point of reference that is politically defined to determine how we are to conceive angles and distance. In navigation we needed a range and bearing to determine our location relative to an agreed upon fixed external location. Location is always relative to units of angular measurement and to units of length and relative to a precisely agreed upon standardized points of location. But what we point to must be in our line of sight, so what we always see is always bound by what we think of as objects. But again objects are usually described in the language of ordinary usage. When we name specifically defined objects the language we use to name those objects finds its way into the language of our ordinary discourse.

It is this same sort of orientation and focus that we find when we search for words to help us eventually find different words that we need to express any point or schematic representation of order or structure that we want to make. But the same circling we find again in moving through synonyms. We are again shifting perspectives or orientations. It is in a comparable way a ring of synonyms. It is just circling around looking for a term that is expressing our fundamental stand and orientation on the point that we are trying to make.

Consequently all communication is dual, **first finding words to say what we want to say** and **second using those words to say what it is that we want to say**. We circle through meanings and definitions, and we find in those word meanings so as to communicate in a grammatical or propositional fashion that can be schematized into a logical order. Communication thus in its beginnings is circling and searching for terms that will help us say what we want to say in an orderly and schematic fashion within a defined reference grid that defines our orientation. Communication starts with defining what it is that we want to say within that orderly oriented vernacular frame that is derived and interpreted from our personal language that we use to tell others where we stand.

What makes us think that definitions are linear and not circular is that the logical terms in *definitions* appear in our linguistic expressions are *propositional,* that is, their grammar is *sentential.* The fact of the matter is that in interpreting terms we are relating terms that are involved in the definition of what we want to say in a propositional or linear order. But finding words in speaking and writing for what we want to say we need to communicate substantive content. We need to precise the interpretations of the words we use or the terms we use in propositions that we want to reason with. We need to put them into statements or sentences that clarify what we want those words to mean for our listener or reader. Our preparing to do so always involves a preliminary circular activity searching through each other's vocabulary to adjust our orientations to what is said.

In sum communication thus always has a dual purpose:

- To **clarify what we are saying to our audience,**
- And after an agreed upon clarification to **state or make a point propositionally about how we want to relate to that audience in a cooperative manner** in getting things done.

6 Modern and postmodern thinking: rational and interpretive thinking

My air force training in a somewhat bizarre way has also helped me clarify distinctions that I find helpful to simplify the differences in what I see between modern and postmodern thinking about cultural criticism of both the natural sciences and the humanities. It seems very strange and a far-reaching way in discussing cultural issues about social and scientific inquiry to talk of all things *the military*.

It is a strange imaginative leap to make in using military culture and military training as a mode of illustration. And especially it is strange to talk about the social dynamics and the politics of fighting wars as a paradigmatic way of talking about cultural criticism when justice and liberty are inherent in any talk about cultural criticism. To talk about culture in terms of military culture for me is in a way an abhorrent but useful metaphor.

But it is thus sufficient to the wise that analyzing abhorrent things can lead to discoveries of certain forms of wisdom about important distinctions useful to human understanding. Fighting wars with complex technology and the politics of war are indeed complex phenomena that we need to think about in simpler terms and in this case using the dyadic simplicity of polarities I hope to show what seems now to be a great intellectual divide between the sciences and the humanities. And such is the distinction that I find in discussing the dichotomy of modern and postmodern thinking in trying to understand military strategy and military organization.

But to begin any clarification of my remarks on modern and postmodern thinking I need to make a number of clarifying distinctions and explanations just even to begin to see, or even to begin to try, to understand how I can make such an apparent outlandish and farfetched distinction about modernism and postmodernism in connection with military culture.

Modernism as many agree starts with the birth of rationalism in the age of Descartes. It is the general consensus of philosophers that much of modern and contemporary philosophy began with *Descartes Rules for the Direction of the Mind* and his *Meditations*. Rationalism as a philosophical movement starts with the belief in the use of deductive reason in giving scientific explanations, especially as Descartes phrases it, explanations of what is true are necessarily based upon clear and distinct ideas. In a way Descartes was recommending the same thing as I am, a program for reducing what we think of as knowledge into simpler terms based upon clear distinctions about differences, especially about those differences and contrasts we find in the uses of terms in our vernacular languages.

But without going into historical scholarship and into any interpretation of Descartes' writings, I want to generalize about the metaphysical and scientific rationalism that Descartes initiated historically. It has its beginnings among the natural philosophers such as Spinoza and Leibniz in their using the new developing mathematics of the 17th century, and their consequent use systems of axioms to lay the foundation for mathematics and the sciences.

Scientific rationalism as I interpret it is based upon ratios, numerical correlations between factors or variables that we want to use to control the world. People who want power and control over the physical and social factors are in search of invariant correlations. And from them they can deduce *invariant theoretical law like explanations* from their scientific theories, which they then can in turn use to manipulate and control events by using algorithms that express these rational ratios to rationalize the steps in their actions and procedures.

And this is why rational numbers as fractions have been so functionally and so distinctively and uniquely important in mathematics. They are used to express correlations that can be used for the command and control of events. The ideal of rationalism is reason and control through a use of 'the logic of natural deduction' and a systematic application of these deductions in mathematical proof. The strategy we need to deal with complex states of affairs is to develop a formal language to express the necessary and sufficient factors that we need to control events to get certain results. And with that formal language we can then apply our knowledge of correlation by the use of algorithms to make things happen the way we want them to happen.

The language of dealing with complex sets of correlations of fact is best expressed in languages where we can make descriptions of correlations, and even correlations of correlations. We need for command and control a language by which we can express those formal functional connections. To express conjunctively procedures we need a language that can combine sets of correlations in ordered sequences, and then we can embed them into models and into maps or lists of procedures so as to outline the steps in the operations and the controls of devices and equipment we use. And once we have these rational models we can then use them to program our computers to have them do what we want them to do. We can press all those buttons in proper sequence and then pop goes the weasels!

The importance of artificial languages and mathematics is the ability we have in their use to talk about conjunctions, disjunctions, and mathematical functions. We need to talk about them without the distractions that come from the value added distractions that come from the emotive-freighted baggage that we use in our normal talk in ordinary language about morality, power, and politics in the using of our vernacular languages. Science and technology have been made possible by our ability to reason, to formalize, to conceptualize, and to visualize complex functional procedures. They have helped us use all those assembly line operations designed by our efficiency experts and technicians using twentieth century mechanical and electrical engineering to design sequenced causal determinate achievements.

In order to be thoroughly modern we need to devise complex designs, patterned sets of matrices, or flow chart maps of procedures by which we address each step, step by step, one step at a time, so as to manage the mechanical means to arrive at our precisely defined concise sought ends. It is the technical mastery of these formal languages, and the mapping and programming of machines that make our mastery and control in this mechanical world ever so easily and so imminently practically feasible.

The major problem in all complex tasks, as I see it, is to order them correctly and efficiently, and to put them in sequences with chains of causal actions and operational procedures. It all ends up in our using formal languages for designing the templates and models for our sequential programming of tasks. And now we have the computer to program the sequencing of these template tasks in overlay and in overlap in patterned and modeled systems of systematically ordered and sequenced complexity. Given the use of artificial intelligence and computer adaptation, it is thought that there will be no damned end to what we will be able to do in time with the programs in our computers.

What struck me in the air corps is that those responsible for complex sets of procedures were given commissions as officers on the basis of their military occupational specialties, that is, their MOS's. Each of these commissioned air flight MOS's had to master and to follow certain complex procedures that defined the task of each of their military specialties. Mine was 0142.

But what also impressed me was a certain ignorance they all had of the equipment that they operated. They simply in their assignments had to master the procedures of their MOS's. Some of their equipment was, as it was for me, simply black boxes with inputs and outputs. When the equipment failed, you understood only that there was something wrong inside a particular black box that was not working. One learned to use whatever was going on in those black boxes by the use of technical manuals with cartoon like drawings that illustrated and outlined the procedures that were to be followed, such as setting dials, flipping switches, turning knobs, and pushing buttons.

One did not need to have to read very well to follow the pictorial outlined procedures in the equipment manuals to learn their specialty MOS tasks. At times one needed to have the literary skills needed to read comic books to be able to follow some of the steps sketched and outlined in the graphically cartooned, plastic bound, colorful comic like book training manuals that we had.

A commissioned flying officer in the air corps was defined by Standard Operational Procedures, SOP's, which were the use of practical algorithms to do the technical tasks. These practical algorithms were discovered by research scientists in the invariant correlations discovered in the physical science laboratories in universities such as with radar at MIT. These invariant correlations of the sciences were also engineered, controlled, applied, and tested in equipment at the military proving grounds.

And these scientists and engineers employed by the military were for the most part definitely rationalists, definitely modern men, creatures of the scientific enlightenment, definitely modern in seeking knowledge in the ratios of reason that control the functions of things. As children of the Enlightenment they were definitely and paradigmatically, and assuredly and confidently thoroughly modern in their designing technical applications for the task of efficiently killing a lot of people.

Not all situations however I found in my experiences in the military contained the requisite control factors amenable to the use of algorithms. And such complex situations were never reducible to the application of knowledgeable ratios. You may read what you should do in a military handbook on how to handle an infantry platoon, but that would be of little help in trying to tell you how to get along with your men in combat. Men and their deployment require interpretations of character, motive, and contextually interpreted facts that were not amenable, nor fully capable of being assessed and determined by formal analytic procedures. What infantry officers did was not simply reducible to the rules and algorithms that operate equipment with precisely ordered standard operational procedures. When you lead a platoon into combat you need interpretive and critical thinking, which is not reducible to reasoning with formal rules and logical procedures. They need in local situations to be creative in innovating local strategies. In Aristotle's terms their need was for *phronesis* (Flyvbjerg, 2001).

Critical thinking on how to relate to men requires imagination and the grasp of complex gestalts for positional involvements and for the assessments of the abilities of your men in various conflict situations. And in that respect the infantry officer is the postmodern paradigm for understanding certain types of military deployment and tactics.

Despite the fact that high tech weaponry and elaborate algorithmic procedures make infantry platoons killing machines, they today still are led by people needing holistic and macroscopic insights using artifice to create strategies in complicated situations, containing biased and tendentious tendencies. They need intuitions of dispositions and awareness of the contrariness of their men to interpret what is going on around them. They need to survey what is going on in fast changing and revolving complex situations. They are expected to interpret the intent and effort of the enemy in their limited and circumscribed perspective of their operational combat sector.

The infantry officer's task has always been postmodern. His worries are permeated by an indeterminate and an irascible *Angst* that is evidenced by a sinking feeling in the lungs, a burning in the stomach, and a lump in the throat that comes from agonizing about things that might be going awry. The infantry officer does not use algorithms or SOP'S with his problems in dealing with his men and now with women. The infantry officer has to use practical judgment as Aristotle (*phronesis*) described it in determining the mean in situations with lethal extremes. He operates in an existential situation where the best he can do is to interpret enemy intent and imaginatively to devise local strategies necessary to counter any deceptive and imaginative enemy with aggressive or defensive dispositions and intentions.

It struck me in the service that it was much more difficult to be a commissioned officer leading a ground operation than to be a flying officer where you simply needed to act automatically like robots. And as a flying officer, when you are under stress and under fire, all you have to do, as best as you can, is to operate your equipment, and then to ignore all that is happening around you so as to better keep your focus on your immediate operational task at hand. You just needed to follow the necessary procedures to get the complex equipment that you were using to operate maximally and optimally as best as you can under the storm and stress of enemy fire in combat conditions.

But the infantry officer has to be deliberate and be cautious, to know his men, to see their weaknesses, and their strengths of character in order to devise his strategies. We do not judge character, as Aristotle would agree, by theoretical reason with algorithms, but we use practical reason to examine the actions of others, which amounts to a fair amount of common sense and a substantial amount of experiential wisdom (virtue or character) as Aristotle said about dealing with the exigencies of practical action.

What struck me always as a radar bombardier was that programmed robots could do what I was doing in the air corps. I understood that eventually robotic equipment would be designed to perform the procedural coordination of the tasks that I performed between my radar set and the Norden Bombsight that I had to do by communicating over the interphone with the bombardier.

I saw in the rudiments of my use of my own technology in World War II the future course of military bombing technology. I could see that in the years to come my equipment would be merged, re-modified, and computerized to obtain the wherewithal to blow the hell out of everybody and everything. It would turn out to be much more elaborate expensive equipment making possible precise dependable first air strikes, geographically coordinated with missile guided attack systems. The tasks I saw performed by the air flight crew would be increasingly replaced by new equipment, making obsolete the manually described tasks that we performed in applying the data we gathered to operate equipment by algorithmically and mechanically guided check list procedures.

Navigators were becoming obsolete with the introduction of Loran and computers, and especially now that early primitive way of using Loran stations that were fixed entirely on earthly spots is obsolete. It has been translated into new ways of tracking and transponding signals from orbital radio positioning satellites. Radar bombardiers would no longer be needed when the computer functions that were internal to the mechanical computer in the bombsights were introduced into radar circuitry. Flight engineers would not be needed when computers could take over the standard operational procedures for checking all the instruments and the optimal parameters of all the engine gages on the instrument panel. They would soon be replaced when the databases of instruments were introduced directly into computer programs to calculate and give immediate read-outs to pilots about what were once the major concerns of the flight engineers.

More and more the function of pilots would be to master new procedures for mastering many more new and complex automated, mechanical functions in automatic guidance and stability mechanisms in newly integrated computer systems. More and more the pilot was becoming less of a pilot and more and more a standby operator of a self-guided robotic aircraft. The pilot was becoming an oversight specialist, a checker-check-checker and a counter check-check checker of read outs on computers that govern the guidance systems to see whether or not they are functioning properly.

And once such systems transmit their control to the ground, there will be no more need for aircrews in air flight systems. But of course I recognized that there must be someone at times needed to take over when all the equipment is in a complete state of collapse. It is a commonplace lament now to hear merchants helplessly excusing your shopping inconvenience by saying to waiting customers, 'Sorry, our computers are down.'

But nevertheless any operational procedure by an individual in guiding and mastering a mechanical system that is operating under a standard operational procedure will shortly and quickly become obsolete. The old SOP's will be added to an enlarged mechanical system, and the new enlarged mechanical systems will have new operational procedures and new manuals of standard operations. One can easily become obsolete in many jobs defined by operational procedures even in a short matter of months.

And the significant character trait for anyone entering into working with new and evolving technologies is having adaptability in mastering as quickly as possible the newly developed standard operational procedures of the new developing fields or tasks. Adaptability requires flexibility. One can never rest easily in one's job in the use of today's new evolving automated technologies without a malleable and plastic, or an adaptable flexible and obedient psyche.

And now when I reflect back on what I did in the air corps, that now after more than sixty-five years later I too am obsolete. We who performed those tasks are as out of date as the standard operational procedures of the Roman phalanx, just as obsolete as the use of medieval armor, the crossbow, and the long bow. We are just as obsolete as the use of horse cavalry became in the twentieth century. Our intelligent use of the technology of World War II is just simply and totally obsolete, and the skill in using it now is for the most part probably forgotten by all, just as civilization has forgotten all those ancient crafts and skills for using those martial arts of using long and cross bows, ax, hammer, and mace that were used against medieval armor.

And in World War II there were none of those questions asked of those dispensing patriotic cant as do the postmodernists now who ask their leading questions today of our politicians. In World War II there was no one to challenge the hegemonic dominations and arrangements of political and economic power. In World War II the questions were simply being patriotically asked: 'What is one willing to die for?'

As I found out in relating to my fellow soldiers, you were willing to accept death when others were willing to accept death. It was the shame of not facing up to it with your buddies that made you do what you did, even though you knew it was morally wrong about what you were doing. Bravery under fire was accepting the responsibility of doing what others would do in your place. It was not bravery beyond the call of duty, nor was it, as it is now so pleasantly and softly, syllabically phrased today in the media, 'Of putting yourself into harm's way.'

The lesson to be learned from the war is that we do not do politics, nor discuss values, or morals, especially about killing using algorithms. That is in part the lesson of Postmodern Criticism. Our hope for understanding and seeking meaning in social politics ultimately rests solely upon one's interpretive skills. It is a hermeneutic skill. It is not a skill reducible to algorithms.

7 Use of different types of graphic display to interpret meaning

As an introductory step what I will have to say about graphic displays and their uses in interpretation will necessarily be sketchy and not fully elaborated. What I propose to do here is to iron out certain conceptual considerations that are fundamental to any description of how visual representations interact with an extended piece of communication that uses the printed or written word.

My method of approach to these problems is in part that of Ludwig Wittgenstein (1955) that is to be found in his discussion of the use of the expression **'seeing'** and **'seeing as'** as these expressions function in our ways of talking about drawings, and how we talk about the perception of our drawings as they relate to interpretations to be found in a written or printed text. I want not only to deal with some of the issues that Wittgenstein raises about interpretation, and especially about illustration, but I also wish to extend my analysis to some other uses of graphics within the context of a written text that were not dealt with by Wittgenstein in discussing drawings.

Diagrams and pictures in most literature on the subject are treated semantically, that is, as affairs of meaning and reference. Map, charts, and statistical tables usually receive this sort of treatment. In history and criticism of the visual arts again, for example, iconology is a semantic affair (Panofsky, 1955). But my interest here is not in the representational and referential functions of graphics. Rather I am concerned mainly in my analysis with the rhetorical uses other than those of simply conveying information or visually inscribing or embedding data. I am interested in how we interpret graphics, not just only those being directed and constructed by a set of concepts to interpret them in our perception or our vision of our graphic model, but how graphics can interact interpretively together in what we see conceptually in what we find in each of them. Note for instance we use titles of paintings to direct our perception and control the focus of our attention to paintings in our interpretations and appreciations of them (See Yoos, 1966).

But I am also interested in how we use visual and graphic schemata to create our own models and our own construction of new drawings in dealing with things that we imagine and construct within the imagery of our minds. We create drawings in novel ways. That is the aim of creative design. Designs can be ours alone. We not only use conventional models generated by concepts, but we create models to create new conceptual patterns that help us arrange matters in ways that fit our own personal adaptive problems. We innovatively create patterns that enable us to adjust them so as to fit them to what we are doing about personal and practical matters at hand. We design graphic models and render them in ways that they can interact and be open to further interpretation either by using the written word or by using other graphic models and their refinements as architects do to understand or explain their own graphic design creations.

In so far as graphics inserted in texts are a separation from a text that is also inserted within a text, it is of some interest to compare the separations, the disjunctions of material within a written text that have been inserted for makings comparisons and searching for correlations (covariance) within a written text. We use maps, charts, and classifications as systems to explore and discover correspondences and relationships not noticed or imagined before. These separations within written texts range in scope from slightly noticeable asides made to the reader by the author to much larger blocks of written interpretations and explanations. We see them in parenthetical elements and transitional sentences and in the more noticeable separations of text from text that we introduce separately, such as interpolations or making further interpretations using extended quotes or footnotes.

All such separations serve to mark divisions of attention for the reader in a written text that have parallels in the interaction of graphics within graphics. We can divide the triangles that we use to construct another triangle, and we combine those triangles to form quadrilaterals. And we can examine a square inscribed within a circle, and then divide the inscribed square again into triangles, both inside the inscribed square and triangles, with one of the vertices which is a point on an arc of a circle and then compare it all with the others points on the arcs attached to the corners of the square.

This sort of interaction of geometric figures in graphic representations occurs just as well in written texts with separate textual insertions so as to make interpretations even of interpretations within a text. This is illustrated by recent trends in the writing of analytical philosophers, especially in use of the schemata of formal logic to focus attention to the logical forms of arguments in ordinary discourse, and in turn to call attention to the use of logical schemata to interpret the processes of argument that are going on from the perspective of the logic of ordinary language.

It is also worthy of note that graphics and visual aids function quite differently in written discourse from the way they interact with oral discourse. In oral discourse graphics interact to interpret what is being said at the moment within the audience's short term memories. But in written discourse they also interact with the long term memory representation that the writer presumes to be in the reader's memory of what he or she has written about. In contrast to oral discourse in written discourse any interaction with long term memory representation can be short circuited by the reader's ability in referencing to the available text in hand. The reader has simply to reference perceptually to the already available text and to place the referenced material back again in short term memory.

Note too that we may put propositions together by accident, and then find in them logical patterns that relate them to each other, and the result then is that we discover processes that alter our perceptions of their diverse connections by different routes of logical proofs. Note then it is not always determinable whether we discover logical patterns in things that we say, or whether or not we present them deliberately to show or to note connections to others that we already perceive. We discover and show logical implications that we know exist. Whether intentional or not, logical analysis discovers whether or not such patterns actually exist in our perception.

Thus, in contrast to oral discourse graphics and written texts can control attention to what is being said in ways much more precise and in a definite manner. Both graphics and written texts enable us to sustain rigorous attention to the structures within written statements. Both graphics and written texts refresh memory perceptually to overcome the constraints and limits of short term memory. Both enable us to avoid the distortions and omissions about what is being said, which is no more than a strategy to remedy the failures of retention of content in our long term memory.

The mnemonic advantages of graphics and written script make possible the skills of analytic reading that is dominated by a singular focus and scrutiny. It helps us slow down and to avoid the flaws that occur with the hasty scanning that we use sometimes in looking too briefly and without scrutiny at holistic frames of graphs, maps, charts, lists, diagrams, or even looking at algebraic or differential equations. Analytic reading involves making perceptual reversals in perceptual uptake. We see reversals that disrupt the habitual controlled perceptual eye movements going from left to right in English script, and analytic reading equally disrupts and magnifies or reduces the scales and directions established by the coordinates of the reference frames of lists and graphics. Analytic reading thus necessarily involves peering and scanning. Both of which are ways of focusing and refocusing and even as ways of indexing and referencing.

The uses of textual cues and graphics to control attention I call rhetorical. They are just as rhetorical in their use as in controlling attention by the rhetorical use of noting and reminding, which need I point out, is the dominant mode of discourse that I have been using in my own personal style of writing. It is a style that I found in my reading of Wittgenstein. The use of these rhetorical cues that direct attention are of special importance in writing that controls attention to logical operations with data, especially in argument and in certain types of explanations.

Unlike with the reading of narration and description, the reading of argument, reasoning, justification, and the use of causal explanations require constant referencing, checking, crosschecking, and counterchecking to insure that all terms, relationships, and steps have been examined. Critical reading like writing can be hard work. We see these very processes rendered explicit in mathematics and in logic about lines of proof that are rendered fully explicit, enumerated, and even annotated. We see the same processes going on in scholarly commentaries where there is a demand for references to lines of a text such as we find in the almost enumerable number of commentaries that have been made about the reading and the criticism of such works as the Bible, the collected works of Plato, and of Shakespeare.

In order to understand the function of graphics we need to analyze the rhetorical function of language in texts that control the modes of attention of readers to the forms and the structure of arguments and explanations contained within them. In so far as both written texts and graphics are both visual, we need to examine the directions of attention that keeps shifting from one aspect to one aspect or to another. We need to examine the direction of attention as it is governed by factors that direct 'our seeing **of something**', or more interpretively important 'our seeing something **as something**', or as Wittgenstein puts it 'our seeing something **plus a thought**', or again as he says 'seeing something **through an interpretation**' (Wittgenstein, 1958).

Wittgenstein explicates these important distinctions in discussing his illustrations of various illustrations. But before commenting on some of these important distinctions made by Wittgenstein, I wish to make a few distinctions of my own about illustration before analyzing further what Wittgenstein says on these matters. My distinctions in discussing these rhetorical strategies in using pictures, drawings may prove to be helpful in sorting some of the complexity of the rhetorical modes of display that we call *illustration*.

Illustrations function in two general rhetorical ways. First, they clarify or specify what is being described verbally in the text. Second, in contrast to this rhetorical use, the verbal text may clarify or specify what is **to be seen in** the illustrations. In the first case illustrations **illustrate text**. In the second case texts **interpret illustrations**.

When we speak of seeing a diagram, a drawing, or a picture as an illustration, it is not at all clear which way we are seeing it. On many occasions there is an interaction between reading the text and seeing the drawing such that the two functions, to illustrate text and to interpret the illustration, are not clearly thought of as distinct and separate modes of attention. When pictures and verbal descriptions perform similar rhetorical functions in discourse, it is easy to assimilate there different functions in our talking about them.

In other words, illustration not only can be spoken of as a visual strategy, but illustration also describes a developmental strategy in prose composition. For example, we illustrate in words what we are saying with other words. Thus, some of the standard means of illustration are through the use of the old traditional rhetorical modes of narration, example, and analogy. Importantly, illustration of words by words clarifies and explains what we might mean in passages that we are choosing to clarify what it is that is being said in them.

Thus, illustrations in texts provide us with interpretations much in the same manner that we might interpret a graphic through the use of a title or through a written descriptive passage. On the other hand, the illustration (e.g. a case study) may be what is focal in a discussion, and what is noticed in the case study as illustration may be what is descriptively in the passage that makes the case study rhetorically an illustration. Function and object in illustration can easily appear reversed. Two passages thus can mutually interact much in the manner that graphics and text interact mutually to illustrate each other. What is illustration and what is illustrated are thus often nominally confused in this joint reciprocity.

In Figure 7.1 I try to illustrate fully these complex dynamics of illustration: graphic with text, text with text, and graphic with graphic. What is called illustration is nominally relative to the context. If we look on illustration as an act of mediation, Figure 7.1 illustrates this relativity of this act of mediation.

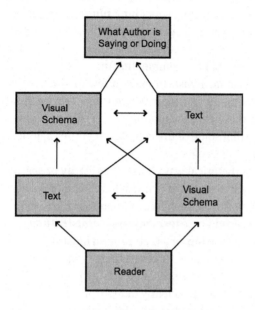

Figure 7.1: Complex Dynamics of Illustration

Now back to Wittgenstein. Note in the following statement in reference to Figure 7.2 found in Wittgenstein's text that Wittgenstein talks about the text as interpreting the illustration and not of the illustration as illustrating the text:

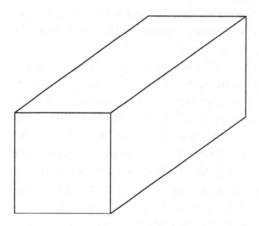

Figure 7.2: Interpretation and Illustration

You could imagine the illustration appearing in several places, in a text book for instance. In the relevant text something is in question every time: here is a glass cube, there and inverted open box, there a wire frame of that shape, or there three boards forming a solid angle. Each time the text supplies the interpretation (*deuten*) of the illustration... But we also see the illustration as one thing, now as another... So we interpret (*deuten*) it, and see it as we interpret (*deuten*) it.

One important issue over interpretation is whether the picture is *eindeutig* or *vieldeutig*. If an illustration lends itself to just one interpretation, we cannot see it other than that way since no other interpretation seems possible. But never can we be certain that alternative interpretations are impossible, so we cannot absolutely rule out the existence of **other possible interpretations** *a priori*.

That we are seeing pictures from the point of view of an interpretation may disappear after a time when there is no suggestion of any other way of interpreting it. Thus, interpretation appears to function primarily in situations where there are alternative interpretations that need to be excluded to see a picture in a certain way. The point of view suggested by the interpretation functions as an intentional way of looking that makes possible the seeing of or the noticing of something as something. Remove the intentional aspects that contribute to the point of view from the act of looking, and the objects are no longer seen **as something**, but they are simply and merely seen **to be something.** In speaking of something as literally there, what we are referring to is something that the description applies to it without the necessity of a mediating act of interpretation, projection, or any act of the creative imagination.

To speak of 'seeing something as something' is one way on the other hand of expressing that there is a change in what is seen. One is saying in this way of speaking that he **sees it** now as X where **before he saw it** as Y. Such changes of aspect do not require an interpretation for Wittgenstein. Wittgenstein speaks of the phenomenon as 'noticing' or the 'dawning' of an aspect rather than a 'continuous' act of seeing. This sort of seeing is illustrated by the duck-rabbit *H-E Kopf.* 'It can be seen as a rabbits head or as a duck's.' Thus, in Figure 7.3 that follows there is no need of an interpretation as in Figure 7.2.

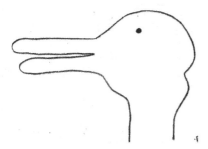

Figure 7.3: Dawning of an Aspect

In Figure 7.2 something more is needed than 'noticing' to see the figure as a glass cube, an inverted box, or as boards forming a solid angle. For Wittgenstein a fertile imagination might do it, but at this point in his remarks it is the written text that does it. In that case the illustrator's intention is usually sufficient to determine how we see the subject. The interpretation of a drawing thus may come from the title or from a verbal description in a text. If these verbalizations enable us to see an abstract drawing now as literally a drawing of the object, then it is puzzling why one would want to speak of the drawing as an interpretation of the subject. Do not the words not just simply name or describe the subject? To see the drawing through an interpretation is to see the drawing **as something** other than the object named in the title or the textual description of it. In such an interpretation we look at the drawing through the interpretation. In either case we look at the subject simply in the drawing. Thus, the viewer takes his point of view not from the drawing, but from the point of view provided by the title or verbal text directing attention to the drawing.

But the important issue for Wittgenstein is that in many cases neither a title nor a verbal description is necessary for noticing the subject of a picture. Neither an inference nor an interpretation is made in noticing that picture is of a given subject. The duck-rabbit in Figure 7.3 exemplifies this sort of seeing or noticing. Wittgenstein's analysis of *seeing something as*, of the dawning of an aspect, or of noticing something reveals to us several of the fundamental operations involved in the use of illustrations.

Turning now from illustration we need to see how graphics and visual schemata give us a different rhetorical mode and a different means of communication that is communicating by indirection. Instead of drawing conclusions for a reader, an author leaves it to the reader to draw his or her own conclusions from what he or she sees in the drawing. Since readers are constrained and limited by the range of possible deductive and inductive inferences that can be made from graphics and visual schemata, the author exercises a measure of control over the case he or she is making to the reader through the use of graphics in communicating.

For example, a map is a schema allowing a reader to make a range of possible deductive inferences using positions, orientation, scales, grids, and certain embedded data such as elevations and so forth. Moreover, maps allow us to make a number of inductive guesses and approximations. If one were arguing, for instance, about the most convenient route for travelling, one might instead of simple outlining alternative routes by making our own verbal recommendations and leave it to the reader to draw his or her own conclusions from the map.

Readers in the same way are thus provided with the means of verifying any claim by using your map. From a judicious combination of your remarks and a map, a reader can form his or her own conclusions by the set of inferences that you may have wished the reader to make, that is, the inferences to the conclusion that you want the reader to accept. Comparably statistical tables and graphs provide readers with the means of making inductive inferences from tabular representations of data, frequencies, and correlations that are sufficient to establish reliable assessments of probabilities. Obviously, in using tables and graphs we use statistical and mathematical computations of correlations which are deductive inferences. But such deductive inferences are auxiliary to the extrapolations of tendencies and projections of correlations that are at the heart of inductive inference.

The weighing of evidence for or against a case that we are trying to make is both holistic and inductive. And in so far as we present charts, tables, and graphs to present a structure or pattern of data, we are controlling the holistic assessments that a reader can possibly make from our presentations of it in graphic or tabular form. The negative side of our rhetorical control of data through graphics is expressed in the phrase 'dammed lies and statistics'. The positive side of our rhetorical control of data through graphics is expressed in the sentence: 'A picture is worth a thousand words.' The rhetorical power of graphic and pictorial representations cannot be understated.

Graphics serve still other rhetorical functions than the three just sketched, that is, illustration, control of deductive inference by the reader by indirection, and control of inductive inferences by the reader by indirection. Graphics also serve to display processes, flow charts, causal connections, classifications, outlined narrative sequences, prescriptive sequences of actions, or algorithms. In addition, they provide us with lists, menus, or options. Graphics perform these functions much in the same manner that these functions can be outlined and described within a written text or in an expository text. But graphics have distinct advantages over written texts in many ways in presenting these descriptions of these complexities that are embodied in graphical representations. Besides providing informational density, they exercise enhanced control over reader attention, perception, and holistic comprehension of the things that you would want the reader to comprehend or understand.

Finally, it needs to be pointed out that a graphic representation need not be auxiliary to a text in communicating. A graphic may itself be the major mode or genre of communication. It is noteworthy that scientific writing, articles, and even dissertations are notoriously briefer than those produced in the humanities. The reason is that the major justifications we have for justifying or relying on hypotheses and theses in the sciences can best be found and discovered or interpreted in mathematical and visual diagrams and schemata. The visual diagrams provide a clearer and perspicuous rendering of what was done in testing a hypothesis than an expository written prose text.

Pictures however at times are merely appendages to the pictorial function of pictures, so a graphic may simply be auxiliary to the message in a textual script. It should be noted, however, that what ought to be focal or primary in discourse, whether it be the written text or the graphic, in the last place analysis should depend on the ends or purposes of a piece of discourse. Graphics in brief are simply more than mere adornments or visual redundancies of written texts. They have many complex communication functions as I have just sketched. They have functions that parallel much of what goes on goes on within and in texts. To treat graphics simplistically and reductively is mistaken. To my mind at least that is the message I have derived from Wittgenstein!

8 Stasis, observation, and facts

A very long time ago I descended into the lower school in a private school when I was principal to substitute for a seventh grade teacher. I had in previous years taught high school science in the upper school. Needing to improvise as I had no lesson plans I thought it best to start a general discussion about science with the class. To stir them up a little I raised the question about the differences between facts and theories. I almost started a class rebellion among those bright little charges when I said to provoke them that it was not a fact that the moon circled the earth.

Every last one of them insisted that I was wrong. It was a statement that countered everything that they had come to learn and believe from the popular astronomy that saturated their everyday pop culture with its Copernican view that the sun was the center of the solar system and that moons circled planets. All statements about these matters were considered by them to be statements of fact. And how, oh how now do so many people think as those young students thought that science is all about facts, and that teachers create tests to measure the extent of student knowledge of a pile of rote learned scientific facts?

How much is the public bamboozled into thinking that some seemingly warranted scientifically conjectures, theories, many scientific concepts are simply facts. Our accepted scientific theories are considered to be simply facts. But how many of these theories turn out to be useful but glorified fictions? Ironically, what I was saying to those students sounded very much like that famous papal contention between the pope and Galileo where the papal view was that it was not a fact but a theory that the sun was the center of the universe. Obviously now the pope at the time was right as no astronomer now that I am aware of considers the sun as standing still in the center of the universe.

The sun moves around the galaxy of the Milky Way. And the Milky Way is going I know not where and in what directions, for directions seem to make no sense when things are moving without any fixed point of reference or point of stability to know exactly in which they are going. But where then in all this commotion going on in the heavens if there is no center? From our everyday perspective now we are now feeling comfortably sitting or standing on a fixed point on the earth within the solar system with the stars and galaxies all about us. At least that perspective gives us our useful everyday sense of stability.

To get those students to start thinking I tried to convince those young boys, as it was the Harvard School for Boys, that when we observe facts we see them happening. They are to be found in our witnessing of events, and that they are found in our observations of things from the position where we stand. They are about events and objects in certain perspectives. They are about the things that we see happening. They are things that get done. But to the contrary what we see as facts in our view of the heavens as I pointed out to them is not the moon circling the earth. The statement that the moon circles the earth is a theory used to explain certain facts, but that point of view of seeing the path of the moon is not actually an observable fact. We do not see exactly what is happening, but can only surmise through hypotheses or conjectures what is possibly happening.

This little incident with students happened many years before the astronauts first landed on the moon. It is interesting to examine what the astronauts saw when they landed on the moon. What the astronauts had to say of what moved in the heavens I have found in my reading has been far too sparse, and what they had to say was not based upon accurately measured descriptions. From the moon the earth, unlike our moon that moves across the sky, displays its rotation while the moon that we see does not rotate as we see it moving across the earth sky. We do not see the moon visibly rotating. We see mostly just one side.

Observation of the sun and the earth on the moon is much the same sort of thing as observations of the sun and the moon on the earth. But they vary depending upon what one sees from different stand points and different places. Just as what we observe of the movements of the moon across the sky at various times and places depends on our geographical locations, we should then expect the same sort of variations of what goes on in the sky to be seen differently from various locations on the lunar landscape.

Note also that what the moon astronauts were also seeing is what astronomers do when they are observing the units of measurements on the instruments that they were using in measuring what they are observing on the moon. There is a radical difference between seeing the qualitative facts and the facts of the measurement that we see recorded on our measuring instruments. Traditionally on earth we used the astrolabe and sextant and a chronometer to make our measurements.

However, in discussing with my students about what we see of the moon in the sky I avoided all talk about making any measurements about movements of the moon. I was simply playing games with them semantically and with the paradoxes of what it means to 'go around' (Yoos, 2009). To illustrate ambiguity I often use that famous paradox discussed by William James about a squirrel going around a tree. Note that what I was doing to the young charges, besides making them think, was proposing to them new ways of talking about what we begin to understand when we propose different technically defined definitions about what are 'facts' and what are 'theories'. I had been in my own teaching of high school science using these very same defined distinctions to help clarify concepts in classes. I did that to make my high school students fully aware of the confusions we get into when we think of certain theories as facts. There arises a great disconnect in ordinary English when we want to say that scientific laws or principles are the true facts about the world.

What I illustrated to my high school students is that in one way of talking, we establish facts in one way directly by the senses and that we use them to warrant our theories quite differently. Theories I indicated are more like **conjectures** that need not be exactly accurate or exactly true. A *conjecture* or an *assumption* in one sense of either of these two terms is simply a hypothesis about which we can never be absolutely certain about, especially when there are ambiguities and vagueness in the statements of theory that make them confusing about the accuracy and truth of what is being conjectured about.

But then to confirm my view to the elementary students that the moon does not in fact circle the earth I attempted to show them that the earth and the moon's orbit with reference to the sun was not exactly a circle, and that earth and the moon were constantly chasing each other in their orbits and that those orbits were not simply and unambiguously a circle, but that both the earth and the moon were said to be rotating together travelling along together in separate ellipses around the sun, both seeming going around the sun whirling, paired together in a constant rotation in a state of equilibrium in the same direction.

And then I tried to show them from that one point of view that the elliptical orbits of the earth and the moon together were undulating curves just moving up and down along interacting changing paths going after and chasing each other around the sun. And then I explained that their movements were attracting each other by gravitation, and that they were actually chasing each other as they moved away from each other, each swerving in orbits that escaped centripetally the path of the other. Moving along the earth and moon in their solar elliptical orbits they were not simply circling but chasing each other as they moved in their orbits around the sun.

What I pointed out, to make my point, was the ambiguity of what we were considering to be a fact, that a *fact* in one sense of the term is what we actually observe to be a fact, what happens, and when we watch the moon we observe certain facts about its movement. What we see as a fact is that the moon circles the earth from our perspective where we are **standing still** and that the moon moves over us from the eastern to the western horizon. And that same so called fact was equally thought to be true in the old Ptolemaic theory in Greek astronomy. The moon circled the earth across the sky very much like the sun. And then I showed them that what was being said about the sun and moon circling the earth depended on what we see from the very place where we stand. Movement as we perceive it is always relative to a stationary perspective. It is all about being static or being in stasis.

Then I tried to explain to them that an explanation or theory depends upon our interpretations of the facts, but many of us think that those statements that logically follow from our theories thought to be true have to be facts. But theories are not facts but conjectures about what happens from certain points of view. What we would see if we were located somewhere else in space where we could observe what follows from our logical interpretations of our theories would then be observed as facts. I suggested to them that theories are about supposed or conjectured facts, that they are not statements about the facts themselves. I was thus proposing to them a different way of thinking that cleared away some of the confusions about the difference between what it is to be considered to be a fact and a theory in ordinary ways of speaking. Theories in this redefined sense are conjectures about what is thought to be true. They are about things we do not directly observe, and our thinking that they are true ultimately depends upon our interpretation of our observations that the theory tries to explain.

Given time if I had been their teacher I could have shown them that the view of the solar system from the view point of Copernican astronomy, which if true, presupposes that the solar system is supposedly in stable equilibrium, either in stasis or standing still. But again to repeat if the sun is moving around the center of the Milky Way, and the Milky Way is moving with respect of the galaxies, where is there any place for an observation of facts of the sort where we could see what is moving and with reference to what? Or to put it in different words, if we want a stable perspective of the universe where would we need to stand? Note that the theory of an expanding universe is a theory that takes the perspective of the earth as the stable center of these measureable expansions that are implied by the red shift in the light spectrums coming from the stars. Note that to say that everything is expanding away from everything is not an observable fact, but a theory that seems to be a theory thought true by astronomical cosmologists in their interpreting the differences in red shifts measurements in the light spectrum that appears to be coming from galaxies.

In discussing astronomical questions about facts and theories we seem to be left only with our quest for stability. We as human beings are seeking a place to stand that defines our own sense of stability as a reference point for making all the other measurable orientations between different things that seem coherently related. Man in that sense is the measure of all things. What seems required is a standpoint for measurement that provides an accurate description of the ultimate changes that seems to be occurring. But that leads to all sorts of messy conceptions of space and time.

If my contention is right, it is not the complexity out there in the world that confuses us, it is the messiness that we have in theories or models that we use to describe what seems to be a random sort of messiness in the universe with no actual boundaries and that has no order. But what actually is messy is the messiness of the mathematical models that we are using to describe the messiness of the facts that we see. What leads to messy contentions about which way the moon moves comes from the inconsistencies found in our formal systems that we use to model what seem us to be correct explanations or theories.

When we talk about the formal inconsistencies of our scientific theories, especially when we try to find a model that contains infinite changing directions and infinite extensions, nothing seems bounded or referenced to a standpoint in them whereby we can build a model or theory that encompasses everything, that is, 'a theory of everything'. In other words, to have a theory that explains 'everything' requires an absolute consideration of all the facts and that those facts are what they purport to be such as the way we observe the moon circling above through the skies that only circles around us from the factual standpoint we have in looking up at it as it traverses the sky.

Note that in looking up in tilting my head it is difficult to maintain stable equilibrium. But note too what happens when I observe things when I am having vertigo. What are the facts that I observe directly when one's horizon is spinning?

What we observe as facts is changing in vertigo from what I observe when I am standing tall and visually stable. Changes in equilibriums, changes of the balances of things around something static, is one way then to measure change.

But the changes we see are also ways that we have of determining our references to things. If I lose my balance I try to stabilize myself by trying to stand up. In starting to fall down I have lost my equilibrium. In its physical descriptions my body in falling down is changing from a stable equilibrium of standing tall into a dynamic equilibrium of being a falling object that no longer is in equilibrium with the gravitational pull of the earth. To regain my feet I either push myself back up, or in my old age someone needs to help me to stand back up again. And if I have a walker I might pull myself up to get back up on my feet. The key to regaining stability or regaining a stable dynamic equilibrium is some sort of **feedback** to regain my equilibrium or stability. You choose the world to describe my stability. *Stasis* is a fancy word for it. Note that observation starts from what we think of as a static or in a set position.

It is obvious in studying mechanics in physics that our models of statics and dynamics interrelate when something is moving. In one way in physics we can study statics as a discipline separately, and in another way we can study dynamics separately. But something moving also can be in stasis or in a stable equilibrium. Feedback is the way we have of maintaining stable equilibrium and of preventing change, or it is the way we have of re-establishing and putting something again back into a stable equilibrium as in dynamics.

In politics the stable equilibrium of economic and legal systems is a view often labeled 'conservatism'. It is a view that in standing tall we never need to move from where we are. We are set in our ways about who we are. What is striking about life are the feed backs that are controlling and monitoring, and that are structured by sensory devices that maintain the equilibriums especially within the cell walls of living things. These walls or membranes allow the passage of what is needed from the outside to bring it into the inside to maintain the equilibriums existing within the enclosures or within the membranes that protect the organisms.

But from another point of view, from the view of those who devise devices to maintain types of **mechanical equilibriums,** we see that these mechanical models are varied and differ in many ways from the models that we make of those **homeostatic creatures** that are said to be alive. Mechanical devices have been produced by artifice, by human ingenuity. They have been devised by an intelligence that simplifies a variety of tasks that maintain different material states of equilibrium. Key then to this sort of designing and engineering of these mechanical types of equilibriums are the construction of technical devices that significantly differ in structure and form from what is monitoring and is going on within those cells that are governing what we think of as life.

It is these models and devices that we think of as machines that are at the heart of science and technology that manages and maintains these mechanisms. For example, we use mechanical electrical devices to create our external environment. They help us create environments within our buildings, or they manage and maintain our flows of transportation or our distribution of electricity. They possess external monitors that regulate feedback to maintain stasis in our external environments. All such stabilizing devices are based upon devices designed by human engineering. They are artifices. They all have feedback systems that are engineered creatively. But to what degree are the forms of life monitored within and not imposed and controlled from the artificers from on the outside?

My first awareness of feedback and equilibrium dawned on me at the age of nine. We lived by the railroad tracks watching the steam engines go by one after the other. My uncles and my dad with whom I lived at the time had all worked around the round houses serving two different railroads around Centralia, Illinois. It was a railroad town. But at that time I had not the good sense to ask them how those steam engines worked. Still I was curious about why all that huffing and puffing of steam that made those drive wheels turn that were pulling all those long and heavy freights and all those fast passenger trains that were flying by night and day on the Illinois Central. I watched those large cylinders connected to those drive shafts. And suddenly to my amazement I noted how that long shaft reversed itself and moved in the opposite direction to redirect the steam in the opposite direction to make the pistons reciprocate back and forth. It was my first sense of feedback and about what a governor is. It governs. But the governing was external to the engine. It regulated steam flow. It was an artificial mechanical invention.

Suddenly it occurred to me that I understood the function of what is now called a camshaft that reverses the direction of the exhaust and the steam, thus resulting in the huffing and puffing noise that was coming from the exhaust of those steam engines. In my youthful imagination I had found to my surprise that I had figured out how to design a steam engine. In my imagination I came to understand an example of a simple device used for reciprocating feedback that kept the train in moving in dynamic equilibrium. And if the engineer wanted more speed, he would release more steam into the cylinders with his throttle and the drive shaft fixed to the wheel would drive those wheels faster as the engine accelerated forward. And to maintain that dynamic equilibrium there was the governor. A spinning set of balls whirling in a circle that regulated the amount of steam that was flowing into those cylinders. It was a mechanical accelerator that allowed the train to speed up and then with the throttle adjusted to hold those rotations at a constant pace, thus maintaining and regulating the equilibrium of the train at a constant velocity.

And later in life before World War II in the dirtiest job I have ever had, I discovered all those intricate soot covered mechanisms that were used to regulate all the various steam engine drivers that regulated the steam pressures, that regulated the air valves on the brakes, and kept that steam engine in various states of equilibrium as it maintained its speed and direction in dynamic equilibrium running down the rail road tracks. And still later in the war I found a much cleaner kind of equilibrium using comparable feedback technology in the air planes in which I flew. Those old bombers were complicated combinations of feedback and backup systems. There I found all those devices that maintained equilibrium that when they were thrown out of equilibrium had to have all those various forms of feedback systems to restore again the flight of those planes to an original stable state of directional equilibrium.

Let me just list of few of those devices: there were Wheatstone bridges and gyros in the autopilots that stabilized the equilibrium of the flight control systems, there were gyros and magnetometers in the compass system, there were oscillators in the radio transmitters and their receivers in our communications systems, and there were oscillators in our radar systems and in our Loran. There were camshafts, carburetors, and distributers regulating different feedback devices in monitoring the engine and prop speeds. And we had pressurized cabins in B-29's that had thermostats and pressure stats that maintained the temperature and pressures in the cabins. And there were automatic feedback systems in the gunnery in the central fire controlled systems. And the optical bombsights were just one complicated set of electrical motors that automated the equilibrium of the bomb sighting that was in turn integrated with the bomb release systems with their timing circuits. Such was my early practical education I had in equilibrium models that explained what was going around me in those monstrous bomb truck carrying vehicles. They were human inventions, artifices that were not a product of biological evolution, but they were designed to kill thousands of people in the name of peace and the hope of a return to normalcy in our society, that is, to return to some sort of stable peaceful equilibrium that never really happened.

The intelligence and ingenuity of designing and testing all those mechanical systems were developed for warfare by the study of prototype models that were a product of the study of military testing and proving grounds. Some of it worked better than expected. But at the time the radar aiming devices were something only practicably applicable. They were designed not for precision bombing as the radar antennae had no vertical stability, and the radar ground returns had no precise definition of the targets. The radar returns were only shifting unstable and large globs of light that gave no accuracy. What were always at issue were their reliability and the overcoming of the imprecision with which these devices regulated the equilibrium needed for the force vectors behind and under the plane to go to where it was aimed and to do what it was supposed to do, and when it got there to dump their fire and demolition bombs on open cities to burn and bomb the hell out of homes and kill helpless people.

In many ways machines act in many ways in the same ways as biological organisms and that raises, as mentioned, the issue discussed whether or not these patterns of these biological functions were as law like just as physicists thought about the motions and the feedbacks of our mechanical mechanisms. Is there something inherently determinate and law like in the nature of beasts just like that which seems to govern machines? Or is it that these patterns used in our machines are just useful in the way as they help us organize our actions in the ways we have of designing machines, testing them, and in using them? In other words are our equilibrium theories about machines are only comparable but they are not the same as our models of human action based upon the functions of human bodies? But nevertheless we do create machines to simplify and help us order and govern our human actions in dealing with the various problems that we have to solve in getting things done.

It has been my contention that instead of thinking of models as representations of things or law like structures in the state of nature as equally the same as the processes of human life, we should look at models first as guides and prototypes by which we exercise command and control in dealing with the problems of life. And it is worth noting that, as we devise these models of human life processes to understand them, that these models in turn become more and more complicated. And using much more complicated models in order to understand life we need in turn to simplify our ways of understanding them so as to discover how we can best use them in ways that make our uses of them less complicated in explaining life functions.

When our schemes and models are too complicated as seems to be the case with life processes for any direct and holistic understanding of them, we need to thread our way through their complexities using the logic and the rules of the ways we have of constructing these models to see how we can in a much simpler fashion interpret our schematic models of life. Especially we need to see whether or not we can interpret them in such a way so as to apply them in economic and efficient ways of making life functions much healthier in living out of our lives.

But in the quest for such simplifications, the problem with using models for both mechanical machines and living processes is that they can be over simplistic, and when over simplified they have only limited applications. On the other hand, as these models become less simplistic they require modes of interpretation that are more and more complicated. And as we try to explain further their complications more and more complications are added to them again and again. When that happens we need again to see these complications in these increasingly complex frames again in simpler terms to better understand them.

To illustrate the problems of thinking about complexity, chess is an interesting model of how we need in overcoming the constraints of memory and our use of chess-clock time to deal with these problem solving issues. Note that chess players do not simply calculate on the basis of the rules that generate the possible configurations of the game and then test them by their calculations using the formation and transformational rules of chess. That task would not be humanly possible within the limitations of human attention and the constraints on human short and long term memory. Even a computer does not have power to make such complicated calculations by simply using the rules of chess (Simon, 1979: 363-403).

Rather the skillful chess player simplifies his conception of play by learning strategies for beginning moves that are simpler and easier to define, and then after the game progresses they learn new strategies to use in the middle game where complications cannot be simply understood except by knowing which different configurations lead to which variations and the complications that develop out of original opening lines of play. Original lines of play hopefully are thought to lead to a set of favorable positions in the end game. It is in the middle of the game that mistakes are usually made as the positions are too complicated to be solved by any set of algorithmic strategic rules. It is at this point of the game that improvisation and difficult calculations have to be made to arrive at desired positions for an end game.

When a game of chess begins to deviate from known opening theories in chess, the players are said to be 'out of book'. In some opening lines the moves considered best for both sides have been worked out for ten to fifteen moves or more. Some analysis goes to thirty or thirty-five moves, as in the classical King's Indian Defense and the variations of the Sicilian Defense. And it is the end game that is aimed at in their studying and exploring the various lines of play that develops in the complexity from the original lines of play. In chess the complications of the endgame are much easier to master as the complexity has been reduced. And since chess must be constrained not only by the structure and pattern of the board, but chess games are constrained when playing in competition by the rules defining the time constraints that alter the possibilities of different strategies in using chess-clock time efficiently to do different calculations.

The need for simplicity in chess strategy is a result of the chess player's limits of memory and the limits of their personal abilities to calculate. Chess as a model illustrates well how there is a need to simplify in order to understand complexity and to predict results. Chess like all complex models needs simplification of our ways of dealing with complexity that again and again require more and more complicated models to deal with the complexity that we do not understand in using the beginning models of lines of play that we have used that are leading us into difficulties.

But the problem then of using simple models is that they mislead us eventually in how we interpret and misunderstand them. In my youth my concept of a bridge was a straight mantel across two pillars. But when I with other kids tried to build a bridge out of oil well cables, we made the mistake of tightening them in a straight line up high between two huge trees. Our bridge that we constructed and built with stretched tight straight line cables between two trees used as our static pillars was a total disaster. What happened is that we were actually using a model of a long or cross bow. We found to our despair that when the clamps that we used to tighten the cables to the opposite trees in a straight line surprisingly slipped, and the kids working on our cable bridge shot up like arrows into the air. We did not recognize that the model we were using was not one for building a suspension bridge, but it was that of a bow that stretches and releases its arrows from a taught string. Using a wrong model we created a disaster. What we believed as the proper way to build a bridge was false. We found knowledge and truth in our mistake.

And that has been a pattern that has often occurred in failures in the history of science. The model of heat as a fluid with negative weight failed to predict. The model of electricity as a positive charge fluid failed to predict. The model of Newton's mechanics did not predict the behavior of nuclear particles. And the model of light as corpuscles failed to predict interference effects of light. But despite these deficiencies in these models, though they are now discounted as theories, they still have turned out to have practical usefulness in certain limited contexts as many of these old models are still used in many technical applications.

What we know now as a result is that models though faulty are still useful in doing certain sorts of things, but they were not useful in telling us how to do certain other things. We know they have false applications. We know that many of their implications are false. That they are false is demonstrably so, and what they are false about has definitely become knowledge. When we work with testable hypotheses about empirical generalizations that we make from observations, we attempt to weigh the evidence that seems to support such generalizations. But that awareness of repetitive events never allows us to prove anything with certainty.

9 The apparent realism of naïve realism
How really naïve is naïve realism?

What I have been maintaining then is that our models, frames, logical and mathematical formulations about structure and our drawings and frames in the sciences and technologies are always originally created and interpreted technically by proposals that start by using terms from our ordinary language. We seem enamored by the wonderful complexity of our scientific models and we feel much the same with the enormous developments in mathematics that underlines them. We are so enamored and in awe of so much of it that many think that this complexity can only be intuitively grasped and understood from some notion of preexisting mental conditions from eternal forms such as we find in the writing of Plato and Aristotle. Some want to maintain that they are creations of the gods and that they are not a product of human artifice and construction.

I take this Platonic position of forms and essences and its philosophical jargon to be what is called 'ontological realism'. This view of eternal forms is to be contrasted with empirical pursuits of knowing where the basic features of reality are to be discovered in and through the sciences, especially in physics and astronomy, where the cognitive aim is to know about stuff and its patterns and arrangement and how it actually is spread out across the universe. The philosophical jargon for this rational quest for the structure of being that is sought in what is external to us through the senses is called 'epistemic realism'. Ontological realism posits forms as an object of thinking. Epistemic realism posits forms as an object of perception through the senses.

Sometimes the ideal modeled constructions of being and its structures seem so beautiful and elegant that we think that their beauty is truth, and their truth beauty, and that all that you need to know are the first principle that determined what is *actually, ultimately* and an *absolutely* real. Note the above strings of intensifying adverbs *actually, ultimately,* and *absolutely* seem to add nothing more of reality to anything of which we speak than when we simply speak of something as simply just real. But yet metaphysicians have maintained that there are different realms of being in the one and only singular universal being. Or again they often speak of reality where some things are more real than other things that are also thought to be real. Note some speak of degrees of reality as if whatever is real can be real as a matter of degree. It is by such play on the grammar of the term 'real', using it as a comparative adjective in characterizing multiple-categories and multiple-orders and rankings that some are able to create a plurality of different realities.

Realists thus in speaking of what is real comparatively are able to multiply the number of the levels of different forms of being as for example the 31 realms of being that are to be found in one version of Buddhist cosmology. Historically it has been no wonder that so many magical religious myths have gotten themselves entangled into such metaphysical speculations about the ground and structure of **Being** or in what is ultimately called the highest reality '**The One**'. They seem in their religious quest interested in what is essentially prior even to God. It is in this quest for ultimate foundations for truth that dominates those who seek God by such faith in their traditional religious myths.

Note how thoughts of cosmology require conceptions of ontology and *visa versa*. As technically defined 'ontology' and 'cosmology' are correlative terms used and interpreted in speculative philosophy about realistic philosophical world views. It is an amazing speculative circle for metaphysicians to bounce between the two terms *ontos* and *cosmos*, and now we even find physicists and astronomers engaged in the same sort of semantic quest in determining which term is the more positive one in defining the other. We find it in their speculating about different levels of being and different levels of reality, and in speculating about the reality of possible worlds and in their speculating about the structure of the world. The basic question for them becomes whether *ontos* or *comos* is the prior term? But when we recognize that the interpretations we make of these models and systems of ultimate entities and their arrangement all have their origins in human artifice and that these conventionally constructed ontologies and cosmologies are very much like many of the verbal semantic games that we play. But however in the game of metaphysics there are no rules to play it as is the case with chess. I found in my experiences with the Metaphysical Society that there were no rules in doing metaphysics.

Chess unlike metaphysical games is a recognized sport defined by the International Olympic Committee. International chess competition is sanctioned by the Fédération Internationale des **Échecs** or World Chess Federation (FIDE). It is an international organization that connects the various national chess federations around the world and acts as the governing body of international chess competition. Chess is a rule governed game made up on earth and not in heaven. There is no chess then played in heaven! And given the nature and structure of the reality that is being sought there also are no philosophers are metaphysicians in heaven. As Whitehead joked, 'The pleasures of philosophy are denied to deity.'

We need to recognize that our ways of dealing with our problems with the world in everyday life are limited by the personal artificial frames of reference that we innovatively construct to deal with the problems of life. It is those things that we speak of in our everyday encounters with each other that are for the most part what we think of as real and fully by consensus are considered to be what is real for us. Noteworthy it is this ground in consensus about what is real that we use in our imaginations when we venture into the abstractions of formal systems. It is this consensus about common sense reality that we use to construct elements in our formal systems as we move away from everyday observations and to terms that we use to talk about the product of these speculations.

The simple descriptions we have of our ways of dealing with the world are for the most part basically simply rules of thumb that we use to guide us as we thread our ways through the games and frames that we create to manage the existential complexity of tensions and conflicts that we do not fully understand. These rules of thumb are just pragmatic ways that we use to live by. They are framed and interpreted and defined by the ordinary language in which we speak.

They are in turn limited in their uses by the constraints of our vernacular language in the ways that we have in using it. What I found striking in the work of Herbert Simon, *Administrative Behavior: Study of the Decision-Making Processes in Administrative Organizations* that in his treating organizational behavior at the time of his writing his first edition that the so called experts in speaking of 'administrative principles', so he maintained, there 'administrative principles' were very much like proverbs. To quote him he says:

> It is a fatal defect of the current principles of administration that, like proverbs, they occur in pairs. For almost every principle one can find an equally plausible and acceptable contradictory principle. Although the two principles of the pair will lead to exactly opposite organizational recommendations, there is nothing in the theory to indicate which is the proper one to apply. To substantiate this criticism, it is necessary to examine briefly some of the leading principles. (1997: 29)

At this point in Simon's text, he goes on to examine four principles that occur in the literature of administration.

Proverbs are then very much like rules of thumb. They function much like algorithms in stating rules that we should act by in certain contexts and cultural situations. Like moral maxims they tell us what to do in practical actions. Whether we speak of **actions** or **behaviors,** they are in the ordinary ways of speaking very much the same thing. But note that the nominal difference of the use of the terms *action* and *behavior* as synonyms. This difference is extremely important to note in talking about human action. Especially this has been the case in the history of psychology where it has been unfortunate that Behaviorism especially that of the B. F. Skinner variety wants to reduce all human actions to human behaviors.

This behavioral way of describing human responses reduces human actions to external descriptions of how human beings act without any considerations about what is related to what is going on that is internal to human beings. Such a behavioral way of describing human actions rules out talk about actions, such as, those involving planning, making decisions, and actions described as thought or thinking. Such a description of human action in terms of behavior as found in Skinner consequently eschews all theory and reduces psychology to a model of inputs and outputs of black boxes. It ends up treating rewards and punishments in terms of reinforcement, positive or negative, of whatever it is that is going on in those black boxes with no intervening variables happily, loudly singing inner thoughts and feelings in between the inputs and outputs.

Simon in his work on administration is all about exposing the limitations of the decision making going on within an organization with a hierarchical structure of command and control wedded together with a rational and an efficient organization of tasks. His work is a study of the limitations of rational control and the limitations of communications that goes on between the various levels of such institutions as corporations or bureaucracies. But what is at issue in Simon's conception of public and private bureaucratic organizations is his realist ways of studying the structure and functions of these organizations. His conceptions of modeling are brought into question in his discussions of modeling in that he interprets these descriptions in terms of ordinary vernacular discourse that varies with different cultures, such as in the different cultures of business, government, science, and technology. He is confronted with the limitations of describing and interpreting the implications of the models that he brings to bear on his own discussion of the way he builds his own theory of administrative organizations.

These limitations in how we use different vernacular languages were recently discussed in an article in the *New York Times* by Guy Deutcher (2010), who maintains the linguistic thesis that the world looks different in other languages, and to express his point he quotes from the linguist, Roman Jakobson, the maxim, 'Languages differ essentially in what they *must* convey, and not in what they *may* convey.' And Deutcher goes on to say in the article, 'This maxim offers us the key to unlocking the real force of the mother tongue: if different languages influence our minds in different ways, this is not because of what our language *allows* us to think but rather because of what it habitually *obliges* us to think *about*.'

He illustrates his point by showing the constraints that gender has in certain languages of obliging us to reveal information about the sex of your companion. Or again he illustrates the different way a remote Australian aboriginal tongue, Guugu Yimithrirr, expresses orientation in small scale spaces that is built into their language not by left or right orientations, but by geographic directions based upon geographic directions such as north, east, south, and west. East is right, and west is left, and the two ways of using languages interfere in expressing orientations only when we have to check out the orientations in the aboriginal tongue when we reorient ourselves to these headings that had been determined by local map makers. Note in tropical latitudes east is where the sun rises. West is where the sun sets.

Much of the worldly wisdom about orientation we find to be over simplistic about the proper working conceptions that we have when our thinking confronts any new problematic complexity such as was found in the basic means and needs of the expertise that is needed in surveying. It is only by processes of simplification that we interpret the complexities of these complex models and the frames created by surveyors that developed much of our local talk about orientation of the local world that we think we know.

In my youth I lived along a street that I always thought ran north and south. It is only recently I put two and two together and recognized that a street farther to the north did not run parallel to it that was originally laid out on a north and south surveyed grid. When you fly over the Middle West the straight lines you see running supposedly north and south were laid out when they were first surveyed by magnetic compasses. Magnetic variation at the time of those original surveys was not truly north and south as would be the basis of a grid whose orientation towards the north is laid out or defined by its relation to the celestial sphere. Where I lived the first few streets were laid out parallel to the direction of the railroad tracks which was north by east.

And it is this simplicity of our ordinary ways of speaking that deceives us about the general application of some of our everyday rules of thumb, proverbs, aphorisms, and simple stories that we live by everyday. When we define technical language and the formal logical and mathematical systems and when we use them, we for the most part forget their origins in the language of everyday speech. In French Poststructuralist jargon the memory of those origins is spoken of as 'eclipsed'. There is a cultural forgetting of the origins of our sense and meaning of terms. It is that original source of meaning which is eclipsed. And too besides this forgetting, we need especially to recognize the pluralism of these multiple frames of reference and the inconsistencies that develop within these maxims or rules in our uses of them. They are in their expression context dependent and in their pluralism independent of the old contexts that were once used.

We are always limited in using conventional wisdom by the fact that our limited and finite perspective on complexity has been limited by the very biological, social, and political limits that constrain and restrict our wisdom. These limitations which constrain us have been introduced into the use of our vernacular languages at the time of the emergent origin of language in biological evolution of which we have no historical awareness. It was at the time of first language use and usage that we originally defined our human condition in our personal relationships to our culturally conditioned conceptions of space and time that have as a result immersed us in the consequent developments that evolved within our language.

But despite the sufficing utilities that we have in dealing with individual situations using general maxims, we need necessarily to expand and work on our difficulties and problems in using them. We need to develop different frames of conventional construction to articulate and calculate new solutions by maximizing and optimizing certain features in the models of logic, science, and math that we have developed to help us clarify and resolve our problems in using our practical maxims and rules, such as used in counting, ordering, and in determining orientation.

We learn to reinterpret our maxims and rules when we use our newly developed complex models in imaginative ways that are in a way reduced and reconstructed in much simpler terms in our using them. We learn to use mathematical and graphic models in ways that enable us to transcend our limitations in apprehending the complexity that occurs when we confine ourselves to the limits established by our ordinary ways of talking. We can by creating new models and new schemata together with new forms of language with new terms learn to rise above these bounded ordinary language limitations that we have in being situated as we are in our common everyday language usage, for that usage which we have come to understand is subject to evolutionary change when its inadequacy is recognized and exposed. It is at that point that our language use and usage moves on.

When we encounter these limits to our understanding in these models and schemata it is our imaginative use of them that helps us escape many of the inconsistencies to be found in our using what we deem only as having *sufficing* utilities and not *optimal* utilities. When our practical applications fail in their use we find then a need to revise them in much more precise and accurate ways. And we find in these revisions that we employ new modes of inquiry and new modes of disconfirmation. These revisions empirically allow us to progress in knowledge as creative creatures. They enable us to move beyond our cognitive limitations of being encased in the limits of our vernacular. We have learned in our use of such newly devised artificial frames that we have developed new ways to discover much better ways to find out how in the past we have been mistaken about the best way to resolve and solve our problems.

Formal schemata enable us to escape the limitations of memory, and they allow us to deal with complexity that overwhelms our normal apprehension of what we thought has happened, what is now happening, and is likely in certain determined ranges of probability likely to happen again. These newly developed models that we use to interpret our experiences are necessary to explore the complexity of our problematic situations that at times tends to overwhelm us.

These newly developed models are the foundation of all expertise. And we find in our interpretations of them that not only are these new models and visual schemata interpreted in many cases in figurative language, but they are often phrased in terms that when taken from literal lexical usage are fraught with multiple senses and imprecision. It is from these language limitations that we have as a result created many of the ambiguities that we find in the uses of terms. These ambiguities tend to confuse us in contexts that differ from those in which we originally learned to apply and use those terms. Such a dependence on models then presents the problem of recognizing how in formal languages that the terms that are used to generate these formal models are often open to various interpretations, which generate the paradoxes and contradictions that we find in our expanded uses of them in different contexts and situations.

The patterns and meanings of terms in formal systems are for the most part generated internally in the growth of our professional languages that are generated by technical definitions. But these technical terms are often reinterpreted and reenter into the vernacular in different ways. Just lately I was astonished as to how the hormone thyroxin as been transformed in my life time by organic chemistry. It is now no longer the simple hormone that my teachers once said it to be. We no longer can think of thyroxin in simpler terms and in the role that it supposedly played in the older models of interactions between it and other hormones.

We especially find this breakdown between those who interpret these models for experimental purposes and those who create these models in formal and theoretical ways. There is a great divide between the language of **experimental scientists** and **theoretical scientists** about these matters. But what people in the end do not seem to recognize is that formal logical and mathematical languages are languages that enable us to exhibit formal complexity, but that they run into serious problems of interpretation when they are applied and used experimentally to test conjectures.

As a result of our human conditions and personal aims we consequently are bound within the limitations of our thinking. We are bound within the boundaries of short-term memory and the constraints of maintaining long term memory. And in addition we are bound within the perceptual limits of attention in our ordinary language use and usage in understanding our human situation as it relates and depends upon other people. We are caught with linguistic skills that have emerged from our biologically innate uses of language. We are embedded in social, cultural, and political conditions that frame our language perspectives. We are as individuals embedded in a life framed by personal choices and commitments. The net result is that we live in a world where our beliefs are questioned by our different uses of the multiple frames by which we relate to other people and how we relate to the culture that we find ourselves within.

Developments in mathematics, the sciences, and in technologies **invert** our conceptions of what is verbally simple. They have done so in the past as we have seen in history of sciences, such as in our revised conceptions of the movement of the sun, the moon, and the planets. They have revised our conceptions of space and time. The implications of such changing perspectives found in the models and schemata of the sciences gradually invert in time our conceptions of what is simple in ordinary everyday language and what is accepted in everyday common sense.

But the major error in using such modified models is to mistake their formal and informal imaginative structures as representations of the real world. Although we conceive and perceive them to be natural representations; yet existentially they are the projections of a linguistically defined emergent and a developing ego that seeks to escape its ignorance. My argument continues to be that the better perspective to take in thinking of the world is to think of models and visual schemata, not as naturalistic representations, but to look at the various patterns and sequences within them as artificial constructions devised from terms in our vernacular, which in the end frame for us what our personal conception of what the **really real** is in the end really like for us. But in the end reality is what is ordinarily thought real for us as we describe what we see happening about us and within us. It is what others can agree with us about in talking to us about what is really real for the both of us.

Human artifice is a development we find originating in the evolutionary development of what we think of as life. This raises all those questions raised about what is life? And since our conceptions of naturalistic processes is framed in artificially developed language and socially constructed schemata, it is a paradox to say just where life begins and emerges from physical and chemical processes that in the fields of biochemistry many purport to describe as externally real life processes. The important point in saying what knowledge is lies in the fact that we feel that we have a certain sense of what it is, but that certain sense of what it is actually is a product of an artificially created language that becomes a medium of exchange for us with others. All the models and schemata developed in math and science equally rest upon artificial creations that have been developed around the innate embedded artifices found in life processes that are emerging in the evolution of human life.

Life creates the emergent changing forms of life that in turn become sufficient for life to adjust and maintain its own form of life by replication. And the human brain especially was a product of that emergent change of new patterns developing in its anatomy for making adjustments. Our brains, as Krishnamurti maintained, are a product of many millennia of readjustments to maintain the species. It is not a machine searching for reality. Its forms and structures were created to maintain the human species. Language is a part of that emergent change of those survival seeking structures. But we as persons are not our brains. As Krishnamurti maintains, and this is the most important point about evolution, our brains belong to the emerging human species and not to us. We as creatures are actively going along with the ride. Evolution historically has been all about the species, that is, whatever it is we mean by what we call a species. A species is at least a name for some of those stabilities we see in the different kinds of life processes.

My argument is that the better perspective to take in thinking of the world is that instead of thinking of models and visual schematic as naturalistic representations, we should instead look upon these patterns and the sequences found in them as linguistic tools developed to exercise command and control. After all they are no more than artificial human constructions. We use them instrumentally as ways of constructing patterns of action in what we see as existential boundless complexity that we have in solving multiple tensions and conflicts. These guiding patterns of action have been generated by the emerging patterns in the brain or in our neural systems that have sufficed, especially in recent biological history in the prefrontal cortex to maintain the human species. But note this conception of the prefrontal cortex is again merely another simplified model of what is happening in this structure that we model and that we think of realistically as the brain. But where anatomically does a brain begin and end. How can we separate what we call a brain from the nervous system? Neurologically what defines a brain?

In interpreting these patterns as representation of fact and reality that is set forth in models and frames we should look upon our interpretations of them in the ordinary language that is used in the first place to shape and construct them. They are no more than artificial constructed frames that we use for the scaffolding our terms and concepts in our language. We use these schemata and frames in order to relate and to correlate our terms and concepts in thinking about the complexity of our lives and the complex problems we face in the world that seem most of the times beyond our rational capabilities. These models then are tools for the mind to think with and to use and to order and aggregate units of things into sets of things.

They are tools to sort out the patterns in the complexity of our thinking. We are severely limited in our ignorance about the facts of occurrence of things both past, present, and future. We are limited by the use of models that do not extend as modes of representation beyond the range of what we can study, as for example many of the micro-anatomical features that stretch beyond our abilities to image them we have no clear conception about. We are limited by not only by the linearity of our thinking, but we are limited in memory about what we think are the so called facts needed to cope with any understanding of our worlds.

And when we think about these artificial frames that we create, we should avoid projecting abstract terms and concepts that we use in different contexts and situations to say anything with certainty about them. We should recognize the limitations of our interpretation in our ways of looking at the world. These models as representation are nothing more than virtual or artificial organizations of experiences that enable us to remember and to recall. As we find in the paradoxes of philosophy, we are using these frames as representations of real structures in the world when in fact they are no more than scaffoldings for our languages that we mistake as being a true structural part of reality.

Our models and frames in the sciences were developed out of our seemingly innate senses of orientation and on our primitive ways of counting which in turn lay the foundations of mathematics. These models shape the way our languages have generated the roles we play in seeking solutions to questions that we believed that we were ignorant about. And when considered from the evolutionary point of view, they are to be found to be found in the very biology of our anatomy that shapes the geometry of our perception. And the net result of all of this is that we end up projecting these artificial constructions into our everyday psychological perceptual and inner experiences, and we end up thinking that they are the patterns to be found in the actual world.

The sum of it is that we are existentially situated in the frames of our ordinary language, which has been biologically and socially constructed. Biologically speaking our evolution has laid the linguistic foundation of our cognitive capabilities. The biological foundations of our language that were first used for making our social adjustments are to be found to exist in the human condition as an emerging social creature. The social interaction and mutual development of our cognitive abilities enable us as human creatures to become very creative creatures. In actuality the models and schemata that we find emerging from our basic innate frames are no more than additional tools and instruments of discovery that emerged out of an added number of new varieties of artifice created in evolution. They are in their creative development just new ways of saying what is normative or ideal in applying the terms of our language in our everyday practical experiences. But our idealism about these norms or ideals is shattered when they result in failure.

What I want now to do in following chapters is to continue to expand in greater depth upon our modes of interpretations of models and frames, logical and mathematical, and to see how they always are interpreted and technically defined in much more complicated ways still using terms of ordinary language. We need to recognize that our different ways of dealing with our problems in dealing with the world are limited by these personal artificial frames of reference that we personally and innovatively construct in our everyday adjustments. And too we need to recognize in the pluralism of these multiple frames of reference the inconsistencies that develop within and between them the incompatible uses we find in our using them. We are always limited in using them by the fact that our limited and finite perspective on complexity is limited by the very biological, social, and political limits we have in using our languages.

But despite the sufficing utilities we use and with which we are able to calculate in using these different models, we can nevertheless in imaginative ways transcend their limitations by creating new models and new schema together with new language and new terms to rise above these bounded limitations. When we encounter these limits in our models and schemata it is our imaginative use of them that helps us escape many of the inconsistencies between them where their practical applications fail in the uses of them. These escapes from our limitations are rendered possible by our uses of the modes of disconfirmation that empirically allow us to progress in knowledge, thus empowering us as living creatures to get beyond our past incapacities.

Formal schemata enable us to escape the limitations of memory, and they allow us to deal with complexity that overwhelms our normal apprehension of what we thought has happened and what is now happening. They are thus necessary to explore the complexity that at times overwhelms us. Not only are models and visual schemata interpreted in many cases in figurative language, but they are often phrased in terms of literal lexical usage that are fraught with imprecision and ambiguities that have been created by the various changing senses of terms in the different contexts in which they are used. Such a dependence on models presents the cognitive problem of recognizing how in formal languages that the terms used to generate these formal models are often open to various interpretations, which in turn generate the paradoxes and contradictions that we find in them. Their formalization quite often is seen as other than what the interpreted defined meaning of the technical terms suggest.

What people in the end do not recognize is that formal logical and mathematical languages are languages that enable us to exhibit formal complexity by rules. They enable us to frame them in a language that allows us to axiomatize statements within them that make it possible for further changes in them that allow for new systems of logical implications to be explored that always have their own determinable logical consequences. We use them to map and to trace the complexity that we have to deal with when we are limited and constrained by ordinary ways of speaking.

In sum as a result of our human condition and our personal aims we are bound within the limitations of our thinking within the language usage that we agree upon.

We are bound within the boundaries of short-term memory and the constraints of maintaining long term memory. And in addition we are bound within the perceptual limits of attention in our uses of ordinary language usage in the understanding of our human situation as it relates and depends upon other people. We are caught with linguistic skills that have emerged from our biologically innate uses of language. We are embedded in social, cultural, and political conditions that frame our language perspectives. We as individuals are embedded in a life framed by personal choices and commitments.

As Herbert Simon suggests we need to look at our communications to see what goes on between us. To me such a suggestion recommends my own outlook that we need to look at the role rhetoric plays in communication very carefully, especially as we use rhetoric in the sciences and technologies to reach cognitive mutual understanding about what to us appears real and functional in our ways of doing things in furthering what is important in our lives.

10 Various types of modeling used for finding correlations, designing structures, discovering contrasts, and making comparisons

The term model has many different senses in a variety of social, industrial, artistic, and profession contexts. Note cars come out in different models, even some have been named that way, such as the old Model T and its successor the Model A. Models are used in the fashion industry. They wear and display clothes at fashion shows and in photographs. Models also pose as bodies often nude to be depicted by artists especially in art schools. Models are also toys such as model cars, airplanes, and ships. Also we speak of models as persons who serve as a behavioral or moral example to other people.

Architects create models of their design proposals. Business models are designs that model the processes of the enterprise. Weather models are used to predict weather. Mathematical and statistical models use mathematical language to construct such things as graphics that describe economic processes, that describe the parameters of distribution such as in population studies, and especially there are all those mathematical models that describe the statics and dynamics of the equilibriums found in machinery.

Note the use of models to display the structures of organs in physiology. Note too, the use of models as mockups of urban design, ecosystems, campus planning, and even such things as stage scenery, landscape design, and even engineering projects such as bridges and dams. But probably the important sense of speaking of models, at least for the aims and purposes of this book, is the use of the term *model* to refer to those conceptual patterns of thought whereby we give organization and structure to the ways we attend and scrutinize our phenomenal experience. Thus when we speak of modeling we are confronted with the multiple variation of the ordinary use of the word 'model' as it shifts usages in context after context. Models are then the different ways of exhibiting certain types of complexity for audiences who have an interest in their use as a display of the simplifications we use to display complexity.

Note the complexity of cataloguing automobile parts. Note the complexity of listing painting materials both for house painters and for artists. Note the complexity of farm equipment and the need for replacement parts. Note the complexity of creating recipes in the culinary arts. Especially note the complexity of architectural design. Architects use new complex patterns of materials in the creative artificing in their design process. They develop new and different models and arrangements to develop new styles of construction, and even they have 'complexified' their architectual expertise by venturing into the new complexities of such arts as landscape design, park and campus design, and urban planning. Note the lack of boundaries in those engaged in modeling for purposes of dealing with different types of complexity.

What is important in organizing and even listing these emerging complexities of new ways of using materials and technology is to think about their uses in the variety of different fields of expertise that we need and use to assist us in doing things. Expertise has been developing historically in the evolution of biological factors by the emergence of new forms of artifice that have brought about the advancement of the human species. The human species has been continuously developing new patterns of expertise in both the social and cultural evolution of the species. We see it entering in different ways into the different forms technology and the different types of creative human artifice that keeps developing in human history.

As J. Krishnamurti said of the human brain that in its evolution that it 'has gathered tremendous experience, knowledge and all the cruelties, vulgarities and brutalities of selfishness' (1985: 2472). It is 'because apparently it is functioning in patterns. Whether it is a religious pattern, a scientific, a business, or a family pattern, it is always operating, functioning in small narrow circles. Those circles are clashing against each other, and there seems to be no end to this.'

What I propose at this point of the discussion of models and mathematical schemata is to show that they consist of a wide variety of separate sets of patterns and arrangements. I do not want to try to show that they are reductive in structure and form to any one simple pattern, to one structure or form, as I find as I interpret Herbert Simon's work. There is a tendency in his work to reduce models to what he describes and defines as one about hierarchical systems. And in addition I want to show in surveying and discussing the different kinds of expertise and the new developments of technology that we have found that we have no single model that unifies or integrates the difference in these models and helps us understand why they and their uses are found in so very many different ways we do things.

Many conceptual models that have been developed to aid in our thinking have been field or discipline specific. But when we try to narrow models to fields or disciplines we have the problems of what constitutes a field or a discipline, for many fields or disciplines as we find them as taught in universities have many different lines of research using different models to teach their subject matters. What adds to and compounds our confusions about this notion that a single set of models define a discipline is our fixation on the use of mathematical models. We begin as a result of their enormous success in their use to think that mathematical models are unitary in method and their application helps to define a discipline. Some want to contend that if a discipline is not reducible to mathematics it is not science.

In one respect then disciplines have been compounded by this sense of having a singular method and a single type of explanation. But in having been a part of the growing development of rhetoric I have been witness to the politics of the development of those who look upon themselves as rhetoricians who are diverse in their methods and types of explanation. The different modes and models that nominal rhetoricians have been developing under the label of rhetoric are obviously plural as we find to be true of what has been going on in the various rhetorical societies, especially the Rhetoric Society of America (RSA).

What I found in the growing development of the Rhetoric Society has been that there are many changing conceptions about who is a rhetorician and what a rhetorician does. And there is openness in the society that allows anyone to join in the name of rhetoric. And now the Rhetoric Society is politically organized to include specialists in many other disciplines that seem related to what has in the past gone on in the traditions of rhetoric, and especially now in what has been recently developed in the New Rhetoric with its new and changing conceptions of what rhetoric is and does. In other words the field of rhetoric becomes less and less a unitary discipline from new and changing conceptions. Prominently it is shown to be pluralistic and interdisciplinary in way it relates to universities and to different types of communication specialists in many different ways in many different fields. The Rhetoric Society as it has developed in its openness is an exercise in social politics that aids and helps advance the different agenda of a wide variety of different specialties.

What I find striking is some of the same parallels that have developed around the so called field of cybernetics. Again the American Society for Cybernetics (ABC) is an organization much like the Rhetoric Society that seemingly defines itself as supporting research and assisting in the theoretical developments in cybernetics as a discipline that in time has found itself to be taught like rhetoric as a subject matter in universities. Both RSA and ASC were founded by significant scholars with achievements in their specialties and disciplines. Although ASC has membership requirements, just as is the case with many other professional societies, it does not admit anyone who wishes to join. Nevertheless there is in the society the same sort of pluralism and interdisciplinary focus among those who deem themselves to be specialists in cybernetics. Just as there is no common definition of what the discipline of rhetoric is we find much the same pattern of description and definition in the pluralism taking place in cybernetics.

Here is the definition of cybernetics used by the University of Reading, UK: 'The acquisition, communication, processing and application of information.' Interestingly, the University on their web site lists definitions by others nominal cyberneticians: 'The science of organization', from Stafford Beer, 'who pioneered the application of cybernetics to management.' 'Control and communication in the animal or in the machine', the early formal definition of cybernetics used by Norbert Wiener in the title of his book that popularized the concept in 1948. And Peter Fellgett, first Professor of Cybernetics at Reading, 'as anything that interested him'. What interested him were Cybernetics and Control Engineering, Cybernetic Science, Computer Science and Cybernetics and Psychology and Cybernetics - whose cybernetic content was consistent with Wiener's definition: control and communication in the animal and the machine. 'A way of thinking', Ernest von Glaserfeld. 'Social constructivist' Sociology. A science concerned with the systems of nature which are capable of receiving, storing, and processing information so as to use it for control,

A. N. Kologorov, mathematician. 'A branch of mathematics dealing with problems of control, excursiveness, and information', Gary Batson. Communications.

What we see in this variety of sentiments is, as with rhetoric, that much of their nominal labeling is socially and politically denominated. In sum cybernetics, noted for its modeling, has applied models used in the studies of various systems in such diverse fields as biology, computer science, engineering, management, mathematics, psychology, sociology, and art.

In outlining the diversity of different types of modeling that follows I have outlined a list of different models that I have found in surveying our modes of thinking. My survey is certainly not complete, nor singularly discrete, nor of any distinctly definable classification into separate types. It simply is a list of models that I have found in the diversity of the disciplines that I have surveyed. It is simply a list of modes of thinking about different forms of technology that I have been exposed to in my academic career. I have said that in my own education I have been a jack of all trades and a master of none, which presumes that there is a multiplicity of trades.

And again who is to say that human enterprise may develop new and different ways of thinking about how we organize our thinking about what we see as complexity. Thus making any list of models are open to new additions, and certainly no list that is open to change as such can be closed or exhaustive. Logicians and mathematicians in their creativity have for over two millennia displayed new and different models to organize our thinking. Their increasing number of models and their newly created formal systems have been shown logically, as Kurt Gödel tried to prove, as necessarily lacking any unified logical coherence. As such the inconsistency proof by Gödel seems to rule out that mathematics is reducible to a single model or system.

Below is a list of models that I have already named before and some others listed within my previous writing. This following list contains many others that I will describe and label in the remaining parts of this book.

Process Models
Backwards and forwards sketches of paths and proof
Narrative models and fictive story telling
Linear process models or algorithms
Process descriptions
Equilibrium and feed-back models
Proximity or catalytic models
Chain reactions

Communication Models
Wells of ignorance
Meta-language models
Rhetorical models
Rhetorical aims

Figurative language metaphor and synecdoche
Proverbs and rules of thumb

Generated by Grammatical Syntax
Role taking 1st, 2nd, and 3rd person
Nominal and verbal phrase structures
Subjunctive conditionals
Reflexive verbs
Prepositions or prepositional prefixes
Predicate nominatives
Passive voice
Active voice
Conjunctive adverbs
Correlative terms
Transitive verbs
Intransitive verbs

Numeracy Models
Counting
Ordering
Orientation
Ratios and proportions
Measurement models
Cartesian model
Circular coordinates
Rotational models
Compass and clock models
Orientation to celestial sphere models
Logical and mathematical models
Digital models
Analogue models

Structural Models
Outside inside models
Bottled up models
Tree models or fractal models
Geometric models
Maps and charts
Structural formulas
Hooks and detachable vectors
Stability models
Restoration and replication models

Corpuscular models
Wave models
Loom, woof and welf
Square of opposition

Mnemonic Models
Digital memory
Classification systems
Lexigraphical models
Encyclopedic modeling
Cataloguing models
Lists
Models for identification
Dictionary modeling

But nevertheless all these listed types of models and ways of modeling listed above I have found for me to be different ways of organizing and programming my thinking. But importantly I have found in my use of them that I have in my extensive survey of them found there are many of them often used in the same way in different sciences. I have found from my own subjective perspective that they are equally used to organize and structure my thinking in different types of disciplines in the social and natural sciences and in the humanities.

To use one example, I noted that in my teaching physics many proofs of physical correlations were not clearly understood by the students. The sketches of the proofs in the texts were too complicated for many of my students to able to reconstruct the intervening steps. What my students failed to see that there are models of proof that sketch only paths and show proofs can work backwards and forwards'. The authors of the text using a sketch of a proof presumed that students could easily see algebraically how to get to B from A. It was thought by the authors of texts that students should know those mathematical steps from their high school algebra. Such sketches of proofs in the text would show how the student could get to C without having to do the algebraic steps to get from B to C.

But note that when the student readily sees the sketch of steps shown of how to get from A to B to C, the student has seen the complexity of getting to C from A in simpler terms than if he had done it rigorously. He or she sees the complex connections in simpler terms. Such sketches of proofs by skipping show, though they might be algebraically complex, yet sketches of proof enable us to see the proof as a whole in simpler terms. There was thus the presumption in my physics text that it should not be necessary for the student to demonstrate each and every step rigorously, which when all added together might seem to involve a great deal of mathematical complexity.

On the other hand in looking at such sketches of proofs, if a student is trying to find a method of proof that would go either forward or backwards from A to E, the student can simplify his or her procedure by finding steps he or she understands full well and put them together. It is like jumping onto larger stones crossing a stream strewn with rocks and boulders. The student cannot see the path to be taken through all the separate steps that he or she does not fully understand, yet that can readily be made exhaustively complete as a whole. Thus one model of doing such proofs of paths to be taken simplifies those complications by working forwards and backwards through the proofs or paths. If a student knows how to get to C from A through B, he or she might find it easier to get to C from E by seeing that one can get to C backwards from E through D thus joining both paths through C.

Note the model for working a proof in mathematics or geometry backwards and forwards is a strategy for simplifying the complexity of doing logical or mathematical proofs. But this same pattern of sketching out a route or path works as well in many other fields that are not just logical, mathematical, or geometric. It works in other fields of endeavor such as how to meet friends or to see patterns in historical explanation. Such a pattern of simplification of perceived complexity is to be found in many different types of human endeavor. It is this perception in this example of the use of models that work in different ways in different fields of human endeavor that helps us recognize that such models are in one way intellectually prior to any adaptation, and their use in new and different novel areas and disciplines that involve problem solving. But as the old saw goes, 'There are many ways to skin a cat!'

Thus my categorization of the different types of models and modeling that I have listed above are I admit quite superficial and possible overlapping. I aggregated them simply in superficial clusters in the lengthy list with somewhat arbitrary labels to keep from overwhelming any reader with the lengthy complex list that I compiled from my personal sense of their different applications in general. My list itself as a type of model is not a simple cataloguing type of model that I use to simplify the complexity of the differences between what I perceive to be types. My list then is too overlapping to classify it as just 'a classifying model or a cataloguing model'.

Some of the complexity generated by some of the different models listed above, and the complexity in seeing what each involves in different applications, will be discussed and expanded upon later in this book. More introductions and illustrations of models will thus follow in the remaining chapters of the book. Some will be more fully discussed and others only superficially. But in all, given the scope of this task my total effort here must be judged to be on the whole a superficial discussion of the complexity of my topic on conceptual models used to pattern ways in our thinking.

The major point in presenting so much diversity in modeling is to show that there is no unifying model that pulls these different ways of modeling together. This seems a warranted conclusion in one respect in that the sciences and the technologies are so plural. And the only way I have of showing the complexity of the models is simply at this point in the beginning to list some of them. And there is no question about the diversity of technologies that are developing as civilization advances. But the list presented does make possible further discussion on the major point of this chapter that we use these models and types of modeling for finding correlations, discovering contrasts, and making comparisons which are necessary for productive thinking.

In developing technology each enterprise becomes a new form of expertise producing and creating new forms of goods and services. Different models and visual schemes are used to list, schematize, classify, and organize. Each involves creative activities and modes of using data and information for new adaptations to changing circumstances that emerge with changing cultures. And the language and graphic representations that we use to describe and to organize these new creative developments in modeling and in simulating them are equally evolving and changing with new forms of visual rhetoric and the new forms of communication technology created today, especially with the electronic computer.

Note the improvements that are going in cartography, computer developments in architectural design, the development of modes and models of transportation, and new models of electrical generation and distribution. Note the language of the sciences and technology follows the same evolutionary pattern that has historically developed among human beings in advancing their tool making technology from their past 'learned-uses' in ancient crafts. Note too we see the important the role that classification has played in the study of anatomy and physiology when we first think of the origins of the biological sciences as we first find them in the work of Aristotle or again as in the medical sciences as we do in the Hippocratic tradition.

I remember the monotony in studying the anatomy of my cat in comparative anatomy in zoology. We had to learn every name of the bumps on a bone to my boring despair. But it was the rote exercise of committing to memory so much anatomical jargon which made it easier to identify what we were observing and to be able to see how that body part related to its anatomical function. How easily is it to forget so much of the technical jargon used in anatomical studies if one is not enthusiastic about medicine or about the biological sciences?

The same sort of memory work I found in my early chemistry where we studied all the chemical properties of agents and reagents. We had to know what reacts with what under certain conditions and with what catalysts. Anatomical drawings and charts and the standardized table of elements in chemistry as I shall later illustrate in talking about theories are the key classification systems of what is quantitative and descriptive about what relates to what in both biology and chemistry.

And when I first encountered nuclear chemistry and physics, in the transformation of the nuclei of elements I became acquainted with the standardized classification table of nuclear particles. These charts and drawings are again not a theoretical model, but they are models that are used to discover analogies, comparisons, correlations, and patterns that have implications for experimental and theoretical developments in the nuclear sciences. They are models again that give us ways of showing what is related to what, especially as we use them to guide our needs for measurement and precision.

The logic of classification developed in Aristotle is based upon one or more defining attributes or predicates that designate a group or a set of objects. Normally in defining in terms using attributes as is characteristic of definitions in using Aristotelian logic, the number of defining attributes for simplicity's sake are never larger than three: *genus*, *species*, and *differentia*. Like in Aristotle given our limitations as thinking beings we have difficulty in relating to four or more attributes attentively when we are using the logic of ordinary language. We need to order and to rank attributes greater than three in an exhaustive list of traits if we want to define or classify items with many numerous different properties. We cannot do that with Venn diagrams. I have illustrated this difficulty in another context in using Venn diagrams (Yoos, 2009).

For example, in the past if we wanted to classify bacteria we needed to set up a system of ordered and ranked attributes to identify different types of bacteria. Note that we do the same thing in using different classifications systems in libraries. We can place all the books of a certain category under a general class description. But importantly when we identify both classes and individuals we try to give unique descriptions to avoid confusion and mistaken identity.

And, for instance if a library has more than one copy of a given edition, it can be indexed to identify that specific book by referring to it as 'Copy 2'. Note it is this above described method of ordering and classifying that has generated the systems that use barcodes for inventory. All such processes of classifying and identification start with a definition in terms of attributes and then attempt by a restricted set of descriptions to develop a classification and a code that is descriptive of one and only one individual or unique item. Thus, in the end identification is based upon unique descriptions emerging out of definitions in terms of attributes or predicates.

In Aristotle the basis of definition is finding a class that is defined grammatically using the predicate nominative grammatical form to which a subject or object belongs. In a way here again this is how the grammar of our language structures our relating of nominalized expressions. Thus, in one way of speaking, nominalized expressions enable us to separate things into types, kinds, sorts, or varieties in our use of ordinary language, and then they enable us to put each of these sorts of classes of things into baskets, pots, barrels, boxes, drawers, containers, lockers, or different piles.

What makes this a way of putting and storing things away is that it serves our needs for identification. We no longer have to depend on a limited memory where we have put something. Instead it makes it practically easy to find what we are looking for, and thus it makes our search for something economically 'time efficient'. When looking for nails, screws, tools, papers, letters, pencils, knives, forks, spoons, or dishes when classified we know where they are located. Finding requires practically then separating things by nominalized named types that make it easy to find them and to use them. And that in sum is the useful purpose of definitions and classifications to order things in useful searchable named frames and categories.

One of my personal faults is that I often put things away, but I forget where I put them. I cannot remember like the birds and the squirrels where I hid my little acorns. To create a prosthetic device as a substitute for long term memory requires us to make some sort of map that tells us where we have or usually put things. One of the great developments in technology is how to handle and account for inventory, to mark its location, and to discover ways to ease its accessibility. Stores involve storage. What is important in seeking any particular item or person is to start organizing them into a system whereby we find it useful to locate things. To do that we need is to analyze and distinguish items or persons by simple differences. Note that even symmetry, though a dyadic relationship can be defined as either as left or right, laterally or vertically. As such all distinctions require contrasting orientations that are indicative of directions in the creating of models that create the patterns used to organize our observations.

It is by these simple divisions that classifications develop. Contrasts are even more important in sorting things than are similarities. We classify tools not by their common properties but by their different uses. Hammers, screw drivers, saws, planes chisels, drills, levels, plumb bobs, squares, and measuring tapes are all carpentry tools. Each is distinguished from other tools by what they do. How we arrange them depends up how we keep them separate in our tool boxes for accessibility and convenience for the different tasks at hand. Note the importance of tools for shaping, cutting, and fastening or attaching wood, Note the importance of tools for measuring and conforming to patterns of structural design. Such is the case with the separation of carpentry skills and their basis for developing from our different uses of them. Other tools are in a way simpler in their uses such as routers, doweling, wedges, hinges, jacks, adhesives, and glues.

Note that carpenters have different skills as their work becomes specialized by the demands of new designs for using new materials in construction. Thus, classification systems for carpenters need alterations as new tools are constantly created and designed to help meet the needs of new types of construction and design. Every expertise develops its own need for ordering and classifying what it uses to master newer tasks. I was amazed at the creative variations that were made on different types of griping tools such as various types of pliers, made for gripping, pinching, and wire cutting tools. It is in this plurality of technologies and the development of new forms of expertise that have created for us the need for developing and the artificing of different models and schema to guide and assist our thinking in the devising and creating new forms of expertise.

One of the first types of schema used for guiding our actions is in the use of sequential lists. Some lists are randomly shaped. Such is the way I make up my 'to-do lists'. I simply put down in a row a list of what I need to do as I search through my memory for all the tasks I have to do either for the day or what I need to do to complete a task that I planned doing within set time lines. But then after making such a random list I need to prioritize what I need to do first of what is on my 'to-do list'. I do it by prescribing the order or sequence I need to follow and to do the set of tasks that meet my immediate needs for that particular day. Note that such 'to do lists' contain more tasks usually than the time that we have to do them within.

Throughout this book I have been introducing for discussion the creation of the models and schemata devised to meet certain basic human needs people have in coping with both their inner and outer world. Let me list below the models and schemata that I have felt to be the ones that in the past I found from my experiences to be the most important in advancing sciences and technologies. These are models I have selected out for their importance for scientific and technological progress that I found in my personal studies. Of course this may be a superficial judgment. They are the ones that I have used as a way of discussing how we think about the everyday tasks that I have found that they keep on expanding into more sophisticated models and schemata that are in use in the advancement of the sciences and technologies.

Important Models Found in Science and Technology
Stability and orientation models
Equilibrium models
Inside outside fenced in models
Top down and bottom up models
Digital models for counting
Digital models for ordering
Box within box models
Flow charts
Evolution and emergent models
Historical and narrative modeling
Algorithms
Coordinate systems both linear and circular
Maps and charts
Recursive and feedback models
Tree and fractal models
Sketches of paths and proofs backwards and forwards

I do not find any unitary theory uniting any of these different important and selected models that have been advancing our knowledge in the sciences and the technologies. Nor do I want to reduce them in a unitary fashion using simple metaphors or figural models, although analogy and conjectures of what it is that I am seeing in using models plays an important part in the discussion of these models. I do not want to say that our world views, our *Weltanschauungen,* determine the methods and patterns of our thinking about sciences and technologies. But they are indeed influenced by them. But such a discussion of world views, *Weltanschauungen,* requires an excursion into the taxonomy of world views. And lately that topic relates to what we find going on among theoretical scientists to keep speculating about their views on TOES or theories of everything. That excursion is another book.

11 A sense of place as fundamental to our thinking about models about equilibriums

When you are old it is your instability that tells you that you are getting old. You stagger. You need a cane. Your blood pressure is out of equilibrium. You get dizzy. You have trouble getting out of bed as things begin to whirl. Your vision does not stand still. To stand up when you are dizzy, much like sea sickness or being air sick, you need a fixed point to stare at on the horizon to reestablish or regain any sense of stability.

In thinking about stability and equilibrium what strikes me is that the two terms *stability* and *equilibrium* are correlative terms. We need one to define the other. As correlatives we need to have a sense of stability to sense that you are in stasis, (*stasis* in Greek is the condition of standing still.) And in a rhetoric about **stasis,** a traditional form of classical type of invention, rhetoric focuses on the stand point of an argument. Stasis as a mode of invention involves the practice of posing and of exploring questions relevant to clarifying the main issues that have a **standing** in the debate.

It is interesting that David Hilbert in his geometry starts by defining his basic axiom about 'a point' by using the ordinary term 'situated'. We are situated on a point. It is out of the stability of a point for Hilbert that systems of lines and planes develop to define our systems of space. We need a point of stability to describe the dynamics that mathematics describes as emerging from the complexity of moving lines, planes, and changing shapes.

And again, as D. H. Lawrence expresses it, 'That I am part of the earth my feet know perfectly, and blood is part of the sea.' He stands on a spot that is part of the earth that is in stable equilibrium, and his blood and its salts are in the same balance or equilibrium as the ratio of the salts dissolved in the sea. He is part of the earth of which the seas served as the original source of life.

There is good evidence that metazoan life evolved in a field of gravity thus making Lawrence as a metazoan a part of the earth, and that his circulatory system evolved by enclosing the sea and then the sea water became a medium for maintaining the circulation of nutrients to the cells of the body that were encased within his skin. Such is my interpretation of the thought of Lawrence in his lyrical outburst in his insisting that he as a living thing is part of the earth and the sea.

Note again that a standpoint is the stance that we take in orienting ourselves. It is as spoken of in French our *point de vue*. But note as mentioned that when we orient ourselves we rotate ourselves from the direction we face to the direction and orientation that is over our right shoulder. In doing so, we have made a right turn nominally to our right. Rotation is always angular, and if we rotate to our right while standing up we rotate clockwise. We make a right turn to our *right line of sight*, and if we continue to make right turns to our next right line of sight, the result is that we make all total four right turns or turnings to the right in rotating back to our original *point of view*.

And if in that **reorientation** we orient out selves to the compass of the celestial sphere we are turning from the north to the right, we are **reorienting** ourselves to the *Orient* the stand point of view of Europeans. Note for Europeans that pointing to the east is pointing to the Orient which includes for them all three regional Easts: the Near East, the Middle East, and the Far East. The very language of orientation in Western Europe is directed towards the east or to the right. How ironic it is for the Chinese to look to the United States as the Far East, and we are the Orient and they are Westerners.

Again there is irony in knowing what is right. To make a pun of our use of the term *right*, we see all the redundancies of our synomyms of 'being right'. 'When we are **right** we are **orient**-ed cor-**rect**-ly or **right**ly in **right**-eous **rect**-itude.' Note that the *correct* turning around our standpoint given our left brain orientation favors the rightness of right-handers in finding their right line of sight. How rightful it is for conservatives to think of themselves as the 'Political right'**?** After all they believe they are right in being right.

The Cartesian coordinate system is a grid or a graph. The point where the axises meet is the common origin of the two number calibrated lines, and it is simply called the *origin* (its stand point of orientation). Note in the following Figure 11.1 the stand point of orientation is often labeled *O*, and if so, then the two axises of orientation are called *Ox* and *Oy*. They shape a **plane** (grid) with *x* and *y*-axises often referred to as the Cartesian plane or *xy* plane. The value of *x* is called the *x*-coordinate or *abscissa* and the value of *y* is called the *y*-coordinate or *ordinate* that moves from a zero degree orientation on the *x*-axis (*the abscissa*) to a right angle rotation towards a 0 on the right that is aligned with the y axis. And that right orientation to the right is the x-axis. It is thus a rotation that generates our concept of an angular measurement.

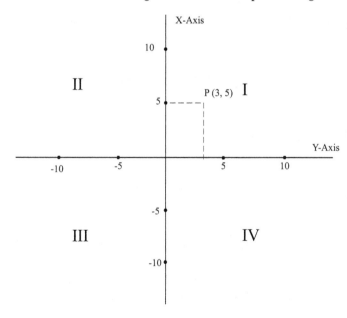

Figure 11.1: Cartesian Coordinate System

Like all measurements, angular measurements are arbitrary until we introduce the notion of a right angle. If we use a 360 degree rotation as a new notion of measurement, we have the number of degrees in a circle, which is a rotation of a turn equal distant from a point or from a standpoint. And since a rotation has four right turns, one right turn is one fourth of the measurement of a 360 degree rotation, which would make a right turn or right angle 90 degrees. And the complete rotation is 360 degrees, the number of degrees on a compass, and thus it becomes another model of angular measurement. The following Figure 11.2 illustrates these compass turns relative to the fixed stars and the line of sight.

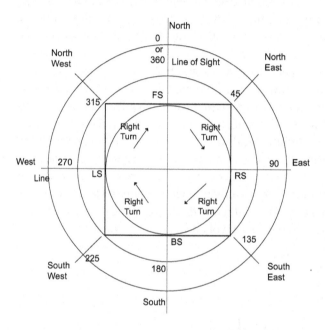

Figure 11.2: Models of Angular Measurement, Foundations of Orientations

And again if we orient our face, *Gesicht*, to the north we have again a new model or frame that is comparable in use to a Cartesian set of coordinates based upon a square and right angles. But the clock is a different sort of grid using a compass set of angles to describe location. It is a different type of mathematical model based upon clock type rotations, right turn rotations, instead of counter clock wise rotations as on the Cartesian grid. At the basis of compass construction is a new grid of rotations based again upon the directions determined by four right turn rotations. Using a calibration based upon a 360 degree division, we are able to swing the compass in four right turns. East is 90 degrees, south 180 degrees, west 270 degrees, and then we return to the north which is 0 degrees, which is a 360 degree turn and which is a return to our original 0 position. The 360 number system is based upon Babylonian concepts of enumeration.

And we can again divide our rotation into units of twelve, which is an angular measurement on a clock. As mentioned in the air corps our gunnery was based on clock angular measurements. 'Coming in at 3 o'clock high.' It has fascinated me as to why we have a twelve hour clock. Why are there 'six sixty (60) degree' angles in a 360 compass? Why would the Babylonians use a scale of 360 to measure angular measurements? It is interesting that the list of factors of 360 are 2, 3, 4, 5, 6, 8, 12, 15, 30, 45, 60, 72, 90, 120, and 180. Segmenting angles in 360 degrees thus gives us many more factors to calculate angular measurements with much more precision. Note the following model of the Babylonian compass Figure 11.3.

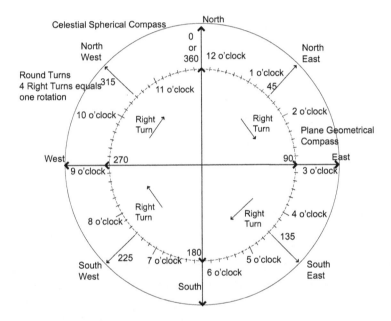

Figure 11.3: Babylonian Compass

Such an advantage in division by factoring makes a number system to the base 360 very precise and efficient. Note that a sextant allows us to divide the compass in six segments of 60 degrees, and note that the pentagon and the five star points of the five pointed star divides the circle in 5-72 degree angles. And note if we go by the clock the heavens move west 15 degrees across the sky in one hour. And note that the patterns of the Zodiac which varies with the ways three different isolated cultures, Mesopotamian, Mayan, and Chinese, divided the heavens in 12 segments. Note that going around the clock is 12 hours. Note in the following Figure 11.4 the directional measurements of a compass diagram of the astrolabe:

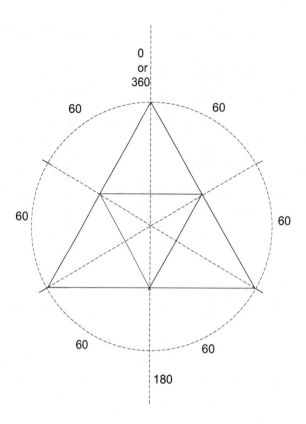

Figure 11.4: Directional Measurements with an Astrolabe

Of course this narrative of the historical account is only a speculative guess, but certainly the Babylonians were using the fixed stars and sidereal angles to measure the angular turn of the celestial sphere. Lunar months most likely were what defined the zodiac. What was the reason of their developing this expertise? It must have been to measure seasons accurately for agriculture that they had a need to generate for these advantageous numerical factors of a rotation of 360 degrees.

Note the nominal appellation of the 'sextant'. Why do sextants as a measuring device use only a range of 60 degrees to measure the declination of the stars? Or what is much the same thing, the angular measurement of a star above a horizon, the *altitude*, which when subtracted from 90 degrees is the *declination*. Interestingly the scale of a sextant has a length of ⅙ of a full circle (60°); hence the sextant's name (*sextāns, -antis* is the Latin word for 'one sixth', 'εξάντας' in Greek.

Note too that an octant is a similar device with a shorter scale (⅛ of a circle or 45°), whereas a quintant (⅕ or 72°) and a quadrant (¼ or 90°) have longer scales. What sort of device could have been used to point in six different directions equally apart in making an angular measurement? I would speculate about the plausibility that the angles of inscribed regular polygons were used by the Babylonians as pointers. And of course that regular polygon would have to be a hexagon with its six equal angles and sides if it measured ⅙ of a full circle (60°). Interestingly note the following construction of a Star of David that is inside Figure 11.5, which becomes the basis of the construction of a regular polygon, the hexagon. It builds up the by construction of an equilateral triangle whose geometrical center is the center of a circumscribed circle around that type of triangle.

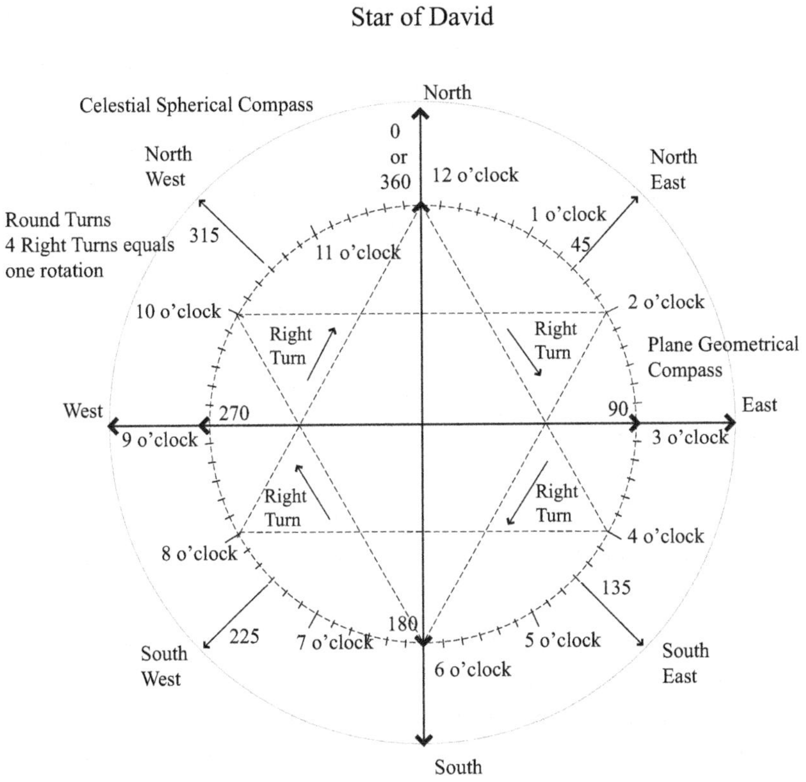

Star of David

Figure 11.5: Star of David

To create the Star of David we construct an overlapping triangle congruent to the first triangle whose geometric center again is also the center of the same circle that equally circumscribes it. Note that the angles between the points of the Star of David have the pattern of an astrolabe or a sextant with 60 degree angles separating the points. Simply drawing straight lines from the points of the Star of David on the circle gives us an inscribed regular hexagon. Note that the perpendicular bisectors of these sides of a hexagon that run through the center of the circle gives us the twelve angular degree measurements that divides into the numerical naming of the hours on the clock. Note each hour marks the movement of fixed stars across the heavenly rotation of the Zodiac.

But there are many ways to measure rotations in sighting or orienting. There is the radian used as an angular measure in mathematics. In the air corps we used it in gunnery, one, two, or three rads. In bombing we used mils. One radian is the angle subtended at the center of a circle (our stand point) by an arc that is equal in length to the radius of the circle.

More generally, the magnitude in radians of such a subtended angle is equal to the ratio of the arc length to the radius of the circle; that is, $\theta = s/r$, where θ is the subtended angle in radians, s is arc length, and r is radius. Conversely, the length of the enclosed arc is equal to the radius multiplied by the magnitude of the angle in radians; that is, $s = r\theta$. It follows from this 'that the magnitude in radians of one complete revolution (360 degrees) is the length of the entire circumference divided by the radius, or $2\pi r/r$, or 2π. Thus 2π radians are equal to 360 degrees, meaning that one radian is equal to $180/\pi$ degrees.' (Bud: 34)

Table 11.1: Radians

		Values						
Turns								
Degrees	°		0°	5°	0°	0°	80°	70°	60°
Radians									π
Grads	ᵍ			0ᵍ		00ᵍ	00ᵍ	00ᵍ	00ᵍ

And consequently also in bombing we used mils to measure our angular off sets in aiming, which were angular measurement of the deviations in our gyros from their vertical line of stability. It is out of the history of war especially using artillery that we find the history of the development (invention) of the concept of the radian that is a reflection of how many of our concerns for measurement emerged from the study of ballistics as a military science.

The milliradian was first identified in the mid 19th Century. „Degrees and minutes were the usual units of angular measurement but others were being proposed, with 'grads' (circle/400) under various names having considerable popularity in much of northern Europe, the grad was based on dividing a right angle into 100 units. However, Imperial Russia used a different approach, dividing a circle into equilateral triangles and hence 600 units to a circle. Around the time of the start of World War I France was experimenting with the use of millemes (circle/6400) for use with artillery sights instead of decigrades (circle/4000). UK was also trialing them to replace degrees and minutes. They were adopted by France, although decigrades also remained in use throughout World War I. Other nations also used decigrades. The United States, which copied many French artillery practices, adopted mils (circle/6400). After the Bolshevik Revolution and the adoption of the metric system of measurement (e.g. artillery replaced 'units of base' with metres) the Red Army expanded the 600 unit circle into a 6000 mil one, hence the Russian mil has nothing to do with milliradians as its origin. In the 1950s NATO adopted metric units of measurement for land and general use. Mils, metres and kilograms became standard, although degrees remained in use for naval and air purposes, reflecting civil practices.' (Renaud, 2002)

Note in German that a point of view is a *Gesichtspunkt*. It is the direction we face. The problem in talking about stability and change depends on our standpoint, our orientation, and the direction that we face. For David Gilbert in his geometry the direction of orientation we face is a line. But note besides that point of view towards the things which we face while looking straight ahead, there is the direction when squared away with our right shoulders that is said in military formation drills to be a 'right turn', 'Right! Face!', 'Right turn! March!', 'Right! Oblique!' Note the first term indicates a command for readiness and the second command describes what it is to be executed. 'At! Ease!'

Drill sergeants are always furious with those who do not know automatically there right from their left. In our squaring things away we are defining our orientation with right angles and right turns, and consequently to be squared away we are oriented as in mental status exams 'times four', 'Four right turns, a complete rotation, makes us mentally oriented.' In aphoristic ways of speaking 'to be squared away is doing things right', 'We are correct, or we have put things right', 'It is all about **rect**itude', 'Our course is cor**rect**', 'What we are doing in reasoning is right', 'We are thinking straight.' Note in the development of our elemental vocabulary in being squared away that we end up knowing what is right. When we get something right, we know what is the correct direction to take from our standpoint, that is, our *Standpunkt*, or *point de vue*.

Just as we need a standpoint to determine what is right, we need a point of stability to establish what is in equilibrium. A pendulum is in dynamic equilibrium when its arm, which is swinging back and forth, is fixed to a **stable** anchoring point. Pendulums like teeter totters need a **fulcrum**. A constant rotating fly wheel needs a fixed axle as a point of rotation. But again, which is the positive term *stability* or *equilibrium*? Is it not a steady state of equilibrium that tells us 'when and where' we are stable? Or, on the other hand, is it the stability of a point or the place where we stand that tells us when we are in equilibrium?

To establish what is in equilibrium note that the terms *equilibrium* and *stability* can be treated as correlatives, and *stability* is the positive term. We know when we are stable from our bodily and sensory experiences. We know when we are out of balance when we are not stable and situated around a point. Like Humpty Dumpty if we lose our stability we fall down. Our equilibium always needs feedback to a reference point to maintain our stability. And like Humpty Dumpty when we are dead, nothing is in equilibrium.

What strikes me in such a task as running, the psychological aspects of how we frame our sense of space and time and how our language of orientation has been incorporated in the way we speak of stability and our points of reference in talking about the way we look at things from our personal perspectives. Personal perspectives in a way are a stable ground for viewing change. For instance it is in ordinary ways of speaking that we have incorporated the ways we talk and interpret what we think of as speed. But it is in the applications and uses of these interpretations of speed that in physics have set up the definitions of the technical terms defining velocity. Nevertheless in defining velocity we have embodied in our formal systems our talk about speed by creating a new technical language by which we are able to say what movement is like, and what is predictable, and what is not about something moving. Being speedy is a contextual interpretation in ordinary ways of talking about speed.

Believing that something is predictable in a determinate way through formal definitions about different states about velocity and distance traveled in a given time is an easy way of exploring any belief we may have about mileage and speed. The physics of it exposes our ignorance and our oversimplifications in talking about speed.

To illustrate let us turn to the use of technical language using a formal language (algebraic) to test hypotheses (empirical generalizations) about correlations of measureable observable phenomena. Let us do a thought experiment testing an hypothesis (empirical generalization) about a correlation between the distance (s) that an object falls and the time (t) it falls: $s = (f) t^2$ Note that the rapid acceleration of a falling object suggests that (s) varies with (t) exponentially.

The question is whether this correlation of s with t^2 is invariant, that is, $s = (f)t = k\,t^2$.

Let's use our algebraic language using $(s = \frac{1}{2}at^2)$. Let us see if we can empirically test (f) or k as a numerical constant where $k = \frac{1}{2}$ a.

Let us suppose the following measurable correlations were observed:

Table 11.2: Thought Experiment

s (in feet)	t (ins seconds)
0.15	0.1
2.55	0.4
7.83	0.7
15.93	1.0
31.31	1.4
46.42	1.7
63.28	2.0

Let's suppose our hypothesis $s = 16^2$ is correct. Using this hypothesis we should have achieved the following results if it were hypothetically correct:

Table 11.3: Comparison of Data with Predictions

t (time)	s (by experiment)	s (by hypothesis)
0.1	0.15	0.16
0.4	2.55	2.56
0.7	7.83	7.84
1.0	15.93	16.0
1.4	31.31	31.36
1.7	46.42	46.24
2.0	63.28	64.00

There are four possible explanations for the difference between the hypothetical predicted data of the dependent variable (s) and the experimental results.
Experimental error
Uncontrolled factors in the experiment
Chance variations

Hypothesis that $s = 16^2$ is in error
1. Possibly there could be an error in the timing device of the controlled variable t. Or there might be a measuring error in our measures of the dependent variable s.
2. There is an uncontrolled variable in this experiment in the friction of the air on the falling object. The data appears to reflect this in the lag in the experimental measure of s at time 1.4.
3. The 'a' is invariant, that is, a = 2k might be in error. 'a' might vary by chance. Or, 'a' might vary if we repeat the experiment. At issue here is the ordinary presumption of everyday experience that the correlation between s and t is invariant. But invariance needs to be tested. Experiments by induction by instantiation tend to confirm this invariance by probability theory.
4. Note the hypothesis $s = \frac{1}{2} g\ t^2$ where g = acceleration, due to gravity, would be inconsistent with Newton's Law of Gravity.
   Newton's Law of Gravity $F = k\ (m^1\ m^2) / d^2$
   Newton's Second Law of Motion $F = (k)\ m\ a$

The force of gravity would increase as the object falls to earth, thus the second law increases as the acceleration of the object approaches the center of gravity of the earth, therefore acceleration due to g would logically not be constant. But it should be noted importantly that for all practical purposes that g as the acceleration due to gravity would experimentally appear to be constant (invariant), especially within the range of the earth's atmosphere. Thus, $s = \frac{1}{2} g\ t^2$ where g = 32 ft / sec^2 is for all measureable and practical purposes descriptively correct. But it is **not** an Absolute Law of Nature. It is approximately apparently invariant in a given type of context.

Note in the tale of the hare and the tortoise that it is inaccurate to talk about the speed of a tortoise, for what is distinctive about tortoises is they have as we ordinarily speak of them as relatively having no speed whatsoever. But when our beliefs about speed as technically defined and derived from formal systems with precise technical definitions of velocity agreed upon by physicists what they say about speed are reinforced by the predictability of time and distance derived from correlations described in the formal systems. Such observations in precisely defined technical terms in physics are a first step in the exposure of the ignorance we have in using vague and ambiguous terms about movement in our use of ordinary language in talking about movement and speed.

Likewise also going into these primitive senses of the meaning of our terms about orientation and direction, I maintain that we can see the basis we have for the invention and construction of formal systems. And to do that construction now, I want first to focus on some of our uses of the term *stability*. Life is all about stability. Where can there be any stability when everything living seems to be changing? What is it for a living thing to be standing still? To change anything there must a beginning and starting place to begin that change. Starting places must be fixed and determinate to identify any change of place. Navigational techniques I have found always involve determining firstly the navigator's starting place IP. He or she does that by comparing what he or she thinks of as his or her place as a fixed location relative to some other known locations.

In dead reckoning the navigator calculates his position relative to the locations of other known places. There is an initial point or starting point IP, and there is a destination that is fixed and determinate relative to other locations. Both are fixed places. Both have determinate locations, places to stand on that are relative to other places or standardized points of defined fixity. We can give names or identifications to these two reference points, that is, our starting point and our destination. The line connecting these two points A and B planned and plotted is thought presumably a straight line between these two points. The problem of the navigator is to determine his or her true actual course that he is actually taking that is relative to that original theoretically planned plotted course. The problem of the navigator is to measure how much he or she has deviated or changed positions in moving away from that true course by wind or current, that is, to correct the error made in moving away from that directly planned course so as to know how to make any course corrections relative to that planned theoretical course.

Note that places sometimes have proper names, for we use proper names to name locations. Locations and places are points of stability. We map or put on charts names of places. Some want to call these places home. And locations are places where we stand even if the ground we stand on is actually moving. We stand on the earth that supposedly is moving much in the same way we might be located sitting still in the third seat from the rear end of a train or bus. We all surely have had the experience of our moving in a train when the train next to us is moving when our car is actually standing still. We are seeing change, but we are confused about what is moving as we are not looking at the ground under the train where we would be standing still. Riding in a car we see the road come at us, but nevertheless we are sitting still in the car. Sitting and standing are locations. Presently I am sitting still before my computer located in my study. My computer screen is moving up and down as I use my formatting keys. The movement thus that we see as change is always relative to standing or sitting still in a position, or it is the perspective we have if we are not moving ourselves.

Note the etymology of the term *understanding*. It is knowing where we stand in understanding where others stand in communication. We reach that understanding even though the other persons are in error about where they stand. Thus, to understand in that case is not to know where we stand, but to know where others think they stand. We can know where we and others stand by confirming our reference points, our places where we stand, by the certitude we have about our standing points and where they are located, and that is one sense of what we think of as knowledge. It is our understanding.

It is the experience of movement that gives us a sense of what it is to be relative. We have no sense that the earth is rotating as we stand still on its surface. But how do we know which way the earth is moving except by comparing our standing still and orienting ourselves to other things that are moving such as the moon, the planets, and the stars. Change is movement away from a point of presumed stability either of the earth, the sun, the Milky Way, or some other location in time and space. But does space have fixity? Is it located, or is location simply a reference to locations in space and time? To measure movement and change you thus need a fixed reference point. All *homeostasis*, that is, maintaining any equilibrium, must have a fixed point of stability or point of reference. What is that point of reference if living things are always changing in the process of surviving and evolving into something new?

Stability starts psychologically from our bodily sense that we have when we are out of balance. We can fall on our face. We can flip over backwards. But balance always requires a steady footing. But to be balanced is always to be in a state of equilibrium. Stability is where the fulcrum is, that is, the fixed point around which a lever rotates. Rotation requires always an axis or axle that is a place to turn around. But actually does an axle turn? Or is the axle fixed to the frame of the vehicle and the wheel rotates on a bushing or bearings around a fixed axle? But to be a fulcrum an axle needs to be attached to a stable platform. Turning wheels require a stable ground for the wheel to roll around. When we measure rotation we need to measure it around a fixed center of stability. For mammals that is always where the mammal is standing.

We find stability in life in the singularity and in the focus of our perceptions. We also find stability in definitions, as I have suggested about the meaning of our conceptions that are generated by the fixity of the usage of the language that we use. Note the sense of location or fixity we have in talking about an 'establishment'. It is a fixed attachment. We are in creating an e**stabl**ishment oriented in a sense to that notion of fixity that psychologically makes us think of it as something standing up upright or standing still. We thus find stability in life in the confidence that there is a sense of stability in the meaning of our usage of the terms of our language. We find stability in our standards and in our codes that we have in our professions and in our vocations. We find stability in the conventions we establish, especially in the laws that we create. And we find stability in the formal models, the graphical languages, and the mathematics that we visually create. We find it too in the foundations of our logic and in our rules and in our definitions based upon agreements.

What is noteworthy then about our sense of the fixity of our language is how the written language fixes our meanings to clarify the ways we rhetorically communicate with each other. Noteworthy is the fact that written language is a visual medium. It has been created and structured by inscriptions of our speech into a visual representation or symbolic notation. Unlike in phonics in talking about phonemes which are never defined with exact precision fixed visual symbols do not change. Important then in understanding our sense of stability is the use of our formal languages. It is the sense of stability that we have in the rigidity of the definitions of our names or terms defined within formal languages that gives us a sense of stability of their meaning.

We find fixity in semantic rules, in our use of logical and mathematical operators, and in the fixity of the rules and operations that shape the grammar of our artificial and formal languages. They are the rigid and determinate patterns that we have created by the rules that we have used in the creation of the patterns and sequences of such artificial created fixed systems of symbolic notations. All such fixity of meaning is thus arrived at by artifice, by cultural acceptance and conventions. They are socially constructed. Visual models, formal systems in conjunction with their use with graphics are designed to be read. They are just scripted vernaculars printed and inscribed in earthly fixed artifacts. Such formal and informal inscriptions then are as visual representation fixed and put into stable and defined symbolic forms that do not change after being imprinted on a page. As such they are products of convention and commitment determined by the politics of our printing and graphic culture.

And in so far as our graphic and formal languages are not scripted phonically we have difficulty in mastering visual languages in conjunction with the use of our spoken language. We do not speak graphics, models, maps, and formal systems of logical and mathematical notation. We rather read and interpret our images of them. Just as we need to have sounds for our alphabet, we need spoken words to interpret and define our symbols in formal languages.

Since we have to translate and interpret printed artifacts in our vernacular phonic or oral patterns of communication, we have visited upon us as a result the difficulties that we have of speaking about them in an oral language, a language that is in flux and that evolves as a product of refinement in its historical changes. And in doing so we fail to see the crucial difference between what seems natural and what seems artificial. We fail to see the differences between the use of our formal languages and the uses of the oral languages that we use in trying to translate them as we interpret them.

Rhetorically in so far as we use graphic or scripted languages, either formal or informally scripted, our use of them is basically to display them visually in a context of rhetorical explanation or argument conducted in an oral vernacular language with questionable presumptions about the fixity of their vernacular meanings. The use of these graphic and scripted languages has many of the same problems that we have in mixing the dialects of our oral vernaculars in communicating.

If we are not competent in our use of a formal or graphic language, we most likely have not internalized our use of it subconsciously by using its formation rules or transformation rules that we have used to create it. To use it and to interpret it however we need to resort to a rhetoric that uses the vernacular language to interpret it by **annotating** what we have done in displaying logical inferences that we make in using an artificial graphic language that we have not internalized in our thinking. Usually in logic we say that people infer and sentences imply. But in so far as we think in formal languages, we display the inferences we wish to make by displaying the logical implications that would follow from the transformation rules of a formal language that we have mastered.

Rhetorically then we see people *inferencing* about what is presented to them in language that displays the *logical implications* that they want to communicate about. We display to them what they themselves will determine that logically exists within and between statements within that formal language. Rhetorically formal languages are often used to communicate the logical implications that we want to display to an audience that exist between other and different symbolic representations of another formal language. But such use of formal languages to interpret another formal language presupposes a comparable competence in our use of those two different formal and graphic systems.

What makes formal language so important is that there is a focus on logical operations and logical syntax of the referencing systems. The simple focus on variables and operators simplifies our human understanding of the complexity that we find in the logical or mathematical operations. The simple focus condenses and abbreviates complexity thus creating simplifications. A simple focus renders visually perspicuous to our attention these logical functions in a ready and in an immediately uptake way. It does so by stripping away all the contextual and situational implications that any vernacular language expresses that tends to distract us from the logical structures of these languages.

Where people go astray in the use of formal and graphic language is that they are led into the distractions caused by the use of a vernacular language as a *metalanguage* (that is the language we use to talk about another language) to interpret our use of formal languages. We circle around in vernacular languages to interpret our formal languages and then we are distracted back again to an interpretation of our vernacular languages using misleading technical language. There can be no fixed stability in this circle of interpretations when they are interacting interpretively. In other words we keep circling around different points of reference where we can find little or no stability.

12 Fenced-off and fenced-in equilibriums: Outside and inside boundaries and fences

One noteworthy way biologists have been looking at living things has been in terms of the forms (morphology) and functions (physiology) that living things exhibit. Especially it is in terms of their anatomy or morphology that we observe living organisms. We find and see membranes that separate an outside from what exists inside of them. We see the forms of all sorts of anatomical structures with boundaries. And it is in morphological structures that we find that what is living (what functions physiologically) and that hides behind these fences. What is living is carrying on functions that separate what is living on the inside from its environmental ecology on the outside.

Living things are said to be cellular. What is outside is outside their skins and the membranes which enclose them to regulate and protect their insides. What is inside is what is said to be alive. What is outside impinges and succors what exists on the inside. What is inside seeks to live by using things, materials and energy that exists outside of them. And it is an interesting chemical property of water that the neutral pH of a solution of salts in water stands midway between the movement between cations and anions. It is by osmosis they pass one way or the other through the protective membrane surrounding living cells. It is this peculiar chemical property of water that allows the metabolic processes of life to take place. Without that chemical property of water life could not be sustained in it especially here on earth.

But there is one important question about being alive. It is, whether or not those protective and selective membranes such as our skin are alive? In so far as hair is a part of our skin it is not alive? But how much of our skin is alive? Certainly there is dead skin on top of our skin. And we can by scrubbing it remove it.

We think of organic individuals as forming barriers and boundaries, that is, fences, yet even behind fences they relate to each other symbiotically and together much of the time in joint actions in interacting societies. Especially this is so of the different levels of tissues and their cells that exist inside the skin of multi-cellular organisms, which in their complex ways create different sorts of fences existing inside that are very much alive together with different levels of inside internal fences. It all seems to be boxes within boxes! Note the variety of peritonea that shield our inside organs. Organisms as individuals or in societies act separately or together to acquire the resources that they need by creating access and modes of selection in dealing with their physical environment.

In my youth when I studied bacteriology, it struck me that a microscope was a tool that had severe limitations about what we could see of what was living on the micro-cellular level of most living creatures. Unfortunately, at that time it was difficult to see the forms and functions of cells and their relations to each other in tissues, for much of what we wanted to see especially in the cytoplasm was invisible and transparent when cells were alive. One had to kill and stain cells and tissue if anyone were to have any visual observation of the changes in the structures and functions that were supposedly going on and functioning within living cells. Therefore, in most of our observations of what we thought were living cells instead we were dealing with specimens on slides under microscopes after the tissues and cells were dead.

At that time to see living structures and their function there were very few visual tags injected into specimens to see actual life functions going on within the cells and tissues. Now however new radioactive tracers enable one to see what is going on now open to visual imaging. We have designed new markers to better to see what we now think of as life processes. And now no longer are we limited in the size of what we can see visually in optical microscopes. The electron microscope has extended the limits of what once was thought impossible to see such things as the images of viruses. Now we use all types of sonic and magnetic and resonating devices that allow us to see visually images produced that are seemingly iconic patterns and structures in cells once thought to be impossible to see. But still we have in the uses of these new devices some of the same problems in imaging in using light as these new and different radiant waves of energy again are still striking the living cells and are altering and killing the life out of whatever it is that we are now seeing.

As I remember from my high school texts what was called *protoplasm* or *cytoplasm* was presumed to be nothing but a simple fluid that constituted the essence of life. And it strikes me now how ironically it was at a time when texts books were saying that protoplasm and cytoplasm were a **simple life substance.** Again what we seem to see now in observations are often to a large degree again merely the inert physical and chemical residues of molecular patterns that no longer are playing an active part in the living processes of the cells. Those living processes have been destroyed either by the prior preparations of specimens or by the absorbed reflected radiation that we see reflected back from the objects imaged. We do not see in living things actual nutritive, reproductive, developmental growth, nor do we see life actually performing in the subjects we image those regenerative and catabolic maintenance functions. What we see in new imaging devices are patterns and slices of physical and chemical functions that seem to play an important part within life processes.

What is at issue about all this imaging is how realistic are these representational models and drawings or schemata that we produce to interpret what it is that we are seeing through these new and various types of image making devices. They are as images simply projections. What is the reality of what we see in so far as we are attempting to describe life processes by using physical descriptions and by using graphic or inscribed formulaic notations? Certainly, it is the images and the descriptions that we make of them that we use to communicate about what it is that we see. It is much the same with all creative imaging in painting and photography that there is a scale expansion or an image reduction. Note that famous portrait painters painted their subjects on their canvases that were larger than life. Note that primitives have feared their photographs for fear that doing so would make them smaller.

There was very much the same problem with the image reduction in radar. I was not seeing Keokuk, Iowa, on one of my missions. It was an image I knew to be coming from Keokuk. But how much of these descriptions of seeing Keokuk on my scope were Keokuk as I was doing in looking at its image? What I was seeing were mostly a result of merely interpretations using my vernacular or ordinary language in interpreting those imaging processes projected on my radar scope. How much of our interpretation of the images that we observe are simply derived from inferences we make from the implications that we derive from our knowledge of what we think our imaging devices are actually doing?

What we see as chemical we cannot easily model as a biological process with its own peculiar functions and with its own evolutionary emergent types of interactions. What we are observing is the outline of unique patterns of physiological processes of what we think goes on within a living *species*. Such imaging now again in part is comparable to how we once used a microscope to picture the different stages of both mitosis and meiosis, which can now be refined step by step in refined photography so as to reproduce in video cinematic simulation the very steps that we thought of as going on as a living process.

Today we simulate living actions by projecting a number of fast moving photographic stills on a strip of film on a screen as we now do using digital photography. Even now we are still using our old style optical microscopes to do the same thing by using digital cameras to create the moving slices of images, and yet we are still thinking that we are again seeing actual life processes not simply images. Just as motion picture frames do not allow us to observe reality. Imaging is still just a mere simulation of life and not an actual observation of what is going on.

It is much the same as in visual perception when we see a flying arrow or the path of a tracer bullet. It is a visual streak. And the artificiality in producing simulations is why biology in its methods has developed those markers that can be visually observed going throughout inner cell processes. It is in an imaging process much like seeing the path of that mentioned tracer bullet. We do not see the bullet. We see a tracer, a burning piece of phosphorus. Thus, questions about reality of what we are seeing begin to fly around and about what we call imaging and all about those paradoxes that we get into when we begin to question the reality of what we are seeing going on in these various imaging processes. As I have suggested what we are seeing becomes a matter of interpretation based upon a great deal of knowledge of medical technology.

Questions begin to be raised about what we are actually describing. They are questions about what we are actually seeing. Questions again arise about how we are describing these perceptions in linguistic terms. To avoid this sort of seemingly endless pursuit of questions about what is real and what we are seeing and what we are not seeing, there is another way of looking at the paradoxes of defining of what it is to be alive. And again using those old positive descriptions of what it is to be alive raises all those serious considerations about stuff and space that were thought to be the stuff of physics and chemistry, and it raises questions about what is it that we are doing in studying biology where we find different sorts of models that are not reducible or simplified into the models and mathematical frames of biochemistry and biophysics.

Let me pursue again somewhat further this detour into these empirical issues about the differences between the living and the dead or what it is to be or not be alive. One noteworthy feature of what some say about what it is to be alive is to say that living things live within fences that allow for the containment of what is going on inside those fences. And as most fences allow access to what is outside, these fences protect and give security to what goes on the inside of them. But not only do these fences act as containers but they also assist though their **selective or semi permeable** functions the maintenance of the processes of life that are said to be in some sort of equilibrium being maintained behind, inside, or within those fences.

This is the view that life seems to aim at some sort of homeostasis. It views life as an *autotelic* process of controlled and managed equilibrium whereby processes inside the fences maintain themselves by the form and function of fences. In addition, in turn these supposedly living things engage with things outside their fences through selective functions with all sorts of things. All living things seem to be made up of cells as do prisons. But even prisons have gates and need to maintain contact with what is outside to keep prisons functioning.

Cells likewise behind their membranes maintain levels of energy. They control access to the material and energy outside their membranes to maintain their inner energy states in equilibrium. All life seems to exist in a bubble within different kinds of ecological types of equilibrium. Living things seem to use or need a somewhat stable environment outside to maintain its own equilibrium within their insides. Life appears to be such that we all seem to live or exist inside of bubbles.

But there are limits to the size of cells in maintaining their inner equilibrium that seems also to characterize life. The smaller the cells the smaller is the ratio of the volume of a cell to its surface area that is needed to absorb what is needed by the cell to maintain its inner equilibrium. When we compare the relative increase of the volume of a cell to the volume of a ball or a sphere, the volume increases by the radius cubed. Note this increasing of volume can be mathematically stated: ($V = \frac{4}{3}\pi r^3$) while the surface area increases only with the radius squared, ($V = 4\pi r^2$). Thus the smaller the radius the smaller is the ratio of the volume of the cell to the surface area of the membrane which thus allows relatively more area for more nutrients and energy to be absorbed into the insides of the cell where the life within the cell is thus relatively smaller in its volume.

The smallest particle with an outside film or membrane covering it would be what is now being termed an 'aerosol.' The word 'aerosol' derives from the fact that matter 'floating' in air is a suspension (a mixture in which solid or liquid or combined solid-liquid particles are suspended in a fluid. To differentiate suspensions from true solutions the term 'sol' evolved its new meaning - it originally meant to cover dispersions of tiny (sub-microscopic) particles in a liquid. With studies of dispersions in air the term *aerosol* has evolved and now embraces liquid droplets, solid particles, and combinations of these. The question arises, 'Can the insides of aerosol ever become the starting point of living things?' What goes on within and inside those aerosols? This thus touches again on those questions about the beginning of life.

Note the following description of cells taken from Wikipedia is often given the standard view of life:

> 'Cells are the basic view of the morphological structure of life in all the various types of living organisms.' The **cell** is the functional basic unit of life. It was discovered by Robert Hooke. It is the functional unit of all known living organisms. It is the smallest unit of life that is classified as a living thing, and is often called the building block of life. Some organisms, such as most bacteria are unicellular (consist of a single cell). Other organisms, such as humans are multi-cellular. Humans have about 100 trillion or 10^{14} cells; a typical cell size is 10 μm and a typical cell mass is 1 nanogram. The largest cells are about 135 μm in the anterior horn in the spinal cord while granular cells in the cerebellum, the smallest, can be some 4 μm and the longest cell can reach from the toe to the lower brain stem.

All this suggests then that the key model to describe what it is to be alive is one where there are cells, where there is feedback and various types of back up to maintain a state of equilibrium within a membrane. Membranes that contain and maintain the equilibrium within living cells are said as mentioned to be *semi-permeable*, that is, living cells allow for *selective* transfer of materials. It is the activities in this transfer of energy from inside to the outside or *visa versa* that seems positively for many to characterize the various the functions of all living things.

But it is a striking fact in dealing with the complexity of things that we see in the world that there are equally other types of equilibrium modeling or framing that goes on in all **the other** sciences. Is this **a law like observation** about all the sciences that in them there are equilibriums in all of them both material and biological? Are equilibrium models the same for what is living and for what is non-living such as machines? Do we not use equilibrium models to discuss catalytic reactions and the stability of proteins, and even of molecules as we do in quantum mechanics?

Or on the contrary might we ask, is it not a simple fact that an equilibrium model is just a human linguistic contrivance and that these 'equilibrium models' are applied in different ways to different things in different sciences and as well in many other different disciplines? Are they as a type of graphic representation simply useful in organizing our practical activities? I find it striking that we use so many different equilibrium models in the sciences and technology in so many diverse graphical and mathematical ways. That we describe so many independent and different human enterprises from politics, to social institutions, to personal relations, to factories, machines, chemical reactions, astronomical phenomena, molecules, subatomic particles, and even solid state physics. Since this is the case, should we not then given our awareness of this wide application of equilibrium models be suspicious of the ontologies and cosmologies that are being used to explain the structures of such stabilities?

Note then this almost seeming universality of the use of equilibrium models in the various disciplines and technologies. What is the basis of this seeming universality of their use in the sciences and technologies? But are not fenced in equilibrium models thus equally used in all the models of politics and in the schematic frames used in the social sciences to model most social interactions? The use of models of equilibrium is equally prevalent as well in economics as well as in the political sciences. They are especially used in ecology and meteorology. Yet it is this same sort of modeling using representations of equilibriums that is equally taking place in most of the natural sciences and technologies, for example in astronomy, physics, chemistry, and biology. To continue we might add such models are used to describe the equilibrium designed into our inventions of machines. They are used in various devices for temperature controls and for devices that control the processes in the maintenance of assembly lines.

But again such equilibrium modeling used in sciences and technologies equally apply as well to business organizations, family dynamics, and the stability of our social and corporate institutions. It applies to legal theory. Note the attempt that is made in rendering and maintaining one kind of justice is to reach a balance such as the one described as a balance between the use of such social and political strategies of carrots and sticks. Many aphoristic and metaphoric images such as this are simple descriptions of equilibrium. It has not been lost on me that my first tranquilizer for my spastic gut was *Librium*, a well-chosen name by a pharmaceutical company for a drug that reestablishes gastric equilibrium in irritable bowel syndromes.

All this leads one to think instead that 'equilibrium models' are human artificial language impositions just the same as the trade name *Librium*. They are useful in providing differently constructed and similar models of explanation. They are useful in different forms of human application of expertise. All this suggests that these models are not descriptive of structures and functions in objective things, but rather these models of different processes are a result of human artifice. They are a product of enterprise that creates schemata to organize how we can deal with the different kinds of physical dynamics and how we organize different forms of human endeavor. As schemata they are useful in coming to terms with the complexity we are trying to understand in what we do so as to be able to carry out human purposes and intentions as we manage to live out our lives.

Using fenced in equilibrium models in all these various and different contexts suggests then that there might be something innate or elemental about the foundations of our linguistic framing and our artificial devising of our thinking tools. By innate here I do not mean genetic, but I mean that these models are basic to the way neurologically that they have developed to assist us in making our descriptions of ordinary perceptions of actions and reaction in the simple ways that we psychologically seem to frame them in our ordinary ways of speaking about our ways of looking at the world.

But are all the ways that we organize human action and thinking framed in equilibrium models? Is it a model that frames all types of modeling? I want to continue to suggest that models of equibriums are just one set of a larger set of graphics and pictorial representations that are used visually to organize human practical experience. What I hope to show as I continue discussing models and graphics is that there are different kinds of graphic representations with which we frame our interpretations and thinking, but in many ways these graphic constructions do interrelate, and we find that equilibrium models do have the potential to explore new and innovative interconnections and correlations in conjunction with other models.

For instance we have primitive senses of orientation such as a sense of stability and balance that relate to fixity and change such as in moving or turning. Such frames are thought to be about stability and balance, which is a state of equilibrium. One sense of stability comes from our vision, another from our inner ear and its semicircular canals, and finally one comes from the neurological balances that come from our muscle coordination. Note the difference in medicine and the technology used by those in medicine who are engaged in treating problems of vision from those who treat problems of hearing, and from those who are in orthopedics. Each clinician uses different models.

Noteworthy although it is out of equilibrium frames that we develop our sense of right and left used in ranking. They still seem to be different forms of graphic representation. We have a sense of up and down that gives us a sense of weight. We have a sense of in and out that is inherent in the way we grammatically indicate relationships. Again we have a sense of balance and stability for centering. We have a sense of front and back for direction. We have a primitive sense of the use of digital units such as fingers for counting that seems to be built into our ordinary language for simple counting, ranking, and ordering. Each of these different ways of visually framing is somewhat related to uses of similar models although they still are quite different ways of viewing things. Note equally the simplicity we have in just counting digitally. Counting can be about balance, but it can serve many functions in generating the functions of numbers. Note also the way we rank things both right and left. We have in speech a simple grammar for describing hierarchies and order. It is these various types of graphical models that allow us to structure how we rank and order things.

Note the anthropological researches of the 'Structuralists' such as Claude Lévi-Strauss, a French anthropologist and ethnologist who argued that the 'savage' mind had the same structures as the 'civilized' mind and that human characteristics are same everywhere. These observations culminated in his famous book *Tristes Tropiques* in which he tried to show the cultural differences in the grammar of human relationships that produce social stability.

But in rejecting Claude Lévi-Strauss's thesis of the universality of the models of structures for human beings I want to illustrate instead their plurality. I contend that it is out of the reduction of these primitive senses of orientation that I have been trying to show how the formal models and mathematical frames grow. It is out of this ordinary language usage about balance and stability with its localized grammar that we artificially develop and construct both socially and linguistically the conventional ways to deal with the complexity of the issues and the problems that we seem to face. And it is then in this plurality of uses of equilibrium models defined by fences that suggests that what we are modeling are not the actual structures that externally exist beyond the range of our ordinary uses of our senses of words in our vernacular language. Rather it is through artificial construction of linguistic and graphical ways of modeling that we have been able to invent new and different creative ways that enable us to come to terms with our practical experiences.

We do it by creating by human artifice conventional frames of reference to deal with the practical side of life. We use such elemental and developmental mathematical schemata to make correlations, which in turn allow us to formulate the logic of conditionals and to transform them into the causal statements. It is by means of these conditionals that we are able to formulate the algorithms that we use to deal with the world. We use the observed correlations to observe and to identify causal connections that are used in command and control. We also use these artificial schemes and graphical schemata to order and to frame our lives. We use them to sort out and categorize. We use them to identify our property and to order and prioritize our everyday concerns. Filing cabinets contain files. They are fenced in models of stable patterns useful to catalogue our various interests and to frame and model our concerns. They fence in classifications which are useful for us to maintain the various selective patterns we find useful in controlling our lives. Note we fence off regions to keep intruders out. We fence off regions to prevent some things from escaping.

But note a dam is a fence that keeps the water back and regulates the water levels by maintaining through various types of locks and spill-ways. We use them to determine just how much water we want to contain and store behind the dam. In establishing water levels we maintain an equilibrium as to what sort of lake levels we want to maintain to make sure that our boat docks are not under or out of the water. Of course with adjustments on the spill ways we can readjust what sort of lake level we want to maintain in new and changed ways. We can revise any stable equilibrium into another form of stable equilibrium. Stabilization often is no more than readjusting our different states of equilibrium.

Equilibrium models then are thus subject to change. And fences that contain just who comes in and whom or what goes out of our domains are subject to alteration. We move our fenced in pastures around. What is noteworthy is the degree to how much of our thinking is guided by our artifice in creating newly designed fenced in areas. And behind those fences we find that there exist various states of equilibrium that are both static and dynamic. What is important to note is that we both create the patterns and the openings in our fences. What windows and doors that we put in our houses are a matter of design. Note the architecture of medieval castles and the choice of their locations.

Note that our bodies are held in static structures by skeletal structures. Note that even in the smallest living cells there is an architecture that maintains its form. Their nutrition comes from energy and materials from their environmental ecology. Noteworthy in single cells, such as *eukaryotes,* their cell membranes are propped up by tubules that allow them to retain their shapes and forms even in such diminutive small cellular wall structures. And too note the muscle structures and fat cells in *metazoans* can also alter the patterns of our skeletal structures and even the features of our face and skin.

But in the smallest cells of *prokaryotes* there is little need for internal structures to maintain their form. Since they do not have forms requiring locomotion, nor mechanisms for ingesting other living organisms or the dead remains of other organisms, their shapes and forms are simple and their enclosing membranes are less complex, much like the shape of our bladders that folds and collapses when the water pressure is down. Since *prokaryotes* are self sustaining in manufacturing their own energy for metabolism, they have no need for forms designed for movements to ingest other forms or dead remains of life.

Note too that the walls that surround gated communities protect the dynamic equilibriums that shape the types of family life and protects the social activities going on within. And too national borders are protected from the intrusion of foreigners for purposes of keeping out unwanted trouble from what we conceive to be toxic intruders entering from other countries. Governments in the name of national security protect their stable institutions and their job markets in equilibrium from outsiders that exist beyond their borders. Note the immigration problem that the United States and Europe have in bringing in others to do their dirty work.

Houses too are designed with skins to protect those who live within them from the elements and the weather. And windows and doors allow for sun and guests to penetrate our households. What is striking in all this walling and fencing is what is allowed in and what we wish to keep out. We need goods to cross borders. We need service providers to enter into gated communities. *Eukaryotic* cells need to ingest inorganic materials or even other organisms. They kill or they eat other organisms alive. Or they are like scavengers they need to ingest the corpses of the dead into their interiors. Eating is bringing something into a community of cells to nourish and sustain the life processes, that is, the *catabolism,* the *metabolism,* or the *anabolism* going on within living bodies.

If a wall happens to be impervious nothing can pass through by definition. It is completely protected from everything that is destructive coming from the outside. For example viruses have an impervious covering to protect their RNA which makes them difficult to kill. Viruses outside the cells need to penetrate other cells to take over, that is, to infect them. But once inside and that virus cell is within another cell, the impenetrable wall comes tumbling down. Interestingly the zygote formed by the union of sperm and eggs at first has an impervious membrane to protect it as it enters and begins its ascent up the fallopian tubes. It is only when it penetrates and grows within the uterus that it opens itself up to its attachment to the mother's blood stream.

The difficulty then of impervious walls is that what is living within them eventually will run out of the sustenance it needs to be able to continue and to maintain itself. Very much like in the social politics of this world, no nation can sustain itself completely isolated despite all such historical isolationist attempts to build fences. Note the history of the Chinese wall and the history of the Maginot line and their circumventions. Note again that quarantines are about building walls to keep people in and to keep people out. Note how political sanctions are attempts to build such walls. Note how politics is about building and tearing down walls.

What is so striking then about talk about fences and walls is that the concept or frame of what it is to be a wall or a fence applies to so many different areas of human experience. And in so far as they are built by the artifice of living things, they are created frames by which we can organize and deal with human problems and situations that require the maintenance of both stability and different sorts of dynamic equilibriums that are able to be maintained within them.

What this suggests is that a model of fencing and a model of balance and stability are intricately used as models that are tied together in most of our other different ways of thinking and in the various ways we use our language and pictorials and graphic representations as we do in the sciences and in the technologies. Such representations are not intimately tied to any ontological realistic structures inherent in the phenomena that we talk about. They become applicable when we determine their uses in terms of the semantics that adjusts our interpretations of what goes on in the terms of our ordinary language and in its use and its applications to projects and concerns for control and production.

And in so far as these barriers are isolated and contain processes within these barriers they are a major concern of human problem solving. A *fenced in equilibrium* is in a way just a symbiotic union of two different sorts of models joined together that are at the heart of cognitive simplification. It is the artificiality and creative design of such models of fenced-in equilibria that are at the very heart of much human thinking and the uses of human intelligence. And as such they are one of the most important models we use in the sciences and technologies. They are as designs modeled to help us deal with our ignorance of complex matters that concern us. In other words we use fenced-in equilibrium models to deal with complexity in simpler terms, especially we do it by using an artificial constructed graphic language that we can interpret in the end in using ordinary language in ways that we need to be able to do things.

We often fail to see that even though these graphics and linguistic representations seem complex that their use is to make things simpler to deal with some of the complexity found in of our language and in our graphic and mathematical representations. Maps and graphics, models of equilibrium are actually in one way often are used to simplify the complexity of the mathematical languages and the pictorial models and graphs that we use to understand what we are doing. This sought after simplicity in our language and our visual schemata is an attempt to make complex models *user friendly*. And when we speak of user friendly computers it is just a way of expressing our need for simplicity in performing seemingly all too complicated tasks by our use of simpler algorithms in place of more complex algorithms.

Looking at the problems of walls from another perspective, that is, a negative one, such as the one facing 'Doctors without Borders' who face quite different problems, for they are vulnerable to the chaotic situations they enter into. When there are no roofs and walls, foreign elements are free to occupy any unprotected space. Note that similar ecological problems happen in the national parks such as Yellowstone. Its porous borders make it difficult to keep invasive species out and to keep its natural fauna and flora denizens in. Wolves and grizzly bears have no protection as they have no conception of what defines their territorial rights. All these boundaries and rights are defined by human artifice and not by the animals, nor are they defined by the plants within. One of the greatest problems facing ecologists is how to protect the boundaries of our sanctuaries and our natural preserves.

Skins, fences, walls, membranes, cell walls, and armed guards form barriers to protect what lives within. Just as we have an up and down by using plumb bobs to create our houses, and just as we have squares to create our rights and lefts, and our fronts and backs, so we have walls to define our outsides and our insides. Just as we have beakers, flasks, and cylinders to give different shapes to our containers, so we have boxes and wrapping to protect their contents. It is all about what is inside and outside and the need for a barrier in between.

Note that such a container model frame is interestingly simply dyadic when we think and contrast an inside with an outside. But when we focus on the barrier the model becomes a simple triad, an outside, a barrier, and an inside. And when we look at rhetoric we note that human communication to be readily understood needs to avoid transcending the use of terms beyond the count of three. Considering dyads factorial 2 (2!) has two permutations. Considering triads factorial 3 (3!) has six permutations, but going four square factorial 4 (4!) has 24. And, when we consider the number of fingers on our hand, factorial five (5!), it has 120. Thus when we are dealing with the complexity beyond three it overwhelms our short term memories when we try to relate to a number of things.

Containment takes many shapes and forms. It is a way to restrain someone or something by boxing them up. What is important is to see is how we create the forms of containment and how we design them by human artifice by such a simple model that is native to our logical syntax that is framed by the prepositions *inside* and *outside*. Such a creation is open and free for new patterns of design. And design is a product of the imagination. It is a product of artifice and calculation that completes the ratios we want to put into whatever we want to build to protect its contents. Simply note the various designs that milk bottles have had in the technological changes in the materials that they were made of. There were changes from glass, to wax paper containers, and now finally to molded plastic containers. Note the different problem solved by each of these changes.

Our design of fences and the equilibrium between the inside and outside of them is an artifact of human evolution, and it is biologically built into our sense of whom and what we are. As a product of human artifice it is the major factor in the modeling of those same biological structures. It is interesting that in the new uses of the biological sciences there are two directions of research going on today in microbiology. The following extended quote by Evelyn Fox Keller describes two different approaches in the study of life:

> One of the most important goals commonly claimed for scientific (biological) explanation in general, and for computation in particular, is predictability. But organisms seen *as* naturally crafted computational machines can be just as effectively be employed for making predictions as can *artificially* crafted machines, and this is just how they are being used in many contemporary research endeavors. Another goal often asserted is the ability to *design and construct* new entities. Yet here, too, real organisms can serve at least as well. The information and technical facility that molecular biologists have acquired over the past several decades makes it possible to employ existing natural organisms in the *design and creation of new kinds of organisms*, genetically modified to perform particular functions and even to conform to particular *design principles* [emphasis added]. (1995: 298-299)

This major division in the direction of the use of models of explanation in biology suggests that the major priority in understanding life is in the redesign of what is living. And the fact that we can by recombinant DNA and RNA and by the use of enzymes and catalysts alter and change life functions suggests the path to understanding of life and its beginnings. But there is the other question as to whether life has actually a beginning? That question leaves us with the question, 'Whether there is such a nominal thing as a beginning of life?' Evolutionary changes in life functions are already existing functions in living beings. We do not alter life functions simply with chemical engineering as we do in developing pharmaceuticals. But the problems we have with drugs and biotech modifications of living things is a **political problem** that requires coming to terms with terms about life and its changing functions, and too about what is valuable about these changes, and especially about any changes through the use of drugs.

13 The rhetoric and politics of standardization: Measurements and needs for precision

Important then to escape the pitfalls of any arbitrariness in understanding what we are doing in counting units of length, weight, or any measurements of areas of space, we need to understand what constitutes the unit of measurement in order to use it practically in what we do when we use measuring tools. Measurements such as sums of units of length, area, of volume, angles, weight, and even sums of units of time are **countable.** In turn we use these measurements to relate to other things that we also define as being **countable**.

How we relate to those countable applications depends upon the measuring tools we create. And what constitutes a unit of measurement is established with these measuring tools within the legal frameworks of what might be considered political power or law, whether laws of the tribe or the sovereign power of a nation. As experts we make political demands that become commands of those that have the political power to standardize measurements in manufacturing, construction, trade, and commerce. They create the law that underpins the technical definitional agreements that are made about measurements by those different social institutional agreements made between social corporate structures and government agencies.

Measurements are always made then within certain social and political frameworks. The definitions of measurable units are usually initiated within the jurisdictions of technological and scientific institutions which with their persuasive power are able to eventually reach their legitimized agreements about standards, and they gain their approvable within law using enforceable legal contracts. Thus, units of measurement for the most part actually have a legal basis such that the technical agreements of interest groups are enacted into laws that lay the foundation of any contractual agreement between those using them.

Let me first illustrate a linear model of the metric system (SI) as standardized and defined internationally by agreement and by political consensus. Next let us compare metric system (SI) with the standardizations of the Imperial/American System established by countries that legally adopt them.

13.1 The Standardization of Metric Measurements

A meter has been officially defined to be the distance traveled by light in a vacuum in 1/299,792.458 second. All other length and distance measurements in the metric system derive from the meter.

Table 13.1: Metric Unit Conversion

Unit	Relation to base
kilometer	10^3 metres
hectometer	10^2 metres
decametre	10^1 metres
decimeter	10^{-1} metres
centimeter	10^{-2} metres
millimeter	10^{-3} metres
micrometer	10^{-6} metres
nanometer	10^{-9} metres
Imperial/American Measurements	

Note the lack of simplicity in converting various units of measures of length in Imperial/American Measurement System. The difficulty lies in the complexity of the conversions and comparisons of units. A yard can be defined as the length of a pendulum that causes its arc to swing in exactly 1 second. Note the nautical mile is the distance across 1' (1/60 of a degree) around the earth's surface. To simplify calculations the practical rule is to transfer Imperial measurements to the metric system when doing complex measurement problems

The metric system makes visible the relative sizes of the comparisons. Note the following model Figure 13.1 using the metric system of measurement illustrates the relative comparative measurable scale of small units of life and units of matter starting with the larger protozoa largest in size and going down the scale to the somewhat smaller eukaryotes that were the progenitors of all muti-cellular life. These units are compared again in size then with the smaller prokaryotes, and then down to the virus and then to the smaller protein molecules, and finally down to the theoretical estimated size of atoms. Note the illustrating model does not extend further down in scale to the theoretical size of nuclear particles. It is through the use of such numerical scalar models that we are able to make relative comparisons in using models and graphs to think of the scale of things and to make relative comparisons more visual perspicuous.

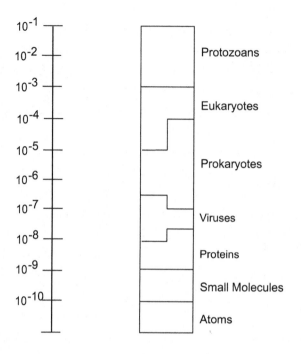

Figure 13.1: Descending Relative Scale of Protazoans, Eukaryotes, Prokaryotes, Viruses, Proteins and Atoms

But note too that the politics and the social politics of measurement have social problems and conflicts. Difficulties arise about the precision and the practical applicability of these legally developed and institutionally technically defined agreed upon standards of measurements. They are issues over values and political power. It is at this point that we see the importance of understanding the rhetoric and the politics of these disputes that take place over the accuracy and the precision of the technical definitions of measurements and the choices that were made in deciding on the standards to be used in differently defined units of measurement. Such negotiations over legalizing the definition of units of measurements present all the measuring complications that create problems between different societies who have their own cultural preferred different accepted standards of measurement to meet their social and political needs.

Difficulties thus arise about the precision and practical applicability of these legally and institutionally defined technically agreed upon standards of measurements. It is at this point that we see the importance of understanding the rhetoric and the politics of these disputes that take place over the technical definitions of measurements and the choices that we make deciding between the different standards that are used to distinguish between the different applications of these defined units of measurement. It presents all the problems of metric conversion that different societies have who still prefer their own cultural standards of measurement over the uses of the metric system. Note the difficulty the United States has in eliminating the penny as a unit of measurement of money. It creates and economy where direct currency exchanges are time consuming. Note how electronic transactions and accounting calculation have eliminated the physical efforts expended in the exchange of worthless pennies.

Note the politics and the history of defining the angstrom unit of light used in spectroscopy:

> Although intended to correspond to 1×10^{-10} metres, for precise spectral analysis the ångström needed to be defined more accurately than with the use of the metre which until 1960 was still defined based on the length of a bar of metal held in Paris. In 1907 the International Astronomical Union defined the international ångström by declaring the wavelength of the red line of cadmium in air equal to 6438.46963 international ångströms, and this definition was endorsed by the International Bureau of Weights and Measures in 1927. From 1927 to 1960, the ångström remained a secondary unit of length for use in spectroscopy, defined separately from the metre, but in 1960, the length unit metre itself was redefined in spectroscopic terms, thus aligning the ångström as a submultiple of the metre. In short, one nanometre is equal to ten ångströms. Today the use of the ångström as a unit is less popular than it used to be, and the nanometre is often used instead. The ångström is officially discouraged by the International Committee for Weights and Measures. (Oxford English Dictionary)

To apply units of measurement then I suggest that we need first to hypothesize about what we directly perceived to be a unit when we try to count anything. We create units literally by taking steps in our thinking to produce or to isolate them. Acts of measurement are based upon our notion that units have boundaries or frames which determine whether something can be perceived as a whole and that such wholes are repeatable and thought identical.

Measurements also involve counting such as we do with the digits of our fingers. We see each finger as a whole and the others like it are also unit appendages of the hand. We line them up to make them separate by contrast. Numbers in one sense then are units or digits that we conceive as counts that we make when we add up our fingers. Primitively counting involved making scratches just as archeologists have found in the early developments of writing. In its elementary form writing had in its very beginning in scratches, which we see in the root historical sense of what it was to write. It first started as a tally of counts. Writers were 'scratchers'. Such was the beginning in the tallying of digits. It was just juxtaposing scratches as symbols of groups of tallies. A count then is based upon combining one unit with another to make an aggregate unit which allows us to keep adding digits by adding each digit to make a new number which we then think of as a new unit, or a tally. One added to one creates a new unit of two, which is a pair, and a pair is a unit as we do in our treating a couple as a unit. And adding a new digit of one to the new unit of two or a pair makes a new unit of three, a trinity, a triple, or a triad. Note the Nicean Creed thinks of the trinity as one. Thus we generate in name a series of new units when we add to each of the previous named aggregate or tally. Thus, in sum we can continually create a new unit by continually adding a new unit or a digit to a previously created digit.

I learned from my four year old son very late in my life with no help from any teacher that adding numbers is simply counting up one number the number of times of the value of the other. And also that subtraction is counting down the number of times the value of the other. And multiplication is no more than counting equal tallies and then counting up by the number of the tally by the number of the tallies. And division is just the reverse of that, which explains why in dividing we are always subtracting from the number that we are dividing. That I should have to find this way of dealing with numbers, which is so obvious to any mathematician, illustrates to me the deficiency of my early parochial school training in learning math.

And to continue in thinking this way it occurred to me also that not only do we count with our hands, with the thumb summing up the tally of five with the closure of our thumb, but that by using both hands we generate our decimal system of numbers by using our hands to create two tallies of five. A hand is a set or tally of additions with its five digits. And the number of hands is a count of the tallies of five which is simply adding hands of fingers by a count that we call multiplication.

We see these processes modeled in the design of an abacus. See the sketch of a Chinese abacus in Figure 13.2 below. This historical account and the picture are a copy of a Chinese organization that sells advertising tours and materials that display Chinese culture.

There are five beads to count the digits and two beads to count two tallies of five digits. And a second row of five beads and two more beads to tally the tallies in the first row. And thus the abacus is aligned by rows of rows to keep tallying our arithmetic operations just as we use an order of prefixs to tally up 10's in our decimal system. It is the model of our first mechanical calculator. The abacus is sometimes called a counting frame. It is a calculating tool still used in parts of Asia for doing arithmetic.

But there are different elemental uses of numbers beside our counting or adding by addition or by multiplication by adding tallies. There is the **ranking** and **ordering** of digits. Ranking and ordering produce quite different type of models than that illustrated by the abacus. Looking at the palm of our left hand the index finger is left next to the middle finger, the middle finger is left and next to the ring finger, and the ring finger is left and next to our pinky or the little finger.

By defining numbers next to each other, not only are we able to count them, but we are able to order them as well. Thus, we create the distinction between cardinal numbers and ordinal numbers. One counts, and the other ranks or orders. Note the importance of thinking of numbers in a definite defined order. First, second, third, who likes to be third? And if you come in fourth in most races, it does not even count. You do not even show. Note that if something does not count, it never matters. Such are the uses of terms surrounding counting and ordering to rank what we think of things as having importance.

content by Mr.Du Feibao

The abacus was a great invention in ancient China and has been called by some Western writers "the earliest calculating machine in the world."

The abacus has a long history behind it. It was already mentioned in a book of the Eastern Han Dynasty, namely Supplementary Notes on the Art of Figures written by Xu Yue about the year 190 A. D. Its popularization occurred at the latest during the Song Dynasty (960-1127), when Zhang Zeduan painted his Riverside Scenes at Qingming Festival. In this famous long scroll, an abacus is clearly seen lying beside an account book and doctor's prescriptions on the counter of an apothecary's. During the Ming Dynasty (1368-1644), the abacus was introduced into Japan.

Abacuses are easy to make, handy to carry around and quick to give the answers, provided one knows how to move the beads. They have been in use, therefore, down to this day. They are made in different sizes, and the largest known abacus, measuring 26 centimetres high by 306 centimetres long with 117 rods (for as many digits), is over a hundred years old and is kept at Darentang, a well-known traditional pharmacy in Tianjin.

The beads on an abacus may be round or rhombus in shape. Traditionally, there are two beads above the horizontal bar and five below. Simplified modern versions have one bead above and four or five below. The methods of calculation remain unchanged.

At a time when the world has entered the age of electronics, the abacus still enjoys undiminished vitality in China. Tests have shown that, for operations of addition and subtraction, the abacus is still faster than the electronic calculator. China developed in 1980 an "electronic abacus " which combines the speed of traditional addition and subtraction methods with those of the modern calculator at multiplication and division. It is a happy example of the integration between the East and West, the native and the modern.

Chinese abacus

Figure 13.2: Chinese Abacus

Units can be counted and ordered. How then do we then recognize or determine a count? Where do we start? How do we describe any order? Temporally we measure time by the regularity of repetition as Galileo supposedly did when he used his pulse to compare the various units of length of a pendulum with the presumed regularity of his pulse. Time in a primitive sense of the term is measured by the number of times that something presumptively regularly repeats itself.

Primitively then we can use our pulse assuming it is regular for short periods of time. But of course we know our pulse rate changes with any increased bodily activity. Thus time requires that we test the regularity of other repetitive events to determine which repetition of the two is more regular or more precise than the other. We can do that by numerous comparisons and correlations with other presumed seemingly regular repetitive pulsing or beating mechanisms or cycling events. Note the waves moving over the surface of lakes and seas when it is not gusting and blustery come in regularly. Such is the notion of regularity that we establish in music. Elementary is the use of the metronome to determine what is a constant rhythm or a beat. Note the musical conductor is a living metronome, who can change any speed of the beat by gesturing faster or slower, thus regulating and 'synchronizing' the beat of the orchestra. The same holds true in military drill. The drill sergeant establishes the cadence or the beat. 'Hup, two, hip, four!'

But note how musicians can defy our expectation by playing an unanticipated beat. Even as in poetry or song there is rhythm that is fundamentally ordered and based on counts of a beat. But the rhythms of language mostly result from our pacing our words in time as we do in our oral interpretation of poetry. But note that for the most part syllabication and words tend to vary in length and in strength with intonation. It is these spoken separate units in poetry that form a rhythm or a beat, or rhythmically interesting variations on a beat.

As Crystal illustrates the origins of language in a growing child starts with intonation and rhythm. Such as stated is the basis of poetry with its rhythm and its numbered beat and its intonations. We can even measure time by the repetition of the rhythm of a set of repeated words. When refereeing a basketball game, as I did years ago, I learned to count one thousand one, one thousand two, one thousand three, that is, the 3 second count in basketball to keep players from posting up too long under the basket in the area at the bottom of the key.

Spatially we usually measure distance or length by our number of steps or strides. We need to avoid shortening or lengthening our stride to make certain that our steps are uniform. Thus, we can pace off a distance. But we can instead of using as a measure a step just mark off the length of our steps with a measuring stick, which serves then as a more refined or precise unit of measurement. But then linear measurement depends on whose measuring stick that we use, a yard stick or a meter stick, or a rod that is 16 ½ feet used for a measuring length in surveying. Note the units that are adopted depend upon what is being measured, the purposes of the measurement, and the demands of the situation.

The ancient Greeks as mentioned first did it with a straight edge and a compass in their geometry. Note the importance of a taut string as a technical procedure to define both a straight edge and a compass. Note then that there are two basic presumptions in geometric constructions in Greek geometry:
1. a straight edge is straight,
2. the compass always draws equal radii when drawing circles.

The very beginning of the construction of lines and figures begins from these static presumptions behind the use of these two primitive instruments. What is most obvious is that Greek geometry in its constructions first focused on circles, triangles, and squares which are not treated numerically but as areas enclosed within lines. Using Figure 13.3 below let me interpret this elementary proto-geometry using elementary modes of construction as the Greeks approached it.

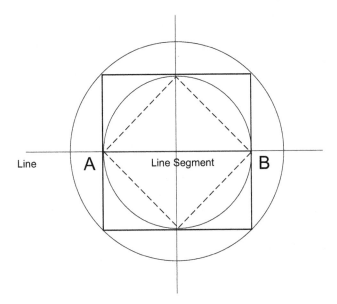

Figure 13.3: Elementary Proto-geometry

Note that when you draw a straight line with a straight edge it is presumed to be straight and when you arbitrarily mark off two points on the straight line using any arbitrary radius of your compass starting from any arbitrary chosen point on that line, such as A, you have by definition marked the end points of line A and B, that is equal distance with the span of the compass. And when you with your compass or divider make the arcs of two larger circles from each of the ends of your line segment, one above and one below from the end points A and B, you create two points of intersection that allows you to draw a line segment CD that passes through line segment AB. The points on the intersection of the line segment CD connecting the two intersecting arcs drawn with a compass is said to be the perpendicular bisector of the arbitrarily marked segment of the line AB. Note that this construction of a perpendicular bisector works on a line, on an arc of a circle, or any other smooth curve.

This construction using a straight line and a line between two points on compass or a string as having the same length seems to be the very basic axiom on which all Greek geometry was based. Such was the beginning of all the interesting constructions of all the different figures that Greek geometers constructed with the straight edge and the compass, and with which they were able to compare the ratios between all the lines, shapes, and volumes in determinate deductive ways. Such was the way Greeks drew circles and used lines to draw linear closed figures with areas both inscribed and circumscribed. Note especially the affinities of squares and circles in the construction of figures.

Much of our rhetoric to express direction and orientation centers on the three basic simplistic ways we have of constructing **three** figures: triangles, squares, and circles. They are the basic simple patterns of the models that we have when we think about what we say. We circle **around** a point. We **divide** our talking points and our concepts in **twos** and **threes**. And we think of triangles combining to form **quadrilaterals**. When we count four sides we need to think of four as two pairs. Four I suggest then is the beginning of our conceptions of complexity that begin to develop when we get beyond structures of triangles.

In one ordinary sense of the term *number*, when we speak of one, two, or three they are not considered a **number** of things. You do not say that there was a number at the party when there were only two or three. And if we think of numbers as describing complexity, that is, a number of things, we need to develop numbers to count the scope of that complexity, thus the rhetorical necessity of measuring by counting to come to terms with the complexity of a number of things.

Quantification in ordinary ways of speaking is both something we communicate by vague estimations or by rigorous enumeration. The weakness of the classical logical syllogism is in the lack of precision in talking about how many and how much and to what degree something is the case. In Medieval logic *some* could mean at least one, a few, many, most, and not all. Such classical logical quantifications are extremely loose and vague when we speak of 'some' in ordinary discourse.

Let me introduce to you the simple Greek way whereby we can construct an endless string of figures simply by constructing figures out of lines and triangles, circles, tetrahedrons, cubes, cones, pyramids, cylinders, and spheres. What this methodology of construction illustrates is our ability to name and create patterns that prior to the Greeks that few, or maybe no one had created or graphically displayed before. It shows how by rule or by deduction from basic rules and axioms, that we can innovatively create new patterns and forms especially in the field of mathematics.

As has been the case in the development of mathematics many mathematicians devised patterns that others were able then to use further to innovate and discover new patterns for themselves. It is much the same in chess. Players in following the moves made, and in using the logic of chess encounter positions probably never seen before. And chess players if they wish can by description of their positions of their pieces give it a new name, which others then in turn can use to identify the same defined positions in using 'standard chess notation'.

To illustrate the nominal deductive nature of plane or area geometry, let me show by example how there have been traditional proofs without numbers to prove one of the most basic theorems of geometry, namely the Pythagorean Theorem, which in its origins was about the areas of square figures constructed using an edge on each side of a right triangle. There are many different ways to prove this theorem, but the following Figure 13.4 demonstrates one simple geometric way without the use of any proofs using numerical algebra.

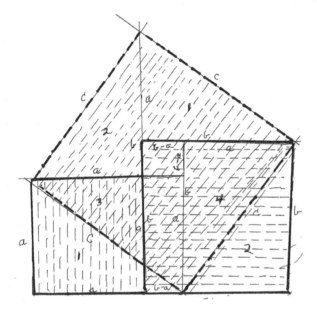

Figure 13.4: Pythagorean Theorem

Given any square with edges c - which is the hypotenuse - and with any rectangle whose area is (a x b) divided along its diagonal with edges a, b, and c to form similar triangles 1, 2, 3, and 4, we can then construct the square with edges c. In doing so we leave open an uncovered little square area in the center with edges (b - a). When we add triangles 1 and 2 opposite the figure to 3 and 4 respectively we can by subtracting and adding the rectangle of edge (b − a) and the edge b, we can construct square (a x a) and the square {(b - a) + a} or (b x b). Thus we have geometrically covered the empty square with edges (b - a), thus showing that the square of a and the square of b are equal in area to the area of the square with the side c. Note our additions and subtractions are of areas and not of numbers. Thus, we visualize geometrically the Pythagorean Theorem in terms of areas not numbers.

However to treat the Pythagorean Theorem numerically algebraically we can illustrate the basic equations give using again Figure 13.4. What results is a simple numerical proof treating a, b, and c as numerical measures of length. From 13.4 we see that the following equation holds:

$$\text{Area of right triangle} = \left(\frac{1}{2}\right)ab$$
$$c^2 = \left[4\left(\frac{1}{2}\right)ab\right] + (b - a)^2$$
$$a^2 + b^2 = c^2$$

Thus we can show from the above equation the Pythagorean Theorem expressed numerically as the measured lengths of the hypotenuse and the other two sides.

$$c^2 = 2ab + b^2 - 2ab + a^2$$
$$c^2 = a^2 + b^2$$

Note then the Greeks did not conceive of their linear segments as numbers, but as having ratios and proportions. This leads to an interesting sense of what the Greeks thought of as a number. As already mentioned in ordinary English when we speak of a number of people we do not ordinarily think of one person as constituting a number of people, nor do we even count two as a number of people. Two people together are a couple such as you and me. We two are not a number in the sense of a multitude of people. And when we come to triads it is interesting that three people, you and me and some other person really are not a multitude or a number of people. We are a couple and another person added together. We form a single triad. Exploring love triangles is a major structure in romantic literature.

Triads are simple configurations that are basic to human intuitions and human reason especially in the role taking as we see reflected in syntax and grammar as first, second, and third person. So three people simply reflects how in communication the way we talk in first, in second, and in third person. Note that G. H. Mead's major contribution in *Mind Self and Society* to social psychology was role taking. There are three that we take: one of self, one of another, and one of that role of that other person outside the self. It is only at four that we need to count what a number of people would be considered as we get outside these basic three roles. It would be two twos, or one against three. $2 + 2 = 4$ or $1 + 3 = 4$.

Counting seems then to be a way of dealing with what might be described as a number of things, which is the beginning of our thoughts about increasing complexity. With two people we have just one pair or set of a relationship, one to one and one to the other. With three people we have only three sets of relationships, but when we come to four we raise the number of relationships to six. And then if we relate the three and four persons asymmetrically, we see we double the number of relationships. It is only then when we reach four that we are confronted in the beginning with a set of multitudinous relationships, which eventually in time leads to too much complexity to grasp in our thinking.

Note how we think of the number of stars as an image of complexity. Who normally thinks ever to be able to count them? And when you speak of crowds of millions, the population of cities, or the casualties of war we have little capacity to image such a large number. It is for that reason that when we consider visible stars as almost enumerable we have made no count. Thus, I was surprised to find out that 'the star catalogue compiled by Claudius Ptolemy in the 2nd century CE lists 1,022 fixed stars visible from Alexandria. This became the standard number of stars in Western culture for hundreds of years. The total number of stars visible to the naked eye is about 6,000; only about half are visible at a given time of night from a given point on the Earth. (Wikipedia). Note our image of the number of stars poetically in not a very big number.

I have tried to illustrate this problem of complexity in dealing with numbers by showing that we rhetorically ordinarily have no clear concepts of the relationships between people in a group when the number in the group has a count of four or more (Yoos, 2009). Clarity in numerosity requires that we have better simplified conceptions and clearer pictures of multitudes. Experiences of numbers require pictures of large groups. Note how difficult it is to estimate the numbers of people in large crowds unless there is some sort of correlation with a number that correlates with a numbered grid such as the number of seats that are filled or empty in an auditorium or maybe how many people occupy an area which we can estimate by the count of such gridded areas that are occupied by people. To be crowded is to be in too dense of a crowd. Note how my terms in talking about crowds circle around proximate meanings and approximations. It is all about finding clearer verbal conceptions about complexity

And it is this reduction of counting to a simple or clearer picture of a number that we initially used the digits of our fingers and our two hands to count either by tallies of fives, or by tallies of tens. Thus it is through digits and by their one to one correspondences between our finger tallies that items can be simplified in counting. We have more familiarity with the pattern of the fingers of our hand than with patterns that we are not so familiar with, such as being together with ten unfamiliar people. It is no accident then that the word *digit* applies both to fingers and the counting of cardinal numbers that are used for counting.

And consequently as importantly mentioned the use of our two hands in counting becomes a frame also to create order as we can order our fingers in sequence: Left thumb, left index finger, left middle finger, left ring finger, and left pinky. This pattern is equally repeated in the names of the fingers of the right hand. Note this pattern is the decimal system that maps the pattern of the decimal numbers. If human beings had had twelve fingers and twelve toes we probably would have had a different number system, first either to the base twelve or by adding toes to the base twenty-four, one with two tallies of six for each hand, or four tallies of six for all our fingers and toes. And thus it was in such counting that units of measurements began: yards of cloth from the stretch of the arms, hands to measure the height of a horse, and feet to measure the distances around enclosures and the areas of enclosures as we do in talking about the size of houses in terms of square feet. Note how inadequate all these measures have become.

Thus, the concept of measurement presumes a unit that is rigid and capable of designation. Rigid designators are instruments that provide us with regulated measures of units. And each designation determines a count. And counts are a matter of digits. As we have seen that in mathematics and trigonometry we have both linear and angular measurements, and that both notions of measurement are developed on the basis of digits or counts. When we measure distance we need a concept of something being straight on a line of sight stretching between two points.

When I was in the air corps we were told in navigating that straight lines were man-made. But of course they were talking about lines in a plane. But there are few lines in nature that are straight in all three dimensions. Trees especially bamboo can grow straight and tall. They grow vertically straight when crowded for lack of light being shaded by the surrounding trees. As such straight lines except for trees and bamboo poles are all artifacts with straight lines of man-made construction. But how then do we ever construct straight lines in a plane? They require two points in a plane, but the problem then is 'Are they in the same plane?'

What has fascinated me of late is a Möbius strip and the lack of any concept of orientation on its surface. The Möbius strip is created by reversing the end of a lengthy flat strip of let us say paper, with straight and parallel sides and then paste-ing the reverse ends of it together. What is created is a surface that slowly curves away from any notion of straight lines. What creates my fascination with this construction is that surface of the strip is the same surface on both sides of the strip. If we follow a line moving forward seemingly parallel to the edges of the strip we find that there is no top or bottom to the surface of the strip, for if we mark a spot opposite on the strip we will eventually reach it by moving along the surface of the strip.

What is seemingly opposite to the starting point on the strip is on the same surface that we are located. In other words there is no directionality on the surface such that it has another side. There is no orientation for a line of sight as there is no conception of a straight line on the strip. In other words the Möbius strip displays the relativity of our concepts about what is nominally a plane or a surface. The Möbius strip is a surface with only one side and only one boundary component. The Möbius strip has the mathematical property of being non-orientable. It contains no straight lines or flat surfaces, in that when we construct it, it exists in three dimensions.

A plane is supposedly flat. But we need to determine if something is flat by a level, and we need to recognize that levels and plumb bobs as tools are based on gravitational pull, and thus we know gravitational fields of equal points of field potential are not flat or straight, but they are centered in a circle surrounding a circular mass of earth. All this suggests that what is straight is a concept that is context dependent. If we fly an air plane for instance using an altimeter that is based upon a measure of air pressure. The plane in flying over a period of time is not strictly flying a straight line but an arc, which is due to its flying around the curvature of the earth in air of equal pressure. And if the plane is flying the shortest distance it is not flying a straight compass heading, for the shortest distance on the earth's surface is a great circle path which requires constantly changing compass headings to follow it. What is a line of sight or a shortest path again is a matter of context and situation.

It is easy to construct a circle; for by definition or by design by strict definition, a circle is a line in a plane that is equal distance from a point. We use a divider to establish an arbitrary unit on a line; and since the divider establishes rigidly a unit of distance between two points, we can rotate that unit of a straight line in a plane to make a circle. But what determines that the point is equidistant is the assumption that an inelastic string or rod rotates around a point is rigid and at a fixed distance. The assumption in using a divider is that we are measuring a straight line. But what is this assumption based upon? It is always questionable whether a surface is flat and our line is rigidly determined.

That assumption of being flat rests upon the notion that two points determine a line and three points determine a plane, and as for three dimensions that depends on four points not being in the same plane. Thus, what is straight and what is circular depend on how we rotate or turn in any direction, whether we are at a fixed point looking at something in a plane or whether we are looking at a point on a circle. It again is based upon assumptions. It is a determination made from a stationary or stable perspective at the point or the axis of rotation.

But how do we ever determine whether a point is fixed or not. The presumption in measurement is that there is a 'here-now' as a point of reference and we can determine a 'there-then' from a rigid designation of an instrument that uses a defined unit of measurement. There must be a constant rotation or a repeated effort using a rigid rod to determine the difference between 'now and then' and between 'here and there'. And that determination must always be a calculation determined from a fixed point of reference.

Such a status of fixity and any change from it presumes that all measurements of time and space are relative to perspective. Such presumptions are at the heart of all modeling and mapping. We used the so called 'fixed stars' to say that time and space were not at all relative, but they were fixed from the perspective of the celestial observer in the ancient world. But there was no measurable conception of distance to the stars held by the ancients. Planets were heavenly bodies moving in fixed patterns found in the mapping of the fixed stars as reference points.

But the Copernican theory changed the whole perspective. It changed what was the fixed point reference of the individual in relation to the stars. What is up was changed with the notion that the earth was no longer the center of reference. And now we have the same problem of reference in modeling the universe since the sun is no longer fixed, nor is the Milky Way as a galaxy fixed, but it is finding its own merry way, assumed to be widening out supposedly with an expanding universe on the way out to somewhere, but out of what spot towards what? There is no way then of looking up and down except in the context of looking at the universe. Note that astronauts have a sense of what is up in their space vehicles if the vehicle has a frame that has a top and a bottom. Note too that what we read gives us a sense of up, for we know that up is at the top of the page. The ancient civilizations developed geometry as earth measurement out of ordinary constructions of lines and their orientations to develop a way of defining boundaries to their land and arable fields. One needs a fixed point of reference to start drawing a line with an orientation to another fixed line assuming that we are on a level plain.

When I first studied Euclid we studied it not algebraically, but with a straight edge and a compass. And the first step in our construction of figures and circles as I have already illustrated was to learn to divide a unit of a line, seemingly a straight line, between two points by learning to draw a perpendicular bisector. To do that required us to draw arcs of a circle with a compass from the two different points on the line. What struck me in doing this is that a perpendicular bisector presumed that the line drawn from the intersection of the two arcs above and below the line did in fact create four right angles around the point that was a bisector of the line, and indeed that the line drawn was a division that actually was a two timing bisector. What justified this presumption?

I never questioned it in my study of Euclid's geometry in high school. But it was out of this original presumption that we were able to construct all sorts of triangles, quadrilaterals and numerous regular and irregular polygons, all too many types to count that we found that we were capable of inscribing and circumscribing figures around circles. And then when we moved into solid geometry later and constructed tetrahedrons inscribed and circumscribed with cubes and spheres, the difficulty of representing such three dimensional figures in two dimensional space strained our ability to study all the different ratios and proportions that were becoming all too complicated to study visually using our two dimensional imaginations.

What struck me in this early study of geometry was the difficulty of representing three dimensional space on a two dimensional plane. There is something planar and level flat in our depictions of complexity in our visual senses. But on the other hand there is something in this reduction of complexity to two dimensions on a flat surface that distorts the way we see accurately multiple dimensions that are full of complexity. This reduction of what we see onto a flat surface distorts the complexity of the phenomena that we wish to depict. In other words it leads to an oversimplification of what we want to depict. It is for this reason that maps are always full of distortions of what we want to display graphically on a flat surface.

How did we know that a right angle has 90 degrees and that a straight line at a point has sides of an angle equally to 180 degrees? How could an angle be straight and still be called an angle, that is, a strait angle? In ordinary ways of speaking there is nothing angular about a straight line. Our ordinary language ways of describing these relationships in geometry were moving away from the conclusions that we were arriving at from our usage of the terms used in our vernacular language. Instead of axiomatizing and finding simpler axioms as mathematicians usually do to define and demonstrate these relationships, it occurred to me that the very language of Euclidean geometry and its axioms and postulates grew out of ordinary ways of speaking as the ancient mathematicians confronted what they were seeing and doing in drawing and creating their new constructions in geometry.

Having experienced the problems of gunnery and sighting especially on a bomb sights, it struck me that as human beings we have trouble seeing straight in having two eyes, and we need to close one eye to determine a line of sight. But how do we know that lining up a gun sight or using a singular tubular telescope confirms that a line of sight is a straight line. What seems to be the opposite is that what we do in lining up in sighting is that we define in sighting what it is to be a straight line by definition as one does in surveying.

What I have been doing in my analysis of orientation is to illustrate how we use ordinary language to create the very foundations of our mathematics. Thus, if we are looking for the foundations of mathematical systems, I suggest that we can find first their basis in ordinary vernacular language usage, which itself is in part an already socially constructed set of usages that we ordinarily use to begin to talk about the formal constructions of logic and the mathematics. My suggestion is that our sense of measurement, counting, and ordering is derived from an innate sense of graphical and pictorial representations that has grown with the biological evolution of our culture.

In a way then the language we used in the creation of our mathematical systems is language already developed with the emergence of language in contexts of communication where language changes, and the terms and their uses are socially and politically constructed in specific and different communities. Much of our language that we use every day has in a reversal emerged out of the technical language that has been constructed by political acceptance as standardized technical vocabulary. As our linguistic skills develop, we find a slow evolving change in ordinary language that is changing with new developing technically defined vocabularies coming from the sciences and technologies

We can see how in the process of digitalization how our sense of numbers developed and how in ordinary ways counting developed. And in so far as we see the basis of what is a straight line in terms of vision and alignment, we can also see that we can use our unit of measurement of a line by constantly extending that line of division by replicating segments of that line in either direction by using a divider to extend it further and further with no end in sight. But in the way we act in the ordinary world we are already limited. We find that our line of sight only extends so far within the limits of our visions. What is practical in sighting is that sighting defines our orientation with things that block our line of sight. We see mountains in the distance, or we face the sides of hills or the trees that can even block our view on the slopes of those hills.

In everyday life we orient ourselves with the reference points that we know to exist in our external environment. Note how often then local directions are determined by mountain peaks. And note that surveyors use fixed points with iron stakes that establish boundary lines, but they also need in addition to make their surveys accurate in orientation or direction from these fixed points. It is by only knowing the location of those iron stakes that are buried in the ground that surveyors establish the perimeters of your property so as to define the extent of your property rights within the law. Your property lines have local orientations that have been locally constructed.

Modeling orientation is thus a social construction as illustrated in Figure 13.5. Note that orientation relates to how we rotate. Note that one complete rotation is to turn around on a point to face again a line of sight from which we originally turned especially as we do it as customary by continuously turning to your right. Note the very meaning of what it is to be a right angle. It is simply a turn in the direction of your right arm. You do not however completely rotate if you just face to the right. To make a complete rotation you keep making other turns to your right until you face again the line of sight from which you started. You have made 4 right turns in all. Thus, orientation in ordinary ways of speaking of it is how we rotate ourselves in a bodily sense to align our self with our bodily sense of what extends out from our right shoulder and arm. A right angle then is a bodily turn to what extends out from our right hand.

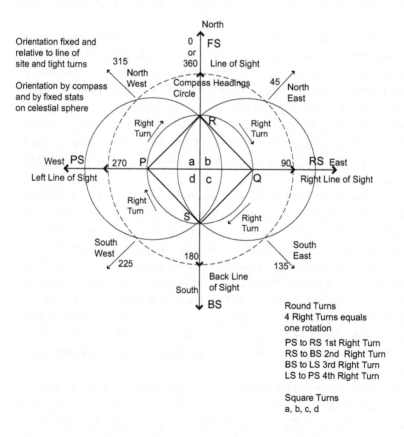

Figure 13.5: Modeling Orientation as a Social Construction

Note as already discussed to say that a right angle has 90 degrees is a social convention on how to count fractions or increments of turns to the right in fractions of 1/90 of a right turn, which becomes a definition of a unit or a degree of an angular scale that is $\frac{1}{360}$ of a complete rotation of the body. Such a scale developed by the Babylonians which, as previously mentioned, is thus a more precise measurement in our talking about directions. In other words our 4 turns to the right is a complete rotation, and when these rotations are based upon a 360 degree scale as illustrated a rotation is 4 x 90, which is the scale of measurement of the degrees in a circle. Thus the 360 degrees of compass headings is defined by a social convention.

Note the four radii of the circle define and determine the length of the intersecting arcs. They are the four directions on a compass, north, east, south, and west which also can be bisected and subdivided again in eight different nominal directions.

(0, 45, 90, 135, 180, 225, 270, 315, and 360 degrees)

or

(north, northeast, east, south east, south, south west, west, northwest, and north again)

Note the difference between the compass headings in degrees and compass headings that are directional with their orientation with the fixed stars. In the air corps on B-29's we had a gyro compass on the flight panel to maintain a straight heading, which was zeroed to measure any angular drift off course. On the other hand, we had a flux gate compass that was calibrated to give celestial headings. The difference between the gyro compass and the flux gate compass was that the gyro compass being a compass whose orientation was toward our line of sight, which to maintain a straight course was straight ahead, while the flux gate compass's orientation was towards true geodesic north. One gave a zero heading. The other indicated the compass heading in relation to the angular difference between our line of sight heading and the heading as related to true north. We could then change this geodesic heading of orientation to a true heading on the radar screen by switching our radar returns to be in phase with the fluxgate compass to give us an image pattern that corresponded to the patterns modeled on maps whose orientation was graphically displayed in relationship to true north.

Note we orient ourselves by saying that something is to the right of something, or saying something about its orientation to north or south or east or west. One orients by sight relationships, and we can also orient ourselves by our knowledge of the location of things on a directional grid determined by landmarks, which one presumes when one says such things as, 'It is located just north of the courthouse.'

The practical way of maintaining planar stability in an air plane is to have the wings on a level horizon. But that is impractical to see when in confined places where there are no visible horizons. Other instrumentation based on levels is needed such as an artificial horizon and a needle and ball. On the ground on which we stand the standard tool for deciding what is up and what is on a level plane is the use of a plumb bob and a carpenter's level. Plumb bobs are based on the assumption that weight makes us all like Humpty Dumpty subject to tipping over and falling down. Without going into the complications of gravity and sticking to our ways of describing what is up and down and what is on a level, we need to see that all these relationships and complications depend on notions of standing in a fixed and in a stable frame.

But note how a level seems to work. The basic common assumption about liquid is that it seeks its own level which is defined by the boundaries or sides of its container. We have no problem with water in containers on ships at sea of knowing what it is in being flat. From the point of the ship on the sea, it is assumed that the sea is level and extends to the horizons. But now we know that is not true. The sea level is a surface on the earth's sphere, so it is spherical. But when we are in a house and want to determine if a beam or a floor is level we need a device or tool called a *level*. We use it based upon the presumption that a liquid seeks its own level when contained on a level flat plane such as on a lake or on the water behind a dam.

Of course a level has a bubble in a liquid, and it has a midpoint to line up the level with the floating bubble. Instead of thinking that the bubble moves and **wants** to determine, what it is to be level by some sort of Spinazoan *conatus* of liquids in seeking their own level, we need to think of a liquid trying to enter into the space that eliminates the bubble. It is not the bubble that rises when we tilt a level, but it is the hydraulic pressure of the liquid trying to occupy the space of the bubble, which it cannot do. It is the hydraulic pressure on each of side of the bubble that seeks a stable equilibrium between the liquid that is exerting pressure on both sides of the bubble. When those two forces are in equilibrium, the bubble is caught between two equal hydraulic pressures created when the liquid is level on the surface upon which the level lies.

Note again what it is to be up and to be down again relates to how our bodies relate to their environment. Up and down depend on how we orient and frame ourselves within terms of our ordinary language. It depends on the everyday forms of speech that has been developed in the evolution of language in our everyday culture in talking about how we relate to each other and how we relate to our environment in the contexts within which we live. Measurements are ways we have of segmenting both our orientations and our linear perspectives. And units of measurement are agreed upon ways of making those divisions so as to be precise about how we act in reference to them in finding ourselves standing in an upright place on this earth.

Note too that the geometry of circles and ellipses as well as parabolas and hyperbolas are divided by the same measurable units the same way that we divide lines, planes, and three dimensional spaces. And those divisions are described ultimately in the language of our vernacular that describes the very methods of their generation. We generate our standardized terms of measurement from the way they have emerged in our describing our stand point of vision in looking at the world. It is language that has emerged from the evolutionary development of language from biological origins. We are upright creatures standing tall. As D. H. Lawrence expressed it, 'We ought to dance with rapture that we should be alive and in the flesh, and part of the living cosmos. That I am part of the earth my feet know perfectly.' Such is our state of equilibrium in being a stabilized point within it. We need to orient ourselves in these elemental formal frames to aid us in maintaining our upright equilibrium. We need to develop these simple frames to construct how we look and visualize the world that we live in and of which we are a part. We do it to show ourselves the way to function in it and to exist so as to be a part of it. We are in it, of it and a part of it.

14 Simple-minded simplicity of simples

One of my teachers in philosophy, Charner Perry, one day in class told me in a discussion with him that the key to understanding Hegel was that there are no simples. And if it is true that there are no simples, why then do we keep on trying to seek simplification and try to find even simpler simples than the things that we already think are so simply simple? Could it be that we innately distrust any notion of simplicity, for we are always inclined to question whether or not there is something even simpler than what we think of as simply simple?

Let me make a point about what geometers have thought geometric points to be. Starting with a straight edge and a divider or compass, using Greek proto-geometry, a line segment of any arbitrary length can be divided and divided without limit. But then there is the problem, or the point, of ever reaching a point where the line drawn cannot be further divided. At that point we have reached what might be considered to be a simple defined point, a part or segment of a line that could no longer be divided. But when we reverse the process and start adding those indivisible points of line segments, we find that they never add up to anything as they have no length to reconstitute a line that has any length. Thus, the source of Zeno's paradox!

A point is a limit to divisions that never can be reached. And if we were ever able to reach that limit of a simple indivisible segment we would never have a way back from that point back to any linear segment. Note the various senses of what it is to be a point in our use of our ordinary vernacular. We always in ordinary ways of speaking speak of simplifying a point that we are making, which means that at any point when we think of it as simple enough to understand, (suffice) then there is no further simplification of it needed.

In talking about simplicity we must agree that when we are talking about complexity that we can often simplify some of the aspects of what we see to be complexity. We find that simplification by analyzing complex patterns into simpler patterns to the point when there is no further need to reduce them any further to understand them. What we think of as simple is simple enough and adequate enough to serve the purposes of the occasion. You have no need to simplify further, for what you have said is simple enough to understand the point that you are talking about. You find that there are no more problems existing in what you say requiring further simplification, or no further need for clarity in determining what you have said. Enough said!

But when we do find simplicity as described above that is satisfying is that ever ultimately sufficient? We are still always open to engage in further analysis if we wish to try to find something 'even more simple' in what we have conceived of as 'simply simple'. Note in one sense then when we say something is simple, it is just an expression that says that one gets it. And as a rhetorician I find that simplification is one mode of clarifying what we say so as to make things simple enough so that our audiences can understand us a little better about what we are talking about.

Simplification rhetorically is just helping someone get it. Our problem then is to know when we have said enough.

One and one are two, what is simpler than that? But we can always challenge what it is to be one and two, for we can always challenge any additions of units when there are questions of what are the names of the units that we denominate and by which we count them one by two. 'East is East, and West is West, and never the twain shall meet.' When we are talking about East and West are we talking here about two regions or cultures? Where is East, and what is West? How do we exactly define them?

Note in a binary number system to the base 2, $1 + 1 = 10$, which nominally as 10 is actually 2 in number systems to the base 10. And note there is no two in a number system to the base 2. And when it comes to counting units what it is to be a unit and what is not said to be a unit is not always that simple. We can always ask, 'Are East and West definable as units?', 'What is unitary about them?'

In one way in writing, simplicity and clarity are all about the ease of reader uptake; and in E. D. Hirsch's terms, it is about *readability* (Hirsch, 1981). With Hirsch it is about how we can rewrite a sentence that says the same thing as another sentence, but that sentence is much easier to read than the other. Or the reader gets it is more easily. In Hirsch's way of expressing it, good writing is all about 'reader uptake'.

But uptake serves a much more integrated rhetorical purpose. It allows us to discover and find out about certain things from others, things which have not been a part of our own experiences of such things. It allows us to find through others that there are things that are not possibly true that we thought to be true from our own personal point of view. Those beliefs that we thought confirmed by our past experiences can turn out to be shown to be actually demonstrably false. In different words, we would say that we do not see things in ways that other people are able to do. Such is the way that we reveal to ourselves a great deal of our ignorance, which others help us remove by showing us that much of what we believe and say is simply wrong.

Noteworthy the term *simple* like the term *perfect* seems to reflect the same type of grammar that is used in making comparisons. Things can be more or less perfect, but never simply perfect. Things can be understood to be more or less simple but never quite simply simple as when it is said that simple things take on different descriptions in different contexts and are always from different perspectives open to interpretation about their simplicity.

Analysis by making comparisons helps us make distinctions to discover the differences between the possible meanings of what we are saying. What I have written about in the past makes the point that differences generate contrasts. Comparing contrasts between our uses of words is at the heart of the enlargement, refinement, and the creation of new linguistic meaning. When we discover the differences in making contrasts we are setting up correlative distinctions that reveal the different senses that words have. Contrasts reveal to us when we interpret our language use that the meaning of the language used in the context differs from what we consider to be conventional usage (Yoos, 2009).

When we turn to looking at similarities, in contrast to the ways of our looking at contrasts, we are looking to find things that have the same attributes, which in turn help us establish identities. If two things are similar in every respect, they are thought by some to be identical, whether it be a set of entities or an individual being. Replication of our body cells in one way is said to be the way we maintain our physical identity. As for establishing identities we use similarity of traits, attributes, qualities, quantities, and numbers to classify so as to place things in files to identify them. Similarity is the way we identify and classify different sets. Since sets are identified by an exhaustive comparison or an enumeration of items in a set, we find that in mathematics that not all sets are closed, which makes it more difficult to identify and define the characteristics of a set that is not **acceptably** named by any definition or technical term that names a unique set of characteristics.

Many paradoxes arise over the different conceptions or different senses of the term *identity*. For example, individuals can be members of uniquely defined sets by giving them unique descriptions. They are thus identified by the definable unique descriptors. When we order and rank things in a unique orderly description, we can name and locate and identify different kinds of unique entities. Note the difference in the different kinds of identity to be found in the use of barcodes. Identity theft starts with your social security number, which legally is intended to be a defined unique inscription of a unique sequence of different ordinal numbers that identifies you as an individual. But note the difficulties arising from some people having the ability to obtain more than one social security number to hide their identity.

On the other hand, barcodes can be used to create places where we can locate inventory, that is, sets of things with common or similar characteristics. We use them in Supermarkets for merchants to identify the prices established for different brands and products that stores have for sale. Note then that the quest for simplicity is equally useful both to take things apart and to identify them as a member of a set or as a unique individual. When we dismantle something note the importance of reassembling or restoring the identity of something when we wish to resemble it without losing any of its parts.

Note the uniqueness of the mapped locations and the generality of classifications that are coded. Note that both mapping and **classification systems** are different kinds of models and frames. We locate in one, and we catalogue in the other. Maps uniquely locate by reference to frames, scales, axises, and orientations. They afford us unique descriptions that identify locations. On the other hand classifications are catalogues and arrangements that allow us to segregate like sets of things into ordered frames so as to locate any stored inventory or to create order in filing systems by segregating like or similar things into unique descriptive sets of things or categories.

Much like in mathematics where we locate points which are the simplest segments of a line or the simplest locations in spatial orientation there is much in the methods of scientific investigation that wants to reduce things to simples: such as chemical elements, physical elements, such as units of momentum or irreducible physical particles. There are many simple unique ratios and quantities that have a unique unit value. They can be found in multiple comparisons and compositions that we find in the world. In physics and chemistry, and especially in mathematics, we find such unit simple values in repeating and unchanging sequences that we can either count or order and even denominate them.

And the same sort of concern for simples or indivisible units is found in biology, the social sciences, and the humanities: biological cells, species, human beings, societies, persons, linguistics terms, phonemes, religions, minds, and works of art. It is noteworthy that in all fields of intellectual endeavor there are controversies over what is irreducibly simple or a unitary, single entity. As mentioned already I remember in high school how my biology book stated that living cells were made up of protoplasm, at which time protoplasm was being described in texts as 'a simple substance that was the basis of life.' How so simply simple? How such a description now sounds stupid and foolish, and that above all it was over simplistic and mythical? It is just a metaphysical simplification of life into a unitary, simply simple, a vital simple sort of stuff.

What strikes me in the origins of what we now speak of as physical science that some earlier natural philosophers such as Democrates and Lucretius said that atoms were simply simple and that we cannot divide them or distinguish any part of them as they have no parts? Corpuscles as simple units were simply indivisible simples. The world of light, matter, and life were all thought to be corpuscular.

Such views eliminated any ability to know what was inside such entities by definition as there was no way of knowing what was inside since we could not physically divide them. Whatever is inside of what is indivisible we can have no notion of what stuff is in the inside. Nor do we have any notion of whether or not that stuff that we do not know about that is said is to be impenetrable or indivisible, is either heterogeneous or homogeneous inside. And if that stuff of which atoms or corpuscles are made up of something is heterogeneous then there would no simple way or conceivable way of knowing whether or not its insides had any complexity inside of it. We would have no way that it could be separated, abstracted, or liquefied, or even purified.

Since we cannot get inside such indivisible atoms or corpuscles, we cannot think of them as having something inside except that what is inside has some sort of reactive properties such as Newton's concept of mass that generates a reaction to something internal to it that equally is said to be internal and measurable. When we divided white light into the colors of the spectrum, white light turned out by refraction not to be simple as Goethe thought. White light as Newton maintained, was a mixture of other simple colors of light in the spectrum. But there is in Goethe's view that white is a simple color a certain amount of indistinguishable, perceptual truth about the perception of it. True colors in a way admit of no variation. But is there any color variation in a patch that is supposedly pure white? Note here in the question again is the presumption of the existence of pure colors as simples.

But note that colors can be distinguished by brightness, hue, and saturation. Off white is such a variation of white. Thinking white as a pure expanse of a color has simplicity. It is such conceptions of expanses of simple undiluted color impressions which caused many philosophers to speak of such patches of color as sense data, which were conceived as simple by the philosophical jargon of the 'sense data school of empiricists' of the time. And note too that we do not often in ordinary speech speak of white as a color just as we do not think of black as a color as both colors in ordinary ways of speaking lack color. But nevertheless in some contexts talking with painters white and black are certainly called colors. There seems no simple descriptive identity named by our terms describing color that does not vary in different ways in existing social contexts where we speak using ordinary terms for color.

Note then that the mixing of light and the seeing of colors differs quite radically as a result of their interference effects as we find in seeing colors that are produced with the mixing of the pigment colors on a painter's palette. Mixing pigments and mixing colored light are two different ways of practically creating new colors. How we mix them has quite different perceptual effects. Note how the two systems of creating colors are at work in explaining the colors in colored photography and in the different way colors are found to an oil painting. There is thus no precise definable concept of color in our ordinary ways of speaking about color in these two different contexts.

I recall arguing with a colleague about the color of the stucco on my house. He said it was tan. I said it was yellow. I consulted my wife, and she said it was cream. It was obvious that our color vocabularies were inferior to my wife's verbal repertoire for colors as we both recognized from her description the differences in color. It is difficult for me to imagine what would be a more precise vocabulary for colors would be like. Paint stores now are able to code colors by numbers to create pigments of every shade, hue, and tint that one can distinguish visually, but numbers as numerical terms do not have meaning unless we are trained to think in them. Note how bathroom talk is reduced to number one and number two. But that is how our ordinary language grows as we integrate numbers from formal systems of numerosity into our oral systems of naming using numbers such the name of Agent 007.

Note the concept of an atom includes a concept of size or a notion of size. Some atoms were thought by the Epicureans so small to be ethereal so as to become quite spiritual. And the assumption is that all atoms are known by features of their exterior, and as already pointed out there can be no known concept of an interior to them. That kind of concept leaves us to conclude that atoms are irreducible units and thus like the digits of our fingers are countable as units or by digits. If we cut off a finger we are left with only nine digits. But atoms of the original atomic theories were indivisible and indestructible as they could not be smashed, and they were unlike any unit of measurement which can be infinitely thought to be divisible indefinitely. But now we know we can penetrate what we think of as atoms with radiation. We are able to image their insides.

But atoms although they were spatially measurable, they were not thought to be divisible like the space that they presumably occupied. Using a little imagination it is easy to think of space as something that when occupied pushes the occupied space away, and if that is so, atoms would have topological spatial properties on their surfaces, but there would be no space where the atom was supposedly located in space. It could simply push away the space it occupied. Note that when we speak of matter occupying space note the different contexts where we speak of not having space when we have too much stuff. How mysterious is our imagination when we have no definite conception of space and of the properties inside impenetrable atoms.

Measurement requires units, which we speak of as units of measurement. But not only can these measurements increase in number compounded additively, but measurements can be divided into lesser units subtractively from any defined unit continuously until we have no remainders. We can multiply measurement units of what is quantifiable additively, and we can divide that unit continuously without limit. We can continuously divide without measure unless we insist on stopping at a point where that unit is not said to be divisible. Thus we are led to the contrasts and the paradoxes of what we cannot multiply and divide in nature, such as the limits of space and the limits of division of simple physical particles, but we have in contrast number theory where we have the formal properties where units can be multiplied and divided continuously.

To illustrate division in math can be represented as fractions, and thus numbers in math for the most part can be divided. For example ½ of ½ is ¼, and ½ of ¼ is 1/8 and we can continue to divide any dividend by splitting it into to two parts or into smaller and smaller units continually. Note that this sort of fractional division is one of the features advantageous to tax collectors and bankers. Tax collectors can tax the money you earn to pay taxes. And bankers can compound their interest by charging interest on what you owe in interest.

Note we are always thinking in measurements when we are thinking about space and time. We are always thinking about space and time both in units of measurement that are continuously divisible. In physics and chemistry quantities seem absolutely necessary to understand what is natural and physical, but unlike the simple measureable units which define particles and time they have their measurable limits in what we think of as points and instants. How many angels can sit on a head of a pin? If we remove our points out of lines or out of planes, how can points exist outside of the space that defines them?

And how is it directly possible to measure and instant? The best way I have of practically defining an instant is through the sense of touch. Note we count time by units of beat or as in military drill in the counting of cadences. It is the moment of coming in contact with an object that we think of as an instantaneous instant. Note how regular the tap-tap tapping, the constantly touching introduces our units for the measurement of time. Note we speak of the **beat** of a pendulum when actually a pendulum does not beat anything. It simply passes regularly through what we think is a set of identifiable points, in two reversals and in a direction straight up and down to the ground.

Thus, to re-cap the gist of what I have been puzzling over, unlike our indivisible atoms of original atomic theories, it appears that it is only the space they occupy and not the matter that is divisible. All we can know about from the history of our conceptions of atoms is that they are indivisible and that they occupy space and that space is divisible, but the stuff that they are made of is not. Note then when it practically comes to dividing particles, we first think of grains of sand, but we know that sand can be fine and coarse, which means we can grind up sand into finer and finer particles of sand and eventually the finest particles of sand we can see only as a cloud of dust. We might see dust particles in the air, but we mostly see dust when it accumulates. But when particles are no longer visible we speak of them technically as **aerosols**. The units of aerosols are only seen as impeding and transforming patterns of light and thus are seen as smog.

Note thefollowing summation from Wikipedia to arrive at a technical sense of the term *aerosol:* Technically, an **aerosol** is a suspension of fine solid particles or liquid droplets in a gas. Examples are smoke, oceanic haze, air pollution, smog, and CS gas (tear gas). In general conversation, *aerosol* usually refers to an aerosol spray can or the output of such a can. The word aerosol derives from the fact that matter 'floating' in air is a suspension (a mixture in which solid or liquid or combined solid-liquid particles are suspended in a fluid. To differentiate suspensions from true solutions the term **sol** evolved—originally meant to cover dispersions of tiny (sub-microscopic) particles in a liquid. With studies of dispersions in air, the term aerosol evolved and now embraces both liquid droplets, solid particles, and combinations of these.

Sand thus comes in variable sizes, and the visible limit only seems to be the indistinguishable particles that we see rise up in a cloud of dust. Note the problems today with volcanic ash erupting being invisible to jet aircraft. What then do we really count as particles are grains of sand? A grain of sand questionably is never simple. It is interesting that Archimedes in *The Sand Reckoner* tried to calculate the number of grains of sand on the earth. But what sort of units could he count in counting grains of sand? Most people who think of sand think of beaches.

According to this story Archimedes calculated that the universe would contain 8 vigintillion, or 8×10^{63}. But when we think of the smallest particles of sand ground to dust it had to be an ancient conception that all matter ground up on the earth (Earth) was reducible to dust just as ashes to ashes dust to dust as we do in speaking about death. Certainly the ancients possessed no tools for dividing up a particle of dust, and they could only speculate that dust could be divided into smaller particles until we reach the limits of division. But if we divide dust into atoms that we cannot see we have reached the limits of division that is atoms, that is non- divisible particles, or that is, we have arrived at simple simples that are the limit we have of discovering any dividable differences.

I found it astounding at the time that my physics book in high school stated, 'The only things that exist in the world are space and matter.' At the time that statement wiped clean for me all my parochial school theology. Again how so simply simple an explanation of how things are! But even the smallest particle of matter in physics, even if we cannot further divide it into further particles, nevertheless it is always an open to question as to whether we still can further divide any particle into more fundamental elements the way we can divide the space that supposedly the particle occupies. Note the paradox of thinking if a particle occupies space, does it move that space aside and as a result there is no space inside that particle? Particle and space do not seem to be miscible. This leads me back to my appendix quote of Mouse's lament to Mole about their cluttered home. You can't have both space and stuff.

All this analysis by division leads to the conclusion that the only things that makes us think that these particles, these atoms, are indivisible is that no one has succeeded in doing it. When we discover that things are ordered in unit values, it is only our conception of the unit that makes us think that we have a simple, but that notion of unit is always divisible in math. And that is what the Standard Model of Particle Physics (see Figure 14.1) illustrates: electrons and protons and neutrons can further be smashed and divided in high energy physics into new and different particles. The following describes the development of the Standard Model of Particle Physics:

> We thus in physics have comparably the Standard Model for particle physics dealing with changes within the atom. The **Standard Model** of particle physics is a theory concerning the electrodynamic, weak, and strong nuclear interactions which mediate the dynamics of the known subatomic particles. Developed throughout the early and middle 20th century, the current formulation was finalized in the mid-1970s upon experimental confirmation of the existence of quarks. Since then, discoveries of the bottom quark (1977), the top quark (1995) and the tau neutrino (2000) have given credence to the standard model. Because of its success in explaining a wide variety of experimental results, the standard model is sometimes regarded as a theory of almost everything. (Oertner, 2006: 2)

What does it mean to give credence to a model? Is it a theory and not a model? But how is the Standard Model of particle physics a theory? It is very much like the Periodic Table in Chemistry which was once thought to be a theory? It is at this point that we need to compare the use of different of models of periodic tables. The Periodic Table in Chemistry although theoretically constructed has proved not to be a theory, but rather a tool for developing hypotheses or theories that have led to the discovery of new chemical elements and the investigation of the chemical properties of the different elements in chemistry. It has rather spawned new chemical theories out the data entries in the table.

On the other hand the evolution of the Standard Model in Particle Physics is even in the short time since its development has been doing pretty much the same things as the Periodic Charts in Chemistry have. As a model or chart of subatomic particles and their combinatory reactions into simpler particles it has been a tool for developing hypotheses that has led to new discoveries in nuclear and particle physics and even new conceptions of chemical reactions. Both models then are not simply theories, but they are more like charts or maps that enable researchers to guide their tests and experiments into chemical and nuclear reactions.

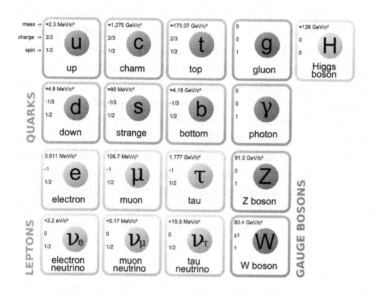

Figure 14.1: Standard Model of Particle Physics

In chemistry the Periodic table has been the Standard Model for the listing of the elements by their combinatory patterns and chemical properties so as to illustrate that they are repeatable. Its invention is generally credited to Russian chemist Dmitri Mendeleev in 1869, who intended the table to illustrate recurring ('periodic') trends in the chemical properties of the elements. What he first noted was the correlation of chemical properties in an ordered sequence of 8 elements repeated in the same pattern in the 2nd and 3rd groups of elements generalizing that it would be repeated. Over the years the layout of the periodic table has been refined and extended especially since the time I studied and taught chemistry in high school. Figure 14.2 below is the periodic table found in my teaching texts in high school and as a very similar chart hung high over my front blackboard. We used the chart to do chemical calculations based upon atomic weights, which was at that time was an empirical concept based upon relative weights of elements which at time was relative to Oxygen standardized at 16.

By relative weights was meant the ratio of the measurable weights of samples of different elements to a standard equal sized weight sample of oxygen. The concept of relative weight was comparable to measures of specific gravity where standard and equal size weight samples of a substance is compared to an equal size weight sample of water standardized at 1. Such a ratio permits the calculations of the weights of matter from the lists or charts of these inductively confirmed standardized ratios. Thus the important use of periodic charts in my long past teaching days was a way of calculating the relative weight of elements compounds in different compounds. In other words it was a measure of combining weights of elements in chemical compounds. The discipline that relied on the periodic table with oxygen as a base standard was at the time spoken of as quantitative analysis.

From the original table of Dmitri Mendeleev in 1869 to the present, the periodic table has been constructed along different lines. What has been significant question about the Periodic Table in its many evolved forms is whether it is a chart or an ordered list of data useful for chemical calculations and discussions of differences in the chemical properties or whether it is an evolving theory about what explains chemical change. What originated the title *Periodic Table* is the theory by Mendeleev that the correlation of chemical properties in an ordered sequence of 8 elements repeated in the same pattern in the 2nd and 3rd groups of elements generalizing that it would be repeated.

But this theory has been demonstrated to be false. What this disconfirmation demonstrates is that the Periodic Table as a theory can be never be a representation of a true account of chemical change. But what has been the case that the table has been used to explore the complexity of chemical change that has lead to new discoveries about elements and chemical change. As such the Periodic Table has been a heuristic that has been successful in developing new modes of inquiry and exploration of chemical change.

Let me illustrate the Periodic Table Figure 14.2 that was essential to the study of chemistry in forties and fifties when I was first exposed to the study of chemistry. I wish to point out the direction of the changes that occurred in its evolution and use.

Many teachers memorized the relative atomic weights at the time to avoid constantly looking at the table to look up the number for their use in illustrating calculations. I found some irony in the fact that when the base of relative of the relative weight of elements was changed from oxygen to hydrogen which had the result that the relative weight values changed in the new periodic tables. The shift to hydrogen reordered the atomic numbers on the base of weight to the number of protons in the nucleus of an atom. In a way then the Periodic Table in its history and usage has been largely responsible for the advances in the science of chemistry which is open to new shifts in the paradigms that we find in the developments in the field. The moment we introduced the notion that atoms have subatomic particles we enter into a new area of mapping especially with the introduction of quantum mechanics where combinatory properties of atoms change and interact with subatomic particles.

Group →1	2	3	4	5	6	7	8	9	10	11	12	13	14	15	16	17	18
↓Period																	
1 H																	2 He
3 Li	4 Be											5 B	6 C	7 N	8 O	9 F	10 Ne
11 Na	12 Mg											13 Al	14 Si	15 P	16 S	17 Cl	18 Ar
19 K	20 Ca	21 Sc	22 Ti	23 V	24 Cr	25 Mn	26 Fe	27 Co	28 Ni	29 Cu	30 Zn	31 Ga	32 Ge	33 As	34 Se	35 Br	36 Kr
37 Rb	38 Sr	39 Y	40 Zr	41 Nb	42 Mo	43 Tc	44 Ru	45 Rh	46 Pd	47 Ag	48 Cd	49 In	50 Sn	51 Sb	52 Te	53 I	54 Xe
55 Cs	56 Ba		72 Hf	73 Ta	74 W	75 Re	76 Os	77 Ir	78 Pt	79 Au	80 Hg	81 Tl	82 Pb	83 Bi	84 Po	85 At	86 Rn
87 Fr	88 Ra		104 Rf	105 Db	106 Sg	107 Bh	108 Hs	109 Mt	110 Ds	111 Rg	112 Cn	113 Uut	114 Fl	115 Uup	116 Lv	117 Uus	118 Uuo

Lanthanides	57 La	58 Ce	59 Pr	60 Nd	61 Pm	62 Sm	63 Eu	64 Gd	65 Tb	66 Dy	67 Ho	68 Er	69 Tm	70 Yb	71 Lu
Actinides	89 Ac	90 Th	91 Pa	92 U	93 Np	94 Pu	95 Am	96 Cm	97 Bk	98 Cf	99 Es	100 Fm	101 Md	102 No	103 Lr

Figure 14.2: The Standard Model of the Periodic Table in Chemistry. A Resource for Elementary, Middle School, and High School Students

15 Rhetorical Unity in Narrative and Exposition

What is striking then in discussing the basis of mathematics as well as physical particles in physics and chemistry is their concept of a unit. Units are the basis of counting and creating definite sequenced orders very much the way a drill sergeant orders and re-arranges individuals in drill formations. We can count similar things, or we can count different things as well, as we can re-order different things so long as these things are said to have a unity, which makes us want to speak of them as units or just as having counts of one.

As already discussed our gesture to indicate a unit is to indicate that it is one of pointing and using our index finger. It is our pointing finger. That finger is a single digit indicator. It is a count of one. It points out one and is in turn one. We count units or digits. But we also can count tallies, which are counts of tallies of digits of the same number of digits or sets of digits. We can count by tallying tallies of equal counts. A group of tallies is simply counted together making it the count of all the indicated digits enumerated. The count then too can be thought of as a unit just as we think of a formation of soldiers in the military as a unit.

But when we start trying to divide any unit in math we find that we can always divide it into further subunits by subtracting tallies of smaller units from our unit of a total tally, and that goes on and on until we reach a limit of our take-aways where there is a smaller number in the remainders than in the tally that we take away. We add and subtract tallies which we call by the names *multiplication* and *division*. Note the irony in dividing one by one. It is truly in one sense not a division at all in our ordinary sense of the word *division*. It is very much like that old saw about clapping with one hand. A division must minimally require two digits. For a denominator to divide into a numerator there cannot by any ordinary sense of the term *division* for a division if there is not anything to divide. When we think of the reciprocal of one, one over one, again nothing is divided. At this point I find that mathematicians' interested in prime numbers have conveniently been for their interest in prime factoring for they have made 2 a prime number even though 2 is divisible.

To be a division we must have something to divide in the numerator by the number or group that constitutes the denominator. It is at this point that we are aware that we have a different vocabulary in talking about dividing with its peculiar definitions in the terminology of arithmetic and algebra that differs from the meaning or the senses of the words that we use to talk about dividing and multiplying in using ordinary language. To divide up something out of a sense of justice does not mean that we divide what we have into equal piles necessarily. And when we increase and multiply by having many children, nothing rules out having an addition of more than one child such as twins or even quintuplets.

We can then think of a collection as a unit composed of units. And we can think of a set of subdivisions as one. We can sum up fractions, and we can think of that sum as a unit. What is curious about this analysis of what it is to be a unit is that it is redundant and analytical to say that a unit is one. In number theory what we are doing in calculating is doing nothing more than constantly circling by definition into the tautologies of what a number actually is nominally in using digits in counting. A number can be a unit of units by counting units. And whatever it is that we do in counting, at least what we do is summing up units into a count that means that it is a sum of units that itself turns into being a unit.

And thus by definition and importantly cardinal numbers are the counting numbers, and each number of the set of cardinal numbers is defined by the addition of one. And since addition is always open to another addition there is no terminus as to how much and how far we can continue to keep adding to any unit sum of additions. Paradoxically what is infinite is the notion of a limit such as that of infinity that by definition can have no limit. Finite means having a limit or boundary, and infinite means having no boundary.

It has always been fascinating to me that billionaires are often said to be people that no longer count how much money they have. They only seem to be alarmed that when they do count up their seeming 'ga-zillions', that they find to their despair their sum of wealth is less than a billion. Such fixation on sums says something how numbers can control our thinking, and how units of measurements control our thinking. Note how easy it is to be a millionaire in Italy. I always wished that I lived in a country with the metric system, for when young I never reached six feet tall when I was growing up and playing basketball. I was never able to enter that basketball honorific status and that was usually granted to six footers.

But note then as stated that we think of particles as units, and so long as we can keep dividing them they are formed of subunits that add up to the whole or the unit that we counted originally as one. But note in rhetoric analogously when we want to give unity to our writing we need to bring it together as a whole to give it unity. A sentence, a paragraph, a chapter, or a book may all be judged to have unity. Each unit has a sense of closure or terminus that helps define that unity. But what is it that defines the unity in each of these different grammatical language structural units in each of these cases where we string words together? Does it have to do with coherence? Note in this case coherence is said to be one way of creating unity in our writing.

Note that cutting anyone off in the midst of what they are saying denies them any unity to what they are trying to say. When we begin sentences we inform someone reading them that we are beginning a sentence by using a capital letter, but in speaking we do it by the intonation of our voice in the beginning. The secret of cutting off someone in the middle of a sentence when we want to interrupt them is to raise your voice over the other person's voice thus interrupting their train of thought, so we can have them hear what we have to say. '**Surprise** I got the floor!' It all starts with an aloud interruption. It is simply cutting someone off from any closure of what would give unity to what one is trying to say. The standard way to stop an interruption is to demand to finish and insist having closure to what one was saying. 'Wait I am still talking!', 'I am not finished.' Such are the strategies we have of dealing with others about their rhetorical interruptions by insisting that you still have the floor.

Note in writing the present day use of bullet points that bullet points introduce statements that are at the same time both the beginning and the closure for the statements that one would want to say and one would want to make in visual presentations, as for instance as we list them in PowerPoint projections. We use bullet points to advertise what follows has a unity in the several points that are being made about a certain topic.

But in writing we do comparable sorts of things by using terms that mark the transitions that we are making in our going from topic to topic. We have words or expressions that mark our shifts from one topic to another in our written texts. We are marking by transitional devices our additions to our sequence of topical unit transitions. In speaking we do not speak in paragraphs, but we do speak by indicating our shift to another topic by using conjunctive adverbs to mark such transitions. Such is the unity we seek in writing sentence by sentence, paragraph by paragraph. These transitional words and phrases are what give coherence in our shaping the bounded unity that we wish to arrive at in whatever we say or write. Our hope when writing is to bring together our unity and purpose in an essay or even in an entire book by combining our steps step by step into a unitary whole.

Note the function of a preface. It is a talk about the book and a description of the context and situation about how the book came about. It expresses the unity of aim and purpose in the writing of that book. The unity of aim and purpose as stated is a promise that is to be fulfilled. But when the book comes together in the very organization and the logic that develops what brings the book together gives it unity in the ending of it. It is in the summation that we create in the end that gives the final focus to what we are speaking or writing about what we have done after we finish. Note how a summary to a book in a way is an addendum much like a preface. Note how a summary can sometimes be used as a preface. A summary is the statement of a promise hopefully we made in the preface.

And as I was writing this book that I first proposed to write as I say in my own preface I was never quite certain about what I wanted to say in any detail about my proposal, and I knew that I wouldn't actually know those details until after I finished writing this book. That achievement in the end, putting together details, I found however in my many revisions that I made of this book. And surprise! My preface now that I have made my revisions of the text as a whole is not my actual summation of what I originally proposed to write. It actually is a prefatory remark I made before actually writing this book.

My original preface was just a poem that I wrote before I even started to write this book. It was what I wanted to talk about. It simply described what I wanted to write about when I first started it. It was not something I had written after I finished. I leave it to my reader to make his or her own summary to see if it matches my proposal in my preface, which is not a description of what I have done, which is what many conventional prefaces or introductions of books usually propose to do, proposing to say what the book says.

Books like dramas and narratives have a beginning, middle, and an end. It is these three parts that give unity to any story being told. But note how we can reverse a story by starting with the ending and go back to the beginning, or by going back to the middle, and then finally concluding it by showing what happened in the beginning or what happened in the middle so as to bring the story together as a whole. Let me illustrate the various changes we can make in narrative form by using what has been claimed to be the shortest story ever told in six words attributed by some to Ernest Hemmingway as a way to illustrate how a few number of words in a context of background knowledge allows the reader to project his or her own interpretation into the story of what happens:

Table 15.1: Hemmingway's Shortest Story Ever

Story	Structure	Function
Baby shoes	Beginning	Normal
For sale	Middle	twist-reversal- *peripeteia*
Never used	End	closure-resolution- denouement

Let me now show how we can shift the above structure into six permutation of this story structure:

Table 15.2: Permutations of the Shortest Story

Permutations 123	132	213	231	312	321
Baby shoes	Baby shoes	For sale	For sale	Never used	Never used
For sale	Never used	Baby shoes	Never used	Baby shoes	For sale
Never used	For sale	Never used	Baby shoes	For sale	Baby shoes

Variation in structure is very much the same in writing and essay or a book. We can start with our conclusion and show how we reached that conclusion, and then finally say what the issue was that originated what we wanted to say, or what generated the purpose of any expository piece of writing. Or again we can trace reasons and connections between topics and show how these reasons as topics apply to an issue of concern, or we can show what conclusions follow from these topics, and then show

how they relate to an issue of concern. Either way we give unity to story or a piece of writing by integrating the beginning, middle, and end in six permutations or Factorial 3!, which we can symbolic represent the variations as BME, BEM, MBE, MEB, EMB, and EBM.

Note that I have used a triad in dividing my concept of possible structures for modeling of storytelling, which was the same for Aristotle, but it is also equally the same in talking about structure in the writing of expositions. As a model of arrangement it is a simple triad. It simplifies how we write a three part theme in composition. An introduction, the three point structure in the middle, and a conclusion $(1 + 3 + 1)$. It is the structure of the 'five star-paper' that pleases so many teachers. It is easy to grade. In simplifying what I have to say in this way, using this standard model as a triad, as I have described before in other contexts, facilitates short term memory for a reader, especially for a teacher. In it there is simplicity in its readability.

So it is that we use dyadic and triadic distinctions in rhetoric to understand the complexity of the many different modes of writing in the writing processes. But note that the unity of a story is limited by its time and place. Stories can only be so long depending on a situation or a context depending on the time constraints involved in the willingness of an audience to listen, or their willingness to spend time reading it. Note how short these constraints are in a television commercial. The time spent reading what a writer has to say is the writer's enemy in saying what he wants to say.

For a writer rhetorically to get his or her points across dyad and triads shorten any sense of time spent by a reader. Note how exceedingly long this chapter on simplicity has been. But key to any talk about simplicity is expanding on the complexity of a topic that Hegel affirmed, 'There is no such a thing as simples. Like the word *perfect* the word *simple* is grammatically used only in the comparative degree.'

And note how long the time spent in a miniseries such as happened on HBO with the Sopranos series. Given its audience willingness to spend so much time on any one episode, each episode had to have its own story integrity. But note the same applies to any piece of adversarial rhetoric. What is necessary is that the length of it needs to conform to the audience's attention span and its holding the audience in captivity in a limited context. How long are people willing to listen? Or how long are they willing to put themselves in captivity where they are obligated to listen. Obviously in some cases not at all! But in some cases it becomes a necessity as in college classes. Holding students in hostage is a problem that both teachers and students need to reckon with especially when seminars are two hours long.

In speaking, writing, reading, and listening note: the importance of the issue, the respect for the author, the consequences of not reading or listening, and how much attention can be expected of audiences in the rhetorical situation. Hopefully, the novelty and importance of understanding what I say about simplicity and unity should require this sort of attention from my own audience in writing this book. In the end I have wanted to be simple even though the trip of anyone reading through the whole lot of important issues about simplicity is lengthy. What there is to say about reducing something complex to a holistic simplicity can never be in the end very simple, exciting, precise, or accurate enough, given the constraints of holding the attention of the audience. The same holds for unity. Topics, themes, and subjects need to have unity, and if points are multiple we have to reorganize them into topical dyads or triads to give them any perspicuous sense of unity.

16 Boolean algebra, Tűring machines, and the Sheffer stroke function

What I put on paper is a record, a note, or a reminder. I think of it as external memory. External memory for me is any notational or schematic device that aids in recall-- such as books, notes, sketches, maps, models, pictures, videotapes, and magnetic or digital memory stored in computer files. Since the beginning of the use of graphics and mathematics and with the development of alphabetical scripted languages, we have supplemented the internal memory of our brains with immense resources of external memory. We have done it on such a scale that at the present time we have no adequate conception of the extent of it. No encyclopedia can be any more than a superficial gloss on it. Who and what we are is determined in large part by the way we access external memory and how we integrate it into our different ways of reflexively mining our own personal memory resources in dealing with other people and the world.

Our internal memories in our brains are linked to our oral discourse. Our external memory of visual and graphic discourse feed, loop, and fold back into our oral resources of short and long term memory. The two forms of memory, external memory and internal reflexive memory link, interact, and feed back into each other, mutually enhancing each other. As a rhetorician I point out the parallels between 'the ancient arts of memory' in oral rhetoric with 'the new arts of managing meaning' in our reading and our writing, and especially in our use of pictorials and charts and graphics. Especially now all of our past symbolic practices now as new ways of visual processing print and drawings utilize video recordings and new computer technology. The old arts of memory were internal to the brain. And the new arts of memory are prosthetics.

I want to think of literature and rhetoric in terms of how we utilize memory as prostheses and as templates for both our ritual and artistic performances and our applications of discourse in everyday practical life. As for our internal memory the amount of what we have forgotten amounts to a gigantic glacial attrition leaving us little more than imagistic scars of past ecstatic and anxious moments of our past to think upon. They are the form of the content of the stories we tell about ourselves. These memory images are selected slices of experience that I think of as synecdoche. As we personally access them they are no more than mnemonic triggers that we use to aggregate our personal memory experiences. As human beings we congratulate ourselves too much when we compare ourselves with animals and think that we have far greater and more comprehensive memories than they. And that comparison simply deflects our attention from the limits of human memory.

We need to look at our internal memories from the perspective of a different measured scale, say r/f, that is, what is remembered over what is forgotten. This diminutive ratio of our remembering to our forgetting speaks to the need of getting our thoughts on paper, or into computer files, into a form of external memory if we do not want to lose them. Such a diminutive ratio of our remembering to our forgetting reflects the minimal scope of internal memory. It reflects the need for clearing the brain of so much clutter.

The great evolution and creative invention of visual marks and recording devices, the invention of written signs and symbols that enable us to represent the oral languages, the development of new graphic techniques to create pictures and graphs, to use charts and maps has been a mark of progress of civilization. The invention of new modes of printing and the invention of logical and graphic schema have been a part of the development of the arts, the sciences, and the technologies.

Important to this development have been the new mechanistic ways these productions of prosthetic memory have been advanced with the development of electronics. Key to this development in the use of electronic computers is the creation and development of the formal languages of logic and mathematics along with the utilization of these developments in creating newly developed languages of graphic and pictorial representations. To note the history of this development one discovers that there is a striking difference between the logic of the formal languages or symbolic logic developed in the 19th century in the work of George Boole and traditional Aristotelian logic.

Aristotle and Plato mark the tradition between an oral culture and a print culture. We find this transition in the interpretation of its symbols. Aristotle and his medieval scholastic followers did not symbolize logical terms such as the *copula*, (**is**) *negation* (**no** and **not**), nor the *quantifiers* (**all** and **some**). The traditional logic they developed only abbreviated symbolically the subject and predicate terms of Aristotelian sentences that were based upon nominalized subjects and nominalized predicate terms that was made possible by transformational grammar. Note the following traditional classification of traditional Aristotelian categorical propositions:

Table 16.1: Reduction of Sentential Operators to Stroke Function

Universal Affirmative		A proposition
All S is P		
Universal Negative	E proposition	No S is P
Particular Affirmative		I proposition
Some S is P		
Particular Negative	O proposition	Some S is not P

When we transition to George Boole in the 19th century and his logical innovations we are dealing with a graphic sign culture that is dealing with visual marks on paper. Note how Boole in his work symbolized not only the Aristotelian terms, but symbolized the logical terms creating new interpretations of the operators that he found in the calculi of algebra, in number theory, and the calculi of probability theory. The net result was that just as in Aristotle symbols presumed a consistent interpretation in syllogisms of subject and predicate terms along with the middle terms, Boole does the same symbolic creation of marks for consistent interpretations of the meaning of the logical terms unlike in Aristotle thus giving them a definite and precise determinate meaning. Note the following definition as stated by Boole: '*Definition* - A sign is an arbitrary mark, having a fixed (consistent) interpretation, and susceptible of combination with other signs in subjection to fixed laws dependent upon their mutual (agreed upon) interpretation.' (Boole, 1951: 25)

Note the following table relating Aristotelian logical forms and symbols to those of Boole: '*Rule* - Express as before the subject and predicate, attach to the latter the indefinite symbol v, and equate the expressions.' (Ibid, 61)

Table 16.2: Translation of Aristotelean Language into Boole's Formal Notation

Universal Affirmative	A proposition	**All** S (Y) **is** P (X)	y = vx
Universal Negative	E proposition	**No** S (Y) **is** P (X)	y = v(1 - x)
Particular Affirmative	I proposition	**Some** S (Y) **is** P (X)	vy = vx
Particular Negative	O proposition	**Some** S (Y) is **not** P (X)	vy = (1 − x)

As illustrated above, note that Boole proposes in his definitions of signs of both elements (x,y, z...) and the signs for logical terms (+, --, x,) that both are subject in reasoning to fixed laws of combination depending upon the nature of their (agreed upon) interpretation. They consequently are by strict definition and consistent interpretations free from ambiguity and equivocation.

Contrast the symbolization of Aristotelian sentences with those of Boole's where Boole substitutes Y for S and W for P with an introduction of a 'v' as an indefinite quantifier. To quote Boole in his interpretation of the proposition '"All men are mortal'. It is clear that our meaning is ''All men are some mortal beings', and we must seek the expression of the predicate 'some mortal beings'.'" Boole proceeds to do this by creating 'v' as new operation which he uses to restrict the quantification of X. Boole in doing this innovation is creating a new sign for new operative distinction, that helps clarified the ambiguous interpretations that Aristotle's logical operations have been found to have in the history of the developments of logic.

By strict definitions (interpretations) of what Boole thinks of as the **laws of thought** (laws of language), Boole was thus able to combine the laws (rules) of arithmetic with the laws (rules) of logic. In this way he was able to set up what today are spoken of as **the formation and transformational rules** of symbolic calculi, which may vary depending on how we define and interpret their symbolic representations of argument and proof.

What Boole achieved by these analytic clarifications is finding a common ground that underpins arithmetic, number theory, theories of probability, and by comparable analytic clarifications of Aristotelian logic the logic of sets (classes) and the logic of propositions (sentential logic). His work thus was used to lay the basis for development or creation of mathematical logic, thus creating new and different modes of strict deduction and proof, which have since become the basis of complex calculations that have proved to be so useful in the language of technology and the sciences.

In my own early attempts to understand the foundations of the syllogism of Aristotelian logic both from Aristotle's and from the Scholastic Medieval logical traditions which developed the rules of the syllogism, which for years formed the basis for the modes of proof in logical text books, I tried much in the same spirit of Boole to give my own strict interpretations of the formation and transformation rules that shaped the rules for determining the validity of the various 256 syllogistic forms traditionally identified (Ibid, 228).

Where Boole maintained that his formation and transformation rules were reflected in our language from the laws of thought, I reversed the pattern and derived the definitions from interpretations from terms of ordinary language, where these patterns and operations were discovered in our rhetoric and the grammar of the communications that we engage with each other. My early sense of logic in my own education I first encountered in my study of Euclidean geometry, which used ordinary language to formulate its definitions and axioms of both arithmetic and geometry. It was only when I encountered David Hilbert's geometry that I discovered a completely developed formal symbolic system of geometry that axiomatized its foundations in formal stipulated definitions.

Hilbert's *The Foundations of Geometry* in speaking of points, straight lines, and planes speaks of them as 'having certain mutual relations, which we can indicate by means of such words as *'are situated'*, *'between'*, *'parallel'*, *'congruent'*, *'continuous'*, etc. The complete and exact description of these relations in abstract terminology that Hilbert defines sets up the terms of the axioms of geometry that Hilbert proposes. 'These axioms', Hilbert continues, 'may be arranged in five groups. Each of these groups expresses by itself certain related fundamental facts of our intuition.'(1950: 2)

In the opening lines of Hilbert's and his co-author's preface to *Anshauliche Geometrie*, translated as *Geometry and the Imagination* in using the English translation we have difficulties in translating the adjective *Anschauliche* into English. What sense does this term have in the text? My interpretation of what Hilbert and his co-author are saying in the English translation is that geometry begins in its origins to arise out of our ordinary concrete expressions. It develops out of the logic of our ordinary language. And equally as I have found that our developing systems of counting and numbers and our senses of rotations and orientations are rooted in the forms of ordinary speech. Our formal or abstract systems have their origins in the psychological roots of the human creative imagination. We find that the growing abstract complexity of logic and mathematics and its almost endless expansion grows out of our primitive senses to be found in our own language growth and development. Let me parse Hilbert and Ackerman's words:

> In mathematics, as in any scientific research, we find two tendencies present. On the one hand, the tendency toward *abstraction* seeks to crystallize the logical relations inherent in the maze of material that is being studied, and to correlate the material in a systematic and orderly manner. On the other hand, the tendency toward intuitive understanding fosters a more immediate grasp of the objects one studies, a live *rapport* with them, so to speak, which stresses the concrete meaning of their relations. (Ibid, iii)

What I find striking in the above quote is the priority given to intuitive understanding expressed in talking about the concrete meanings (for me expressed in ordinary language) that we use to express our immediate grasp of the objects of geometric studies. It was my lack of any interest in the concrete formalizations of geometry that was my curse that severely limited me in my own pursuit of any advanced knowledge of logic and mathematics. Personally, I always had difficulty in making the transition to any calculus based on formalized axioms, and I showed little interest in carrying out any formal derivations of proof that were using precisely defined steps in proofs in mathematical and logical terms. It was a rabbit whole I chose not to enter.

Not being interested in following faithfully along the multitude of explorative pathways of derivations through so many systems of calculations frankly made me at times feel that I was ignorant and stupid about logic and mathematics. In other words, in my lack of intellectual fortitude to follow symbolic proofs I lacked the enthusiasm to work out the logical implications of the complex multitude of so many logical and mathematical formal proofs. Thus, I failed in my own education to engage in the long expenditures of time what were required in working out any calculus using abstract mathematical operators and symbols that did not depend on ordinary language based intuitions.

The key expressions in the above quote by Hilbert and Ackerman are for me 'fosters a more immediate grasp of the objects' and 'a live *rapport*... which stresses the concrete meaning of their relations.' As I interpret these phrases they are immediate descriptions of geometric relations that we find in expressions that are derivative of the concrete descriptions of the language we speak. In other words, we find in the very innate and ordinary spoken language we have acquired in our vernacular the very expressions that give rise to the formal concepts and conceptions of proof that develop into formal systems in logic and mathematics that are quickly forgotten (eclipsed) and that are not held in our attention in using a calculus that we no longer intuitively grasp or follow. We just learn to follow the rules and 'crank' the machine of mastered transpositions and translations that makes a calculus appear to be nothing but a thinking machine just as we find to be the case in the use of the old mechanical calculators and adding machines, and now in our new amazing uses of electronic computers.

And later the two authors state with Hilbert in the lead:

> In this book, it is our purpose to give a presentation of geometry, as it stands today, in its visual and intuitive aspects. With the aid of the visual imagination we can illuminate the manifold facts and problems of geometry, and beyond this, it is possible in many cases to depict the geometric outline of the methods of investigation and proof, without necessarily entering into the details connected with the strict definition of concepts and with the actual calculations. (Ibid, iii)

What we find in this description of logical methods of proof is a statement of the ground of what we have come to understand to be immensely complicated, extensive, and complex in the formal expansion and extension of mathematics. It is the patterns of mathematical and logical complexity that our scientific and mathematical cultures have developed in several millennia that overwhelms most the common lot of us. We have no concept or any sense, nor any intellectual grasp of the extent of so much of the complexity and diversity of it all. All we need to confirm this amazing development is to simply glance at the *Oxford users' guide to mathematics*. We find there the complexity that has developed in the development of symbolic operations and their use in derivations that has evolved in the continued intellectual growth of them and applications of them for humanity and any knowledge of them as the basis for achievements of human civilization. The further invention and the pursuit and expansion of it all require an ever increasing number of mathematical specialists to continue to explore every aspect and detail of this ever growing expansive complexity that in many ways may prove cases fruitful in the future.

And given that this extended complexity is in part a product of the human imagination, it will continue and continue to grow beyond the limits of any one person or any select groups of persons, especially among those who aspire to be generalists and intellectuals so as to enable them to comprehend at least in part the scope of it all. The more civilization grows the more complex it becomes, and the more it grows more people have had to depend on one another to remedy their own limitations generated by their own personal ignorance of the complexity of it.

What is interesting about the use of logical and mathematical calculators is that in using them there must be an input and output. Data entry can be temporary just for short term access. Let us refer to this data retention as a form of short term memory. However, there are devices and tapes that allows now for longer term short term memory preservation. Remember that old adding machines had paper tapes that allowed accountants to check all the operations performed in using them. Those paper tapes were the long term memories that allowed the accountants to preserve them as a form of prosthetic memory or as a physical record to check the short term memory calculations that were made by the machine.

When we use an abacus or a slide rule, there is an accumulation of the results of data from the input in doing single calculations. Note we are doing the same in making tally sheets. Note again that cuneiform writing originated in the use of clay tablets to do accounting. A navigation log is again a recording of all the data inputs and calculations that a navigator computes as I had to do in the past using an E6B as a circular slide rule to calculate my true course and position. In various forms of technology there are records even diaries and notes kept to give a history of all the procedures done in accomplishing short term memory calculation tasks. Human memory is not to be trusted when tasks are complicated and subject to mistakes. Preservation of long term memory is needed. A flight data recorder is a form of long term memory preservation about aircraft performance.

Note that electronic calculators have short-term memories to record the results of operations. When we are using a calculus of numbers or a logical calculus to record logical steps we need both short term memory devices and long term memory devices if we are to exercise and follow the steps in the proofs that we do. Note that chess players and golfers record each and every step of their play. Golfers record the number of strokes on a hole. FIDE master players in chess have all their games recorded such that all players have access to many if not all their past lines of play. Now chess tournament-play have chess boards that record electronically the moves on chess boards.

In a way then all print is just a recording of a history. It is a mnemonic device that allows us to recall past events, especially about what people have said and done. It is obvious that history, and history is memory, begins with the mnemonics of print. And likewise scholarship is an activity where someone searches and finds things that they deem important to be found to be recorded in print. Note the thin line then that separates archeology from history. And note how they interact and supplement each other when you consider that the printed word is just another human artifact that leaves something for the historical record.

What we have with the development of technology are new ways of overcoming the limits of human memory. And with the development of formal systems of logic and mathematics we have created a new way of linking, sorting, introducing, and showing the connections between past observations and making these recorded observations readily and efficiently available to what is going on in the present. What has been created by computer developments are new methods of book keeping and new ways of accessing without any great effort what has been recorded in print.

It is no historical accident that those who invented or created the electronic computer were mathematicians engaged in cryptography, inscription, and crypto-analysis. Their successful efforts during the war were in deciphering Enigma messages during the war to break the German code machines. Foremost among them were British cryptographers such as Max Newman and Alan Turing, who too many were the conceptual founders of modern computing. After the war Newman established the renowned Royal Society Computing Machine Laboratory at the University of Manchester where he with others built the world's first electronic stored-program using digital computer based on Turing's ideas.

Note that the development of electric calculators was based upon a dependable mistake proof electronic storage by inscribing mathematical and logically formatted data. It was a mode of inscription that unlike human memory was not subject, nor was it prone to logical or semantic errors of interpretation as formal languages are based on perfect mathematical rule defining dictionaries.

What fascinates me is that Turing like Simon tried to design computer programs to play chess. If we treat chess as a competitive game, it is a game only so far as there is no way of always becoming a clear winner. There is a certain amount of psychology at play in competitive games. There are deceptions going on as is the case in playing poker. Note that in gambling games in casinos that there are house rules on payoffs that are to the house's advantage. There comes a time when players of games come to recognize that certain rules give certain players and a clear disadvantage. There is something foolish about gambling against someone who is able to set the rules with the odds in their favor. Much the way that stock transactions can be made by certain players who control stock and commodities exchanges we find that there is very little difference between such markets and casinos.

The following excerpt is from an article published by the New York Times in a column reprinted as 'Watson Still Can't Think' by Stanley Fisch submitted by Sean Dorrance Kelly and Hubert Dreyfus (NY Times, 2011).

The new, embodied paradigm in AI, deriving primarily from the work of roboticist Rodney Brooks, insists that the body is required for intelligence. Indeed, Brooks's classic 1990 paper, *Elephants Don't Play Chess*, rejected the very symbolic computation paradigm against which Dreyfus had railed, favoring instead a range of biologically inspired robots that could solve apparently simple, but actually quite complicated, problems like locomotion, grasping, navigation through physical environments and so on. To solve these problems, Brooks discovered that it was actually a disadvantage for the system to represent the status of the environment and respond to it on the basis of pre-programmed rules about what to do, as the traditional GOFAI systems had. Instead, Brooks insisted, 'It is better to use the world as its own model.'

Although the new model embodies a world in its model, it is a world constructed not by a human body, but the body of a world with information taken from the knowledge that a computer finds on line with giant data bases constructed on all the knowledge it finds such as in its arrogance the NY Times says is 'fit to print'. What is pointed out in this article by Kelly and Dreyfus is that the computer's world was not aware of what its competitors were saying in giving an answer. It is a form of AI that socially constructs its world from the world that search engines scan.

The same problem with Watson occurred with IBM's Deep Blue. They have created a game with competitors where each can act supposedly in response to another human when in fact it is a response to a problem or a question that is prompted by how the game is played. But a game as a game between live contestants has bodies that have problem skills involving invention and creativity. When faced with a real competitor psychologically there is the problem of knowing what the other is thinking.

In the history of games we often find that those who decide the rules of game want to change the rules to make their game more competitive. They are changing the rules to remove the disadvantages that make games one-sided. It is in such features of competitive games that questions are raised about computers playing games against live players. Note that just as there are algorithms that make tic tack toe unwinnable the same now is true for checkers. Knowing such algorithms removes all competition for those who know them. Note that computers do not have the capacity as yet to calculate all chess configuration possible in games of chess.

But the question about computer competitive chess is the way a computer is configured to give an unfair advantage to the computer in playing a game of chess. When chess players participate in rules with computers there are certain features of computers that make them have distinct advantages over human beings who are playing each other with over-the-board with competitive rules. Certainly, in the forefront of those advantages is the issue of the speed of calculation. But that is not the real issue as designers of computers know. Their use of mechanical calculators is really not the issue in computers playing games with human beings.

Accountants had no complaints against adding machines or the using of computers to do tedious tasks. But it is just not the tedium and the stress of calculating in one's head that makes the computer unfair in the game of chess, for chess is not just about computing possibilities. What is so unfair and one sided is that the computer specialist manipulated the rules of chess and have taken advantage of chess players since the rules of competitive chess put severe constraints on chess players in accessing memory banks, or in their consulting with outside players or coaches in making their plays. A computer is allowed to put into storage all the lines of play that a chess player of any caliber has played. It frames into its memory all the critiques players have used in playing a player with a known history of a style of play. IBM used hired consultants and their commentary which was stored away for the computer to access it. But the player is not permitted to consult with his or her coaches.

In addition a human player in over-the-board play was not allowed to access *Informants* (published accounts of games played) or use another computer while playing, but the computer has in its memory storage all those records that a human player is prohibited by the rules from accessing during play. And after all a computer can have multiple calculators computing for it, while on the other hand the computer is not itself permitted to enter the play from the outside and used during a game by the human player. What the computer can do is consult multiple other computer designers' programming, thus forming a virtual committee of chess players, and then program their anticipations into the computer design. The chess computer program is the fruit of multiple chess players. The identity of a computer is not as uniquely defined as is the single human brain. Computers in their design may have stacks of computers interacting compounding their computer power and their memories.

Note the very existence of computers has made over the board chess competitions change. Mail chess was completely changed by the existence of computers. Likewise chess games have been changed to make the time constraints change so that chess needs to be played now within the time constraints of a single day and not to be adjourned to be continued later. The computer now has changed the way that chess players study chess. Their search for innovations has changed, and the way chess players study the game has been completely altered by the computer being used as a tool to explore lines of play. Primarily then the computer in over the board play has an unfair advantage in how it has been permitted within the rules to have a clear disadvantage in the uses of its memory storage. Not only does it have an advantage in its multiple sources of different forms of memory, it has by its design multiple calculators simultaneously performing services that normally that computer coaches and teachers cannot give to players during play.

The study of chess by computer experts and mathematicians and logicians to simulate human thinking (artificial intelligence) was the primary aim of men like Turing. As founders of artificial intelligence (AI), they in thinking about machines that simulated steps in thinking began to ask whether the computer as theorized by Turing as a machine was no different from thinking. The key to Turing's theory of the computer is the notion of a computer program combined with an inscribed added inscribed code data base that is used by it in selecting and performing logical operations on that data base. Turing described his theoretical conception of what he called a Logical Computing Machine, which is the answer to a question put by Newman 'Whether there is a *mechanical process* which could be applied to a mathematical statement, and which would come up with the answer as to whether it was provable.' Turing's response is as follows that theoretically there could be such a machine:

> ...with an infinite memory capacity obtained in the form of an infinite tape marked out into squares, on each of which a symbol could be printed. At any moment there is one symbol in the machine; it is called the scanned symbol. The machine can alter the scanned symbol and its behavior is in part determined by that symbol, but the symbols on the tape elsewhere do not affect the behavior of the machine. However, the tape can be moved back and forth through the machine, this being one of the elementary operations of the machine. Any symbol on the tape may therefore eventually have an innings [emphasis added to indicate Turing's personal use of the term]. (1948: 61)

Key to the simplicity of using logic and mathematical proofs on the database is the development of the logical languages of such a base and the mathematical device that scans that database. It is these developments of computer languages that are at the heart of Artificial Intelligence or of a machine that derives solvable or provable conclusions from its memory of its inputs. The complexity of computer science is in part in the fact that the operations of computers and their programming require complex codified languages that need to be mastered to use them. It is for this reason that in the development of computers there were developed programs that would make computers user friendly and make the users oblivious to all the underlying complexity of the computer languages being used in the machine.

But all this computer complexity and all the mathematical and logical algorithms that have been developed in the creative construction of these formal languages developed for the computer can be seen as complex codifications resting on a simple base of spaces, squares (*innings*). These spaces or innings can be full or empty of electrical impulses, and as a result we can reduce such codifications to definitions of operations to a single operation on pairs of sequential digital operations 'on 0 or on 1', 'on or off', 'true or false' as the basis of interpreted codifications.

Such a reduction can be actually seen as a simple artifice in a logic with a single operation created by an interpretation of a sequence of dyads or sequences of pairs in codifications. It was the simplification of logical operations what were developed in set theory or the propositional calculus, that is, in 'term logic' or 'sentential logic', by using an even simpler logical language that lay the possible basis of such codifications as a basis for proof. These logical sentences of set theory or the propositional calculus can be reduced to a single operation of utmost simplicity. The language of set theory and the operators of formal mathematical systems and their logics can be eliminated by unitary dyadic codifications such as developed by Henry M. Sheffer that enabled logicians to reduce logical operations to a single stroke function called the Sheffer Stroke Function.

To see this reduction of so much computer complexity to simple digital dyads as a basis of encoding complex logical and mathematical operations allows us to see the basic simplicity that underlies the complex logical and mathematical algorithms that make computer technological developments so enormously complex and creative. This reduction can be illustrated in the innovation of the Sheffer stroke function pq or what is now referred to as the NAND operator, which is interpreted to mean that not both p and q are true, and this makes possible the reduction of complex logical systems and graphic models to simple pluses and minuses, zeros and ones, that is, the binary operations so famously exploited in computer development. The Sheffer stroke function or the Nand function is sometimes also written as A | B or A ↑ B). The truth table of **A NAND B** is as follows:

Table 16.3: The truth table of A NAND B

INPUT		OUTPUT
A	B	A NAND B
0	0	1
0	1	1
1	0	1
1	1	0

The NAND gate has the property of functional completeness. That is, any other logic function (AND, OR, etc.) can be implemented by using only NAND gates. An entire processor can be created using NAND gates alone. The basis of computer technology is the machine language that evolves out of the use of the NAND gate, the device that permits coding and decoding of the machine language. The NAND gate allows for the interpretation of a signal as being false, that is, if both squares or innings are full or both empty. Both signal spaces cannot be filled with true or false entries in data recording.

What makes the Sheffer Stroke so simple is that there are no need for any codification of punctuation as the sequence of coding can use Polish notation that defines the scope of an operator. For example, KKpqr in Polish notation is a combination of a conjunct both p and q in conjunction with another conjunct r, that is, Kpq within a conjunct (Kpq and r). It would read, the conjunction with both the conjunction 'p and q' as the first term and r as the second term of a conjunction. Polish notation simply uses the first term of correlative logical operators with the assumption that there is no need to use the second term, ((pvq) v r) thus removing any need for punctuation such as parentheses and brackets to determine scope of logical operators in machine language. In sum notation thus is again simplified by eliminating any punctuation by using Polish Notation.

Note that the following examples of Sheffer stroke functions with only parenthesis could be rewritten using only strokes as follows:

$(p(p(q(q((pq)(pq))))))$ becomes
$p|p|q|q||pq|pq$, and
$(p(p((qq)(pp))))$ becomes,
$p|p||qq|pp.$

This follows the same rules as those found in the parenthesis version, with opening parenthesis replaced with a Sheffer stroke and the (redundant) closing parenthesis removed.

What makes Polish notation so difficult in reading or in interpreting it as a logical notation is that it is not readable visually because of limitations of human memory. It is difficult to read due to the difficulties that we have in short term memory in holding in our attention the overly complex grammatical syntax that prolongs closure. It is the very same difficulty we have in readings a system of numbers to the base 2. It is difficult to deal with the problems of visualizing scope of 'numerical place' in numbers to the base 2. Note that $2 \times 2 = 4$ in base 10 contrasts with the same operation of $10 \times 10 = 100$ in base 2 calculations.

Let me illustrate all the logical reductions or eliminations of operators from a standard type of 'term logic' or a 'sentential logic' by reducing them to the Sheffer stroke function. For example the Sheffer stroke '|' is equivalent to the negation of conjunction. Expressed in terms of NAND ↑, the usual operators such as negation

'—', material conditional '→', conjunction 'V', and disjunction '∧', of propositional logic are defined as follows by substitutional equivalents '←' for well-formed formulae wwf's using only **NAND ↑ operators**

Introduction, elimination, and equivalencies

The Sheffer stroke ↑ is the negation of the conjunction:

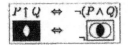

$P \uparrow Q \leftrightarrow \neg(P \wedge Q)$

Expressed in terms of NAND ↑, the usual operators of propositional logic are:

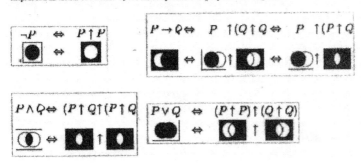

Figure 16.1: Reduction of Sentential Operators to Stroke Function

One can thus use the sentential calculus as the basis of encoding and utilizing many more formal languages and mathematical systems into computer processing of information and data. Importantly what can be embedded in the data base of computer memory can be nothing more than encoded blanks or 'innings', which becomes the basis for entering data into the machine language which is at the heart of the computer's inscribed memory or data bank.

Given the complexity of the data bank and the possibilities of what can be inscribed in that memory, the computer more and more can simulate more and more patterns that are a result of human creation or design. The questions then are: 'How far these patterns can simulate thinking and human behavior?', 'Can we ever look upon a computer as nothing more than a machine and not as a living human being?'

The heart of computer operations looking at the process from rhetorical frames is that rhetoric at its heart is a way of using rhetorical actions or rhetorical strategies in utilizing fragments of human memory to communicate with other people. We rhetorically note and remind other people. We use figurative language as modes of indirection to call attention to this accumulated set of life experiences in our biological, cultural, and personal memories subconscious and conscious that each of us has.

And just as we develop a set of rhetorical actions to access those personal reservoirs of psychological memory, those who develop and program computers devise comparable guides to actions that can access, discover or recover, what is in the memory of the computer. But the computer in its way of creating memory has not the capacity to simulate and interpret the complexity of human memory especially of a single individual. But in a way computer memory surpasses human memory in being able to transcend many of the aspects defined by human limitations and so much human ignorance about so much of the existential complexity that human beings face.

Appendix

Topical Quotes on Ignorance and Simplicity/Complexity:

Flattery and insult are born out of ignorance. Receive them both kindly.

The human being is irrational. Right? And as long as he is functioning irrationally, he says of any rational factor, 'I refuse to see it.'

I can't go back. If for example, if I see all the religious nonsense, it is finished.

I think the human brain is not a particular brain; it doesn't belong to me, or to anyone else. It is the human brain which evolved over millions of years. And in that evolution it has gathered tremendous experience, knowledge and all the cruelties, vulgarities and brutalities of selfishness. Is there a possibility of its sloughing off all this, and becoming something else? Because apparently it is functioning in patterns. Whether it is a religious pattern, a scientific, a business, or a family pattern, it is always operating, functioning in small narrow circles. Those circles are clashing against each other, and there seems to be no end to this. So what will breakdown this forming of patterns, so that there is no falling into other new patterns, but breaking down the whole system of patterns, whether pleasant or unpleasant? After all, the brain has many shocks, challenges and pressures upon it, and if it is not capable or renewing or rejuvenating itself, there is very little hope.

> Verbal statements made by J. Krishnamurti, an Indian Philosopher

Stupidity and pride grow on the same tree.

> A proverb quoted by Robert Musil
> *On stupidity, Precision and Soul, Addresses*

While we can no doubt state some things we do not know, we cannot in general state with confidence what it is that we do not know. There are limits in principle to the extent that we can know what we do not know.

> Bernard Williams
> *Understanding Ignorance, Philosophy as a Humanistic Discipline*

If the purpose of critical thinking is not to help us decide what to believe, what can that purpose be? Insofar as the question of knowledge and belief are concerned, I would say that the role of critical thinking is defensive: to protect us from being coerced or brainwashed into believing what others want us to believe without our having the opportunity to inquire for ourselves. There are great and powerful forces ranged against the individual in every society—the political, the military, and the economic are the obvious examples—and their aim is often to get us to acquiesce without reflection in the views they want us to have.

Matthew Lipman
Thinking in Education

The aim of science is to seek the simplest explanations of complex facts. We are apt to fall into the error of thinking that the facts are simple because simplicity is the goal of our quest. The guiding motto in the life of every natural philosopher should be, Seek simplicity and distrust it.

Alfred North Whitehead
Concept of Nature

Each of us sits in a long dark hall within a circle of light cast by a small lamp. The lamplight penetrates a few feet up and down the hall, then rapidly attenuates, diluted by the vast darkness of future and past that surrounds us.

Herbert Simon
Social Planning, The Sciences of the artificial

Mouse to Mole: 'If you want to have stuff, you can't have space. And if you want to have space you cannot have stuff.'

Mouse and Mole
The Wind and the Willows

For he who attempts to view a multitude of objects with one and the same glance, sees none of them distinctly; and similarly the man who is wont to attend to many things at the same time by means of a single act of thought is confused in the mind. But just as workmen, who are employed in very fine and delicate operations are accustomed to direct their eyesight attentively to separate points, by practice have acquired a capacity for distinguishing objects of extreme minuteness and subtlety; so likewise people, who do not allow their thought to be distracted by various objects at the same time, but always concentrate it in attending to the simplest particulars, are clear headed.

René Descartes
Rules for the Directions of the Mind

The world judges things well, because it is in that state of natural ignorance which is the true place of the human. The sciences have two extremities, which converge: the first is that state of pure ignorance, in which we are left by nature; the other extremity is that at which great minds arrive, which, having traversed everything which man can know, discover that they know nothing, and recognize once more the point from which they set out. But this is a learned ignorance, which knows itself. Those who have set out from the stage of natural ignorance, and have not yet been able to arrive at the other, have but a hint of that real and adequate knowledge; and these are the assumers and pretenders to reason. These disquiet the world: and judge everything worse than the others.

Le monde juge bien des choses, car il est dans l'ignorance naturelle qui est le vrai siège de l'homme. Les sciences ont deux extrémités qui se touchent, la première est la pure ignorance naturelle où se trouvent tous les hommes en naissant, l'autre extrémité est celle où arrivent les grandes âmes qui ayant parcouru tout ce que les hommes peuvent savoir trouvent qu'ils ne savent rien et se rencontrent en cette même ignorance d'où ils étaient partis, mais c'est une ignorance savante qui se connaît. Ceux d'entre deux qui sont sortis de l'ignorance naturelle et n'ont pu arriver à l'autre, ont quelque teinture de cette science suffisante, et font les entendus. Ceux-là troublent le monde et jugent mal de tout.

Blaise Pascal
Pensées pt 1, art vi, sec 25, pensee No 327b (308) (Frag. Sel. No. 117)
(ca. 1649) in the OEuvres completes p. 1166 (J. Chevalier ed. 1954) (S.H. transl.)

I argue that ethnography aims at interpretation and anthropology at explanation, in order to achieve these aims, and to entertain more fruitful relations, the two disciplines should first free themselves from one another.

The project of a scientific anthropology meets with a major difficulty: it is impossible to describe a cultural phenomenon, an election, a mass, or a football game for instance, without taking into account the ideas of the participants. However, ideas cannot be observed, but only intuitively understood; they cannot be described but only interpreted. Thus description of cultural phenomena raises epistemological issues without counterpart in the sciences.

Dan Sperber
On Anthropological Knowledge: Three Essays

Phronetic (*phronesis*) social science explores historical circumstances and current practices to find avenues to praxis. The task of phronetic science is to clarify and deliberate about the problems and risks we face and to outline how things may be done differently, in the full knowledge we cannot find ultimate answers to these questions or even a single version of what the questions are.

As with phronesis the main object of genealogy (historical narrative) is to produce input for ongoing dialogue and social praxis rather than definitive empirically verifiable knowledge, even though rigorous empirical study and verification of data are central to genealogy....Thus the results of genealogy may be confirmed, revised or rejected according to the most rigorous standards of historiographic inquiry and such results are open for testing in relation to other interpretations. This does not mean that one interpretation is as good as the next, for each interpretation must be based on certain validity requirements. It does mean, however, that genealogical studies will be prepared to defend such requirements as any other study.

Discourse, therefore, must be viewed as a series of interrupted segments whose tactical function is neither uniform nor stable. One ought to view the universe of discourses as divided into accepted and excluded discourses, into dominant and dominated discourses, or into successful and fallacious discourses. Rather, one should operate with a multiplicity of discursive elements, which can be put together in various strategies.

Bent Flyvbjerg
Making social science matter

Charner Perry, an old teacher of mine, told the following story in class in discussing price as a measure of value: In Arkansas they used to measure the weight of a hog by balancing the hog on a pole with a sack of rocks, and then they would dump the rocks on the ground, and guess the weight of the rocks.

George Yoos

Bibliography

Ackermann, R. J. (1988). Wittgenstein's city. Amherst. Ma: The University of Massachusetts Press.

Alberts, B. at al. (2008). Molecular Biology of the Cell. 5th Ed. New York: Garland Science, Taylor Francis Group.

American Psychiatric Association. (2000). DSM-IV-TR: Diagnostic and statistical manual of mental disorders. 4th Ed. Arlington. VA: American Psychiatric Association.

Aristotle. (1941). The basic works of Aristotle: Categories, On interpretation, Prior analytics, Posterior analytics, Topics, On sophistical refutations, Nicomachean ethics, Politics, Rhetoric, and Poetics. Ed. Richard McKeon. New York: Random House.

Austin, J. L. (1962). How to do things with words. Cambridge, MA: Harvard University Press.

Austin, J. L. (1970). Philosophical papers. Ed. J. O. Urmson and G. J. Warnock. 2nd Ed. Oxford: Oxford University Press.

Bacon, Sir F. (1955). Novum organum. Chicago: Encyclopedia Britannica.

Barthes, R. (1988). The semiotic challenge. Trans. Richard Howard. New York: Hill and Wang.

Baudrillard, J. (1968). Le système des objets. Paris: Gallimard.

Baudrillard, J. (1981). For a critique of the political economy of the sign. Trans. Charles Levin. St. Louis, MO: Telos Press.

Beardsley, M. C. (1950). Thinking straight: A guide to readers and writers. New York: Prentice Hall.

Beardsley, M. C. (1958). Aesthetics: The problems in the philosophy of criticism. New York: Harcourt, Brace, and World.

Beardsley, M. C. (1966). Thinking straight: Principles of reasoning for readers and writers. 4th Ed. Englewood Cliffs, NJ: Prentice Hall.

Beardsley, M. C. (2007). Thinking straight. Amherst, NJ: Oliphant Press.

Berndtson, A. (1975). A theory of radical creativity. The Modern Schoolman. LIII, 1-19.

Berndtson, A. (1981). Power, form, and mind. Lewisburg, PA: Bucknell University Press.

Bitzer, L. (1968). The rhetorical situation. Philosophy and Rhetoric, 1, 1-14.

Black, M. (1949). Language and philosophy: Studies in method. Ithaca, New York: Cornell University Press.

Black, M. (1962a). Models and metaphors: Studies in language and philosophy. Ithaca, NY: Cornell University Press.

Black, M. (1962b). The importance of language. Englewood Cliffs, NJ: Prentice-Hall.

Bloom, A. (1987). Closing of the American mind. New York: Simon and Schuster.

Bloomfield, L. (1933). Language. New York: Henry Holt.

Bohm, D., at al. (1964). Quanta and reality: A symposium. Stephen Toulmin, Introduction. NY: Meridian Books.

Boole, G. (1951). An investigation of the laws of thought, on which are founded the mathematical theories of logic and probabilities. New York: Dover publications.

Boole, G. (1952). Studies in logic and probability. La Salle, IL: The Open Court Publishing Company.

Booth, W. (1961). The rhetoric of fiction. Chicago: University of Chicago Press.

Booth, W. (1978). Modern dogma and the rhetoric of assent. Notre Dame, IN: University of Notre Dame Press.

Booth, W. (1979). Critical understanding: The powers and limits of pluralism. Chicago: University of Chicago Press.

Booth, W. (2004). The rhetoric of rhetoric: The quest for effective communication. Oxford: Blackwell.

Bourdieu, P. (1991). Language and symbolic power. Cambridge, MA: Harvard University Press.

Bridgeman, P. W. (1927). The logic of modern physics. New York: Macmillan.

Brooks, C. (1947). The well wrought urn: Studies in the structure of poetry. New York: Reynaland Hitchcock.

Brummett, B. (2003). The world and how we describe it: Rhetorics of reality, representation, simulation. Westport, CT: Prager.

Bruner, J. (1990). Acts of meaning. Cambridge, MA: Harvard University Press.

Bruner, J. (2002). Making stories: law, literature, life. New York: Farrar, Straus, and Giroux.

Bud, Robert and Deborah Jean Warner. Eds. (1998). Instruments of Science: An Historical Encyclopedia. London: Routledge.

Burke, K. (1965). Permanence and change: an anatomy of purpose. Indianapolis, IN: The Library of Liberal Arts.

Burke, K. (1966). Language as symbolic action: essays on life, literature, and method. Berkeley, CA: University of California Press.

Burke, K. (1969a). A grammar of motives. Berkeley, CA: University of California Press.

Burke, K. (1969b). A rhetoric of motives. Berkeley, CA: University of California Press.

Burnyeat, M. (2006). The sense of the past: Essays in the history of philosophy. Princeton, NJ: Princeton University Press.

Butchvarov, P. (1970). The concept of knowledge. Evanston, IL: Northwestern University Press.

Carnap, R. (1935). The logical syntax of language. London: Psychical Miniatures.

Carnap, R. (1948). Introduction to semantics. Cambridge, MA: Harvard University Press.

Carnap, R. (1969). The logical structure of the world and pseudo problems of philosophy. Berkley, CA: University of California Press.

Cassirer, E. (1979). Symbol, myth, and culture: Essays and lectures of Ernst Cassirer, 1935–1945. Ed. Donald Phillip Verene. New Haven: Yale University Press.

Cicero, M. T. (1986). Cicero on oratory and orators. Trans. J. S. Watson.

Cole, P., Morgan, J. L. (1975). Speech Acts. Vol. 3 of Syntax and semantics. New York: Academic Press.

Corbett, E. P. J. (1999). Classical rhetoric for the modern student. 4th Ed. Oxford: Oxford University Press.

Croce, B. (1963). Aesthetics and science of expression and general linguistic. Trans. Douglas Ainslie. New York: Noonday Press.

Crozier, M. (1984). The Trouble with America. Trans. Peter Heinegg. Berkeley, CA: University of California Press.

Crozier, M. (1964). Bureaucratic phenomena. Chicago: The University of Chicago Press.

Crystal, D. (1997). The Cambridge encyclopedia of language. 2nd Ed. Cambridge, UK: Cambridge University Press.

Crystal, D. (2005). How language works: How babies babble, words change meaning, and languages live and die. New York: Penguin Group.

Crystal, D. (2008a). Think on my words: exploring Shakespeare's language. Cambridge, UK: Cambridge University Press.

Crystal, D. (2008b). By hook or by crook: A journey in search of English. New York: The Overlook.

Davidson, D. (2001). Inquiries into truth and interpretation. 2nd Ed. Oxford, UK: Clarendon Press.

Deleuze, G., & Guattari, F. (1994). What is philosophy? New York: Columbia University Press.

Derrida, J. (1974). Of grammatology. Baltimore, MD: John Hopkins University Press.

Derrida, J. (1978). Writing and difference. Trans. Alan Bass. Chicago: University of Chicago Press.

Dewey, J. (1929). The quest for certainty: A study of the relation of knowledge to action. New York: C. P. Putnam's and Sons.

Drucker, P. (1946). The concept of the corporation. Boston: Beacon Press.

Drucker, P. (2006). Classic Drucker: Essential wisdom of Peter Drucker from the pages of Harvard Business Review. Boston: Harvard Business School Publishing Corporation.

Ducrot, O., & Todorov, T. (1979). Encyclopedic dictionary of the sciences of language. Trans. Catherine Porter. Baltimore, MD: John's Hopkins University Press.

Eco, U. (1992). Interpretation and overinterpretation. With Richard Rorty, Jonathan Culler, and Christine Brooke-Rose. Ed. Stefan Collini. New York: Cambridge University Press.

Empson, W. (1930). Seven types of ambiguity. London: Chato and Windus.

Fisch, S. (2001). Watson Still Can't Think, submitted by Sean Dorrance Kelly and Hubert Dreyfus: NY Times.

Flyvbjerg, B. (2001). Making social science matter: Why social inquiry fails and how it can succeed again. Trans. Steven Sampson. Cambridge, UK: Cambridge University Press.

Foucault, M. (1973). The order of things: An archeology of the human sciences. New York: Vintage Books.

Frankfurt, H. G. (2005). On bullshit. Princeton, NJ: Princeton University Press.

Frege, G. (1964). The basic laws of arithmetic: Exposition of the system. Translated and edited by Montgomery Furth. Berkeley. CA: University of California Press.

Gadamer, H.-G. (1994). Truth and method. Trans. Joel Weinsheimer and Donald G. Marshall. New York: Continuum.

Gaonkar, D. P. (1993). The idea of rhetoric in the rhetoric of science. Southern Communication Journal, 58, 258–95.

Geertz, C. (1973). The interpretation of culture: selected essays. New York: Basic Books.

Goffman, E. (1959). The presentation of self-in everyday life. Garden City, NJ: Anchor Books Edition.

Goffman, E. (1974). Frame analysis: An essay on the organization of experience. Cambridge, MA: Harvard University Press.

Gove, P. B. (1961). Webster's third new international dictionary of the English language unabridged. Springfield, MA: Merriam-Webster Inc.

Grice, P. (1989). Studies in the way of words. Cambridge, MA: Harvard University Press.

Habermas, J. (1987). The philosophical discourse of modernity: Twelve lectures. Cambridge, MA: MIT Press.

Habermas, J. (1991). The structural transformation of the public sphere: An inquiry into a category of bourgeois society. Trans. Thomas Burger. Cambridge, MA: MIT Press.

Hacking, I. (1999). The social construction of what? Cambridge, MA: Harvard University Press.

Hartshorne, C. (1937). Beyond humanism: Essays in the philosophy of nature. Chicago/New York: Willett, Clark & Co.

Hartshorne, C. (1948). The divine relativity: A social conception of God. New Haven: Yale University Press.

Hartshorne, C. (1953). Reality as social process: Studies in metaphysics and religion. Glencoe, IL: The Free Press.

Heidegger, M. (1962). Being and time. Trans. Jody Macquarrie and Edward Robinson. San Francisco: Harper.

Hilbert, D. (1950). The Foundations of Geometry. La Salle, IL: The Open Book Publishing Company.

Hilbert, D., & Cohn-Vossen, S. (1952). Geometry and the imagination. Translation of Anschauliche geometrie. Trans. P. Nemenyi. New York: Chelsea Publishing Co.

Hirsch, E. D. (1967). Validity and interpretation. New Haven, CT: Yale University Press.

Hirsch, E. D. (1981). The philosophy of composition. Chicago: University of Chicago Press.

Hirsch, E. D. (1988). Cultural literacy: What every American needs to know. New York: Vintage Books.

Husserl, E. (1977). Cartesian meditations: An introduction to phenomenology. Trans. Dorion Cairns. The Hague: Martinus Nijhoff.

Huxley, A. (1940). Words and their meanings. Los Angeles: Jake Zeitlin.

Johnson-Laird, P. N. (1988). The computer and the mind: An introduction to cognitive science. Cambridge, MA: Harvard University Press.

Johnson, R. H. (1996). The rise of informal logic: Essays on argumentation, critical thinking, reasoning, and politics. Newport, VA: Vale Press.

Jones, G. E. (1995). How to lie with charts. San Francisco: Sybex.

Joseph, Sister Miriam. (2002). The trivium: The liberal arts of logic, grammar, and rhetoric. Philadelphia: Paul Dry.

Keller, E. F. (1983). A feeling for the organism: The life and work of Barbara McClintock. New York: W. H. Freeman.

Keller, E. F. (1992). Secrets of life, Secrets of Death: Essays on language, gender and science. New York: Routledge.

Keller, E. F. (1995). Refiguring life: Metaphors of twentieth century biology. New York: Columbia University Press.

Keller, E. F. (2000). The century of the gene. Cambridge, MA: Harvard University Press.

Keller, E. F. (2002). Making sense of life: Explaining biological development with models, metaphors, and machines. Cambridge, MA: Harvard University Press.

Keller, E. F. (2010).The mirage of space between nature and nurture. Durham, NC: Duke University Press.

Kennedy, G. (1980). Classical rhetoric and its Christian and secular tradition from ancient to modern times. Chapel Hill: University of North Carolina Press.

Kinneavy, J. L. (1971). A theory of discourse: The aims of discourse. Englewood Cliffs, NJ: Prentice-Hall.

Kirsten, M. Ed. n.d. The linguistics encyclopedia. London: Routledge.

Kneale, W., & Kneale, M. (1962). The development of logic. London: Oxford University Press.

Korzybski, A. (1933). Science and sanity: An introduction to non-Aristotelian systems and general semantics. Lancaster, PA: Science Press.

Kripke, S. A. (1980). Naming and necessity. Cambridge, MA: Harvard University Press.

Krishnamurti, J., & Bohm, D. (1985). The Ending of time. New York: Harpers Collins Publishers.

Kuhn, T. S. (1996). The structure of scientific revolutions. 3rd ed. Chicago: University of Chicago Press. (Orig. pub. 1962).

Lakoff, G., & Johnson, M. (1980). Metaphors we live by. Chicago: University of Chicago Press.

Langer, S. (1942). Philosophy in a new key: A study in the symbolism of reason, rite, and art. Cambridge, MA: Harvard University Press.

Lawrence, D. H. (1974). Apocalypse. London: Penguin.

Leff, M. (2000). Rhetorical disciplines and rhetorical disciplinarity: A response to Mailloux. Rhetoric Society Quarterly, 30 (4), 83–93.

Leibniz, G. W. (1947). Discourse on metaphysics, Correspondence with Arnauld, Mondadology. La Salle, IL: Open Court.

Leibniz, G. W. (1949). New essays concerning Understanding. La Salle, IL: Open Court.

Levi, A. W. (1959). Philosophy and the modern world. Bloomington, IN: Indiana University

Levi, A. W. (1969). Humanism & politics: Studies in the relationship of power and value in the western tradition. Bloomington, IN: Indiana University Press.

Levi, A. W. (1970). The Humanites today. Bloomington, IN: Indiana University Press.

Levi, A. W. (1974). Philosophy as social expression. Chicago: University of Chicago Press. Press.

Lipman, M. (2003). Thinking in education. 2nd Ed. Cambridge, UK: Cambridge University Press.

McDowell, J. (1994). Mind and the world. Cambridge, MA: Harvard University Press.

McKeon, R. (1987). Rhetoric: Essays in invention and discovery. Ed. Mark Backman. Woodridge, CT: Ox Bow Press.

McLuhan, M. (1967). Understanding media: The extensions of man. New York: Bantam Books.

Mead, G. H. (1932). The Philosophy of the Present. Ed. Arthur E. Murray. Chicago: Open Court.

Mead, G. H. (1934). Mind Self and society: From the standpoint of the behaviorist. Ed. Charles W. Morris. Chicago: University of Chicago Press.

Mead, G. H. (1956). On social psychology: Selected papers. Edited by Anselm Strauss. Chicago: University of Chicago Press.

Mailloux, S. (2000). Disciplining identities: On the rhetorical paths between English and communication studies. Rhetoric Society Quarterly, 30 (2), 5–29.

McCloskey, D. (1997). Big rhetoric, little rhetoric: Gaonkar on the rhetoric of science. In Rhetorical Hermeneutics: Invention and Interpretation in the Age of Science, ed. Alan Gross and William M. Keith. Albany: State University of New York Press, 101–112.

Menand, L. (1997). Pragmatism: A reader. New York: Vintage.

Menand, L. (2002). The metaphysical club: A story of ideas in America. New York: Farrar, Straus, and Giroux.

Morehead, P. D. (2002). New American Roget's college thesaurus in dictionary form. New York: Penguin.

Morris, C. W. (1938). Foundation of the theory of signs. Vol. 1, no. 2 of Encyclopedia of unified science. Chicago: University of Chicago Press.

Morris, C. W. (1946). Signs, language, and behavior. New York: Prentice-Hall.

Nagel, E. (1956). Logic without metaphysics: And other essays in the philosophy of science. Glencoe, IL: The Free Press.

Nagel, E. (1961). The structure of science: Problems in the logic of scientific explanation. New York: Harcourt, Brace.

Oerter, R. (2006). The Theory of Almost Everything: The Standard Model, the Unsung Triumph of Modern Physics (Kindle Ed.). Penguin Group.

Ogden, C. K., & Richards, I. A. (1947). The meaning of meaning: A study of the influence of language upon thought and the science of symbolism. New York: Harcourt, Brace.

Oxford users' guide to mathematics. (2004). Ed. Eberhard Zeidler. Oxford. Oxford University Press.

Palmer, R. E. (1969). Hermeneutics: Interpretation theory in Schleiermacher, Dilthey, Heidegger, and Gadamer. Evanston, IL: Northwestern University Press.

Panofsky, E. (1955). Meaning in the visual arts. Garden City, NY: Anchor Books.

Parsons, T. (1949). The structure of social action. Glencoe, IL: The Free Press.

Paulos, J. A. (1992). Beyond numeracy: Ruminations of a numbers man. New York: Vintage Books.

Peirce, C. S. (1960). Collected papers of Charles Sanders Peirce. Vol. 1, Principles of philosophy, Vol. 2, Elements of logic. Vol. 3, Exact Logic. In C. Hartshorne, & P. Weiss (Eds). Cambridge, MA: Belknap Press of Harvard University Press.

Pepper, S. C. (1948). World hypotheses: A study in evidence. Berkeley, CA: University of California Press.

Perlman, C., & Olbrechts-Tyteca, L. (1968). The new rhetoric: A treatise on argumentation. Trans. John Wilkenson and Purcell Weaver. Notre Dame, IN: University of Notre Dame Press.

Petraglia, J. (2003). Identity Crisis: Rhetoric as a pedagogic and as epistemic discipline. In The realms of rhetoric: The prospects for rhetoric education. New York: State University of New York Press, 151-170.

Pinker, S. (1995). The language instinct: How the mind creates language. New York: Harper Perennial.

Pinker, S. (2007). The stuff of thought: Language as a window into human nature. New York: Viking.

Plato. (1969). The collected dialogues of Plato: Republic,Euthyphro,Phaedo, and Phaedrus. Ed. Edith Hamilton and Huntington Cairns. Princeton, NJ: Princeton University Press.

Polanyi, M. (1958). Personal knowledge: Towards a post-critical philosophy. New York: Torch Books.

Popper, K. (1959). The logic of scientific discovery. London: Hutchitson.

Popper, K. (2004). Conjectures and refutations: The growth of scientific knowledge. London: Routledge and Kegan Paul.

Potter, R. W. (2000). The art of measurement: Theory and practice. Upper Saddle River, NJ: Prentice Hall.

Putnam, H. (1992). Renewing Philosophy. Cambridge, MA: Harvard University Press.

Bohm, D., et. al (1964). Quanta and reality. A symposium for the non-scientist on the physical and philosophical implications of quantum mechanics. New York: Meridian Books.

Quine, W. O. (1953). From a logical point of view: Logico-philosophical essays. Cambridge, MA: Harvard University Press.

Quine, W. O. (1960). Word and object. Cambridge, MA: MIT Press.

Quine, W. O. (1981). Theories and things. Cambridge, MA: Harvard University Press. Renaud, Hugues Dictionnaire historique de la Suisse. Fonds, AV Laussane. 'Dapples: ...Charles-Marc (1837-1920)'.

Rescher, N. (1975). A theory of possibility: A constructivistic and conceptualistic account of possible individual and possible worlds. Oxford: Basil Blackwell.

Rescher, N. (1993). Pluralism: Against the demand for consensus. Oxford: Clarendon Press.

Rescher, N. (1998). Complexity: A philosophical overview. New Brunswick, NJ: Transaction Publishers.

Rescher, N. (1999). The limits of science. Revised edition. Pittsburg, PA: University of Pittsburg Press.

Richards, I. A. (1965). The philosophy of rhetoric. New York: Oxford University Press.

Ronell, A. (2002). Stupidity. Urbana and Chicago, IL: University of Illinois Press.

Rorty, R. (1982). Philosophy and the mirror of nature. Princeton, NJ: Princeton University Press.

Rorty, R. (1998). Truth and progress. Vol. 3 of Philosophical papers. Cambridge, UK: Cambridge University Press.

Safire, W. (2003). No uncertain terms: More writing from the popular 'On language' column in The New York Times Magazine. New York: Simon & Shuster.

Safire, W. (2008). Safire's Political Dictionary. New York: Oxford University Press.

Saussure, F.de. (1972). Course in general linguistics. Trans. Roy Harris. LaSalle, IL: Open Court.

Saddock, J. M. (1974). Toward a linguistic theory of speech acts. New York; Academic Press.

Schiappa, E. (2001). Second thoughts on the critiques of big rhetoric. Philosophy and Rhetoric 34(3), 260–74.

Schiappa, E. (2003). Defining reality: Definitions and the politics of meaning. Carbondale, IL: Southern Illinois University Press.

Schon, D. A. (1967). Technology and change: The new Heracitus. New York: Delacorte Press.

Schon, D. A. (1963). Displacement of concepts. London: Tavistock Publications.

Scott, R. L. (1967). On viewing rhetoric as epistemic. Central States Speech Journal, 18, 9–16.

Scott, R. L. (1976). On viewing rhetoric as epistemic: Ten years later. Central States Speech Journal 27, 258–66.

Searle, J. (1969). Speech acts: An essay in the philosophy of language. Cambridge, UK: Cambridge University Press.

Searle, J. (1995). Construction of social reality. New York: Simon and Schuster.

Simon, H. A. (1997). Administrative behavior: A study of decision-making processes in administrative organizations, 4th ed. New York: Free Press.

Simon, H. A. (1996). The sciences of the artificial, 3rd ed. Cambridge, MA: MIT Press.

Simon, H. A. (1979). Models of thought. New Haven, CT; Yale University Press.

Sobel, D. (1995). Longitude: The true story of a lone genius who solved the greatest scientific problem of his time. New York; Walker and Company.

Sontag, S. (1966). Against interpretation. New York: Dell Publishing.

Sperber, D., & Deirdre, W. (1986). Relevance: Communication and cognition. Cambridge, MA: Harvard University Press.

Stevenson, C. L. (1944). Ethics and language. New Haven, CT: Yale University Press.

Stiegler, B. (1998). Technics and time, In Translation by B. Rich. & G. Collins, The fault of Epimetheus. Standford, CA: Standford University Press.

Tarski, A. (1941). Introduction to logic and to the methodology of deductive sciences. New York: Oxford University Press.

Toulmin, S. E. (1984). An introduction to reasoning. 2nd Ed. New York: Macmillan.

Toulmin, S. E. (2001). Return to reason. Cambridge, MA: Harvard University Press.

Trask, R. L. (2007). Language and linguistics: The key concepts. 2nd Ed. P. Stockwell (Ed). New York: Routledge.

Turing, A. M. (2004). The essential Turing: Seminal writings in computing, logic, philosophy, artificial intelligence, and artificial life plus the secrets of Enigma. J. Copeland (Ed). Oxford: Clarendon Press.

Urdang, L., Hunsinger, W. W., & LaRoche, N. (1991). A fine kettle of fish and other figurative phrases. Detroit, MI: Viking Ink Press.

Urdang, L. (1966). The Random House dictionary of the English language (unabridged). New York: Random House.

Urdang, L. (1975). The basic book of synonyms and antonyms. 2nd Ed. New York: Signet.

Urdang, L. (1983). Literary, rhetorical, and linguistics terms index. Frank R. Abate, managing editor. Detroit: Gale Research Company.

Urdang, L. (1986). -Ologies & -Isms. 3rd Ed. Anne Ryan and Tanya H. Lee, editors. Detroit: Gale Research Inc.

Urdang, L. (1998). Suffixes and other word-final elements in English. Old Lyme, CT: Verbatim.

Urdang, L. (2008). The last word: The English language, opinions and prejudices. Detroit: Omnidata Research.

Veblen, T. (1958). The theory of business enterprise. New York: Mentor Book.

Voltaire, F. M. A. de. (1947). Candide or optimism. Trans. John Butt. New York: Penquin Books.

Voltaire, F. M. A. de. (1951). Choix de contes. F. C. Green, Introduction and notes. Cambridge, UK: Cambridge University Press.

Vygotsky, L. S. (1962). Thought and language. New York: Wiley.

Walton, D. (2001). Persuasive definitions and public policy arguments. Argumentation and Advocacy, 37 (3), 117–132.

Waismann, F. (1965). The principles of linguistic philosophy. R. Harre (Ed). New York: Macmillan.

Ward, E. C. (1996). Reconfiguring truth: Postmodernism, science studies, and the search for a new model of knowledge. New York: Rowman & Littlefield.

Watson, P. (2006). Ideas: A history of thought and invention from fire to Freud. New York: Harper Perennial.

Webster's dictionary of synonyms: A dictionary of discriminated synonyms with antonyms and contrasted words. (1942). Eds. editorial board of G. & C. Merriam. Menasha. Wisconsin: G. & C. Merriam Co.

Williams, B. (1995). Making sense of humanity: And other philosophical papers 1982-1993. Cambridge, UK: Cambridge University Press.

Williams, B. (2002). Truth and truthfulness: An essay in genealogy. Princeton, NJ: Princeton University Press.

Williams, B. (2005). In the beginning was the deed: Realism and moralism in political argument. Princeton, NJ: Princeton University Press.

Williams, B. (2006a). Philosophy of a humanistic discipline. Ed. A. W. Moore. Princeton, NJ: Princeton University Press.

Wittgenstein, L. (1958a). Tractatus logico-philosophicus. London: Kegan Paul, Trench, Truber.

Wittgenstein, L. (1958b). Philosophical investigations. Trans. G. E. M. Anscombe. 2nd Ed. Oxford: Basil Blackwell.

Wittgenstein, L. (1960). The blue and brown books. Oxford: Basil Blackwell.

Wittgenstein, L. (1970). Lectures and conversations on aesthetics, psychology and religious belief. Ed. Cyril Barrett. Oxford: Basil Blackwell.

Wittgenstein, L. (1972). On certainty. Ed. G. E. M. Anscombe and G. H. von Wright. New York: Harper and Row.

Wollheim, R. (1980). Art and its objects. 2nd Ed. New York: Cambridge University Press.

Worf, B. L. (1956). Language, thought, and reality: Selected writings. Ed. John C. Carroll. Technology Press of Massachusetts Institute of Technology.

Yoos, G. E. (1967). A work of art as a standard of itself. The Journal of Aesthetics and Art Criticism, 26 (Fall), 81-89.

Yoos, G. E. (1968). On being literally false. Philosophy and Rhetoric, 1 (Fall), 21-227.

Yoos, G. E. (1971a). An analysis of three studies of pictorial representation' M. C. Beardsley, Gombrich, E. H. & Wittegenstein, L. Doctoral dissertation at University of Missouri, Columbia.

Yoos, G. E. (1971b). A phenomenological look at metaphor. Philosophy and Phenomenological Research, 32 (September), 78-88.

Yoos, G. E. (1975). Review of The concept of knowledge, by Panayot Butchvarov. Theory and Decision, 6 (3), 71-375.

Yoos, G. E. (1975). An analysis of some rhetorical uses of subjunctive conditionals. Philosophy and Rhetoric, 8 (Fall); 203-12.

Knowlson, J. (1975). Universal Language Schemes in England and France 1600-1800. Toronto: University of Toronto Press, The Eighteenth Century: Current Biography.

Yoos, G. E. (1979). Rules, Conventions, and Constraints in Rhetorical Action. Rhetoric Society Quarterly, 9 (Winter), 28-34.

Yoos, G. E. (1987a). Rhetoric of appeal and rhetoric of response. Philosophy and Rhetoric, 20, 107-117.

Yoos, G. E. (1987b). The pragmatics of graphics within written discourse. Visions of rhetoric: History, Theory and Criticisms. Edited by Charles W. Kneupper, The University of Texas. Arlington. Arlington, Texas: Rhetoric Society of America.

Yoos, G. E. (1994). Style, invention, and indirection: Aphorisms. In Composition and context: Festschrift for Don Stewart. Carbondale: Southern Illinois University Press.

Yoos, G. E. (1995a). Pragmatics and critical thinking. Inquiry: Critical Thinking across the Disciplines, 14 (Summer), 19-28.

Yoos, G. E. (1995b). A review of western philosophic systems and their transformations. Robert S. Brumbaugh. The Journal of Speculative Philosophy, Vol IX, No 4.

Yoos, G. E. (1996). Logos. In Encyclopedia of rhetoric and composition. T. Enos (Ed.). New York: Garland.

Yoos, G. E. (2003a). Review of 'Truth and truthfulness: An essay in genealogy', by Bernard Williams. Rhetoric Review, 22 (2).

Yoos, G. E. (2003b). Review of Making stories: Law, literature, life, by Jerome Bruner. Journal of Advanced Composition, 23 (2), 459-463.

Yoos, G. E. (2007). Reframing rhetoric: A liberal politics without dogma. New York: Palgrave Macmillan.

Yoos, G. E. (2009). Politics & rhetoric: Coming to terms with terms. New York: Palgrave MacMillan.

Young, R. E., Becker, A. L., & Pike, K. L. (1970). Rhetoric: Discovery and change. New York: Harcourt, Brace, and World.

Ziman, J. (1968). Public knowledge: The social dimension of science. London: Cambridge University Press.

List of Figures

List of Tables

Index

CPSIA information can be obtained
at www.ICGtesting.com
Printed in the USA
LVOW02*2249250216
476769LV00011B/48/P